3

Compact
ACTUAL iBT Reading & Listening Book 3

Publisher Chung Kyudo
Editors Cho Sangik, Hong Inpyo
Authors Darakwon TOEFL Research Team
Proofreader Michael A. Putlack
Designers Zo Hwayoun, Park Sunyoung

First published in November 2011
By Darakwon, Inc.
Darakwon Bldg., 211, Munbal-ro, Paju-si, Gyeonggi-do 10881
Republic of Korea
Tel: 82-2-736-2031 (Ext. 250)
Fax: 82-2-732-2037

Copyright © 2011 Darakwon, Inc.

All rights reserved. No part of this publication may be reproduced, stored in a retrieval system, or transmitted in any form or by any means, electronic, mechanical, photocopying or otherwise, without the prior consent of the copyright owner. Refund after purchase is possible only according to the company regulations. Contact the above telephone number for any inquiries. Consumer damages caused by loss, damage, etc. can be compensated according to the consumer dispute resolution standards announced by the Korea Fair Trade Commission. An incorrectly collated book will be exchanged.

ISBN 978-89-277-0606-9 18740
    978-89-277-0581-9 18740 (set)

www.darakwon.co.kr

Components Main Book / Answer Book
12 11 10 9 8 7 6   23 24 25 26 27

Contents

- Introduction — 6
- Actual Test **01** — 8
- Actual Test **02** — 20
- Actual Test **03** — 32
- Actual Test **04** — 44
- Actual Test **05** — 56
- Actual Test **06** — 68
- Actual Test **07** — 80
- Actual Test **08** — 92
- Actual Test **09** — 104
- Actual Test **10** — 116

Introduction

One of the most important standardized tests students of the English language may ever take is the TOEFL® iBT. Because getting a high score on the test is so crucial, it is important to prepare for the test as much as possible prior to taking it.

That is the purpose of *Compact Actual iBT Reading & Listening* series. This book focuses on two of the four sections on the TOEFL® iBT: the Reading and Listening sections. These are arguably the two most difficult parts of the TOEFL® iBT. In both the Reading and the Listening sections, test takers will face passages and lectures that cover a wide variety of topics. These include subjects in the arts, social sciences, physical sciences, and life sciences. For that reason, a familiarity with many of these topics is crucial. So is having an extensive vocabulary that includes knowledge of specialized words in each of the fields. Fortunately, *Compact Actual iBT Reading & Listening* provides exactly what students need. The Reading passages and Listening lectures cover many of the very topics that often appear on the TOEFL® iBT. In addition, the Listening conversations do the same: They cover topics that frequently appear on the TOEFL® iBT, which can only serve to assist test takers when they sit for the actual test.

Compact Actual iBT Reading & Listening has been designed to be used both in the classroom and by test takers working on an individual basis. Each compact test consists of one Reading passage, one Listening conversation, and one Listening lecture. All three of them are the standard length of actual TOEFL® iBT passages, conversations, and lectures. In addition, they all have the same number of questions and the same types of questions that are found on the actual test. By using this book, test takers will be more prepared for the test when they actually take it.

This book, however, is merely a tool. Both students and teachers must make use of this tool in the best possible manner so that test takers may do as well as possible when they take the TOEFL® iBT.

About This Book

Compact Actual iBT Reading & Listening consists of ten units. Each unit consists of one compact test. A single compact test contains one Reading passage, one Listening conversation, and one Listening lecture. The passage, conversation, and lecture are followed by questions. These questions are of the same type and number that are found on the TOEFL® iBT.

In addition, the subjects of the passages in the Reading section are those that have all appeared on recent TOEFL® iBT tests. As many topics on the TOEFL® iBT Reading section tend to repeat, this can be a great benefit to test takers. By familiarizing themselves with the topics, subject matter, and vocabulary used in the passages in the Reading section of each compact test, test takers can be more confident when they take the Reading section of the TOEFL® iBT.

The same is true of the conversation and lectures in the Listening section. The Listening conversations contain situations that have appeared on recent TOEFL® iBT tests while the Listening lectures are all on topics that have occurred recently as well. By familiarizing themselves with the topics, subject matter, situations, and vocabulary used in the conversations and lectures, test takers can be more confident when they take the Listening section of the TOEFL® iBT.

Reading Section

The Reading section of each compact test consists of one full-length Reading passage followed by either thirteen or fourteen questions. Each passage covers a field that commonly occurs on the TOEFL® iBT. This includes fields such as history, archaeology, biology, and art.

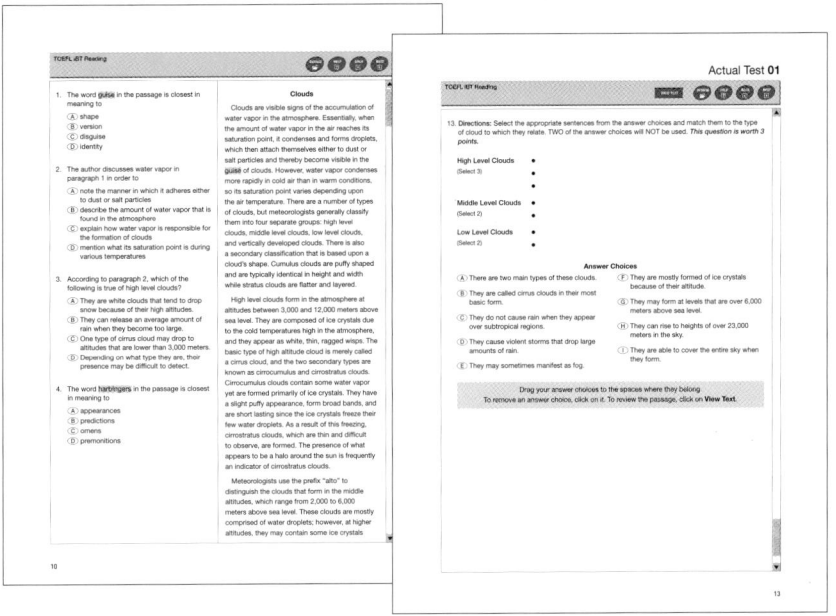

Listening Section

The Listening section of each compact test consists of one full-length Listening conversation followed by five questions and one full-length Listening lecture followed by six questions. Each conversation concerns either an office hours situation or a service situation whereas each lecture covers a topic that commonly occurs on the TOEFL® iBT. These topics are in the following four categories: arts, life sciences, physical sciences, and social sciences.

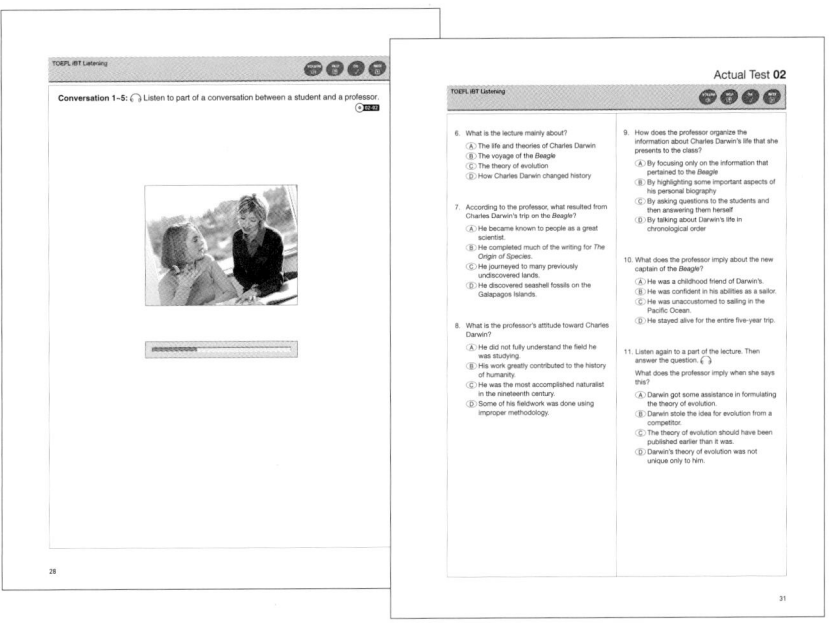

Actual Test
01

TOEFL iBT Reading

Reading
Section Directions

This section measures your ability to understand academic passages in English.

In this part, you will read 1 passage and answer reading comprehension questions about the passage. Most questions are worth one point, but the last question is worth more than one point. The directions indicate how many points you may receive.

Some passages include a word or phrase that is underlined in blue. Click on the word or phrase to see a definition or an explanation.

When you want to move on to the next question, click on **Next**. You may skip questions and go back to them later. If you want to return to previous questions, click on **Back**. You can click on **Review** at any time and the review screen will show you which questions you have answered and which you have not answered. From this review screen, you may go directly to any question you have already seen in the Reading section.

You may now begin the Reading section. You will read 1 reading passage. You will have **20 minutes** to read the passage and answer the questions.

Click on **Continue** to go on.

TOEFL iBT Reading

1. The word guise in the passage is closest in meaning to

   A shape
   B version
   C disguise
   D identity

2. The author discusses water vapor in paragraph 1 in order to

   A note the manner in which it adheres either to dust or salt particles
   B describe the amount of water vapor that is found in the atmosphere
   C explain how water vapor is responsible for the formation of clouds
   D mention what its saturation point is during various temperatures

3. According to paragraph 2, which of the following is true of high level clouds?

   A They are white clouds that tend to drop snow because of their high altitudes.
   B They can release an average amount of rain when they become too large.
   C One type of cirrus cloud may drop to altitudes that are lower than 3,000 meters.
   D Depending on what type they are, their presence may be difficult to detect.

4. The word harbingers in the passage is closest in meaning to

   A appearances
   B predictions
   C omens
   D premonitions

Clouds

Clouds are visible signs of the accumulation of water vapor in the atmosphere. Essentially, when the amount of water vapor in the air reaches its saturation point, it condenses and forms droplets, which then attach themselves either to dust or salt particles and thereby become visible in the guise of clouds. However, water vapor condenses more rapidly in cold air than in warm conditions, so its saturation point varies depending upon the air temperature. There are a number of types of clouds, but meteorologists generally classify them into four separate groups: high level clouds, middle level clouds, low level clouds, and vertically developed clouds. There is also a secondary classification that is based upon a cloud's shape. Cumulus clouds are puffy shaped and are typically identical in height and width while stratus clouds are flatter and layered.

High level clouds form in the atmosphere at altitudes between 3,000 and 12,000 meters above sea level. They are composed of ice crystals due to the cold temperatures high in the atmosphere, and they appear as white, thin, ragged wisps. The basic type of high altitude cloud is merely called a cirrus cloud, and the two secondary types are known as cirrocumulus and cirrostratus clouds. Cirrocumulus clouds contain some water vapor yet are formed primarily of ice crystals. They have a slight puffy appearance, form broad bands, and are short lasting since the ice crystals freeze their few water droplets. As a result of this freezing, cirrostratus clouds, which are thin and difficult to observe, are formed. The presence of what appears to be a halo around the sun is frequently an indicator of cirrostratus clouds.

Meteorologists use the prefix "alto" to distinguish the clouds that form in the middle altitudes, which range from 2,000 to 6,000 meters above sea level. These clouds are mostly comprised of water droplets; however, at higher altitudes, they may contain some ice crystals

5. The author's description of clouds that form in the middle altitudes mentions all of the following EXCEPT:
   Ⓐ They may be so large that they cover the entire sky as seen from the ground.
   Ⓑ They frequently drop large amounts of rain whenever they appear.
   Ⓒ They cover a range of 4,000 meters in the middle of the atmosphere.
   Ⓓ They may result in people on the ground barely being able to see the sun.

6. The word it in the passage refers to
   Ⓐ convection
   Ⓑ air
   Ⓒ land
   Ⓓ a heaped or piled-up appearance

7. The word hazy in the passage is closest in meaning to
   Ⓐ polluted
   Ⓑ weathered
   Ⓒ distinct
   Ⓓ unclear

8. The author's description of low level clouds mentions which of the following?
   Ⓐ The most common manifestation of this category of cloud is fog.
   Ⓑ Some of these clouds may stretch from the ground up to 2,000 meters high.
   Ⓒ Including fog, there are five different types of these clouds.
   Ⓓ Among these clouds are nimbostratus and altostratus clouds.

9. Which of the following can be inferred from paragraph 4 about cumulus clouds?
   Ⓐ They are rarely seen in places that often experience cold winters.
   Ⓑ Some of the precipitation they cause can develop into violent storms.
   Ⓒ They may rise into the middle altitudes and become altostratus clouds.
   Ⓓ Sometimes, they are formed because of excessive pollution in an area.

as well. The two main types are altostratus and altocumulus clouds. Altostratus clouds, which are mostly ice crystals, typically cover the entire sky and may be whitish-gray or blue-gray in color. The sun is normally only dimly visible through altostratus clouds. On the other hand, altocumulus clouds are white rather than gray and are puffier than altostratus clouds. They are made of water droplets and may form long bands that move in step with one another. As a general rule, these clouds are harbingers of approaching rain fronts or thunderstorms.

Low level clouds, which come in a variety of types, manifest between the ground and 2,000 meters above sea level. Fog forms at the lowest levels and is commonly seen near the ocean or sea, where water vapor condenses on salt particles. Above the ground, there are four primary types of low level clouds: cumulus, nimbostratus, stratocumulus, and stratus clouds. Cumulus clouds are the result of convection— rising warm air. On hot days, they are common when the air over land heats up and rises. As it ascends, it cools, condenses, and forms cumulus clouds, which have a heaped or piled-up appearance that makes them resemble a piece of cotton. Nimbostratus clouds cover the entire sky at extremely low levels and are gray in color and smooth in appearance. They almost always result in some form of precipitation. Stratocumulus clouds form in large groups and are dark and puffy. They are not particularly high because of the stable layers of air above them. Stratocumulus clouds frequently appear in subtropical regions over water and rarely produce precipitation. The last type of low level cloud—stratus clouds— covers the sky at low levels and is white in appearance. The clouds give the sky a hazy appearance, and, except for the fact that they are located above the ground, they resemble fog.

The final group of clouds is perhaps the most dangerous: vertically developed clouds, of which

10. According to paragraph 4, which of the following is NOT true of stratocumulus clouds?

   Ⓐ They are prone to producing rain showers.
   Ⓑ They are found at relatively low altitudes.
   Ⓒ They are known to manifest over water in hot places.
   Ⓓ They are dark clouds that have a puffy appearance.

11. Which of the sentences below best expresses the essential information in the highlighted sentence in the passage? *Incorrect* answer choices change the meaning in important ways or leave out essential information.

   Ⓐ At 23,000 meters above sea level, the conditions are so unstable that water vapor can form clouds that stretch all the way down to the ground.
   Ⓑ When there are unstable air conditions, water vapor begins to form, and then it goes up to around 23,000 meters in height, where it then forms clouds.
   Ⓒ When clouds reach up to 23,000 meters high, they may make the air so unstable that water vapor enters the atmosphere in extremely large amounts.
   Ⓓ Instability in the air results in water vapor going to high altitudes, so the clouds may stretch up to 23,000 meters above sea level while their bottoms are close to the ground.

12. According to paragraph 5, vertically developed clouds can be dangerous because

   Ⓐ they may form tornadoes as well as tropical storms such as hurricanes
   Ⓑ they form at altitudes that are very high above the ground
   Ⓒ they can result in weather that is of a violent nature
   Ⓓ their unpredictability can disrupt regular weather patterns

thunderclouds are the primary type. **These clouds are created in unstable air conditions, which allow convection to drive water vapor high into the atmosphere, and the result is clouds with a very low base that can also reach as high as 23,000 meters in altitude.** Vertically developed clouds are associated with violent weather, for they may bring sudden <u>torrents</u> of rain, strong gusts of wind, and flashes of lightning.

Glossary
dimly: faintly; vaguely
ascend: to rise; to go up
torrent: a strong downpour of rain

Actual Test 01

TOEFL iBT Reading

13. **Directions:** Select the appropriate sentences from the answer choices and match them to the type of cloud to which they relate. TWO of the answer choices will NOT be used. *This question is worth 3 points.*

High Level Clouds
(Select 3)
-
-
-

Middle Level Clouds
(Select 2)
-
-

Low Level Clouds
(Select 2)
-
-

Answer Choices

(A) There are two main types of these clouds.

(B) They are called cirrus clouds in their most basic form.

(C) They do not cause rain when they appear over subtropical regions.

(D) They cause violent storms that drop large amounts of rain.

(E) They may sometimes manifest as fog.

(F) They are mostly formed of ice crystals because of their altitude.

(G) They may form at levels that are over 6,000 meters above sea level.

(H) They can rise to heights of over 23,000 meters in the sky.

(I) They are able to cover the entire sky when they form.

Drag your answer choices to the spaces where they belong.
To remove an answer choice, click on it. To review the passage, click on **View Text**.

Listening
Section Directions

This section measures your ability to understand conversations and lectures in English.

In this part, you will listen to 1 conversation and 1 lecture. You will hear the conversation or lecture only **one** time. After the conversation or lecture, you will answer some questions about it. The questions typically ask about the main idea and supporting details. Some questions ask about a speaker's purpose or attitude. Answer the questions based on what is stated or implied by the speakers.

You may take notes while you listen. You may use your notes to help you answer the questions. Your notes will **not** be scored.

If you need to change the volume while you listen, click on the **Volume** icon at the top of the screen.

In some questions, you will see this icon: 🎧 This means that you will hear, but not see, part of the question.

Some of the questions have special directions. These directions appear in a gray box on the screen.

Most questions are worth one point. If a question is worth more than one point, it will have special directions that indicate how many points you can receive.

You must answer each question. After you answer, click on **Next**. Then click on **OK** to confirm your answer and go on to the next question. After you click on **OK**, you cannot return to previous questions.

A clock at the top of the screen will show you how much time is remaining. The clock will not count down while you are listening. The clock will count down only while you are answering the questions.

Now you may begin the Listening section.

Conversation 1~5: Listen to part of a conversation between a student and a student services employee.

Actual Test 01

TOEFL iBT Listening

1. What problem does the student have?
   - Ⓐ She locked herself out of her dormitory room.
   - Ⓑ She cannot find her key to her dormitory room.
   - Ⓒ She does not know where her roommate is.
   - Ⓓ She lacks enough money for a replacement key.

2. Why does the student want to come back before the student services office closes?
   - Ⓐ She would like to receive her schedule by the end of the day.
   - Ⓑ She needs to talk to the man's supervisor as soon as possible.
   - Ⓒ She has to pay for her purchase before she receives her key.
   - Ⓓ She wants to receive her replacement key before the weekend.

3. Why does the student mention her roommate's weekend plans?
   - Ⓐ To tell the man why she is going to be busy over the weekend
   - Ⓑ To explain why she does not want to wait until Monday
   - Ⓒ To try to get the man to give her a discount
   - Ⓓ To encourage the man to keep the office open until late

4. Listen again to a part of the conversation. Then answer the question.

   What can be inferred about the student when she says this?
   - Ⓐ Her recent action is abnormal for her.
   - Ⓑ She feels awkward talking to the man.
   - Ⓒ She is angry about her misbehavior.
   - Ⓓ She needs to try to improve her attitude.

5. Listen again to a part of the conversation. Then answer the question.

   What is the purpose of the man's response?
   - Ⓐ To tell the student she has no choice in the matter
   - Ⓑ To apologize for the problem he is causing her
   - Ⓒ To compliment the student for her attitude
   - Ⓓ To encourage the student to calm down a little

Lecture 6~11: Listen to part of a lecture in a history class.

6. What aspect of the Silk Road does the professor mainly discuss?

   Ⓐ The manner in which it was constructed
   Ⓑ Its effects on people all throughout history
   Ⓒ The ways that the Mongols managed it
   Ⓓ The fastest routes people took along it

7. Why does the professor explain the connection between the Mongols and the Silk Road?

   Ⓐ To compare their actions on the Silk Road with those of Alexander the Great
   Ⓑ To name the century in which travel on the Silk Road became more difficult
   Ⓒ To discuss the Mongols' role in the downfall of the Byzantine Empire
   Ⓓ To describe their role in permitting trade on the Silk Road to continue

8. According to the professor, what contribution did the Persian Empire make to the Silk Road?

   Ⓐ They constructed a number of actual roads on it.
   Ⓑ They patrolled the Silk Road for highwaymen and robbers.
   Ⓒ They charged tolls to people using the road.
   Ⓓ They encouraged the spread of Hellenism along it.

9. Why does the professor discuss the use of pack animals on the Silk Road?

   Ⓐ To claim that people first domesticated them on the Silk Road
   Ⓑ To explain how they managed to eat while traveling on the Silk Road
   Ⓒ To note why trade on the Silk Road was able to expand
   Ⓓ To emphasize the cost of taking them on trading ventures on the Silk Road

10. What will the professor probably do next?

    Ⓐ Dismiss the class for the day
    Ⓑ Ask the students some questions
    Ⓒ Continue lecturing on the same topic
    Ⓓ Discuss the discovery of the Americas

11. Listen again to a part of the lecture. Then answer the question.

    What does the professor imply when he says this?

    Ⓐ The Chinese military lacked the strength to defeat the robbers on the Silk Road.
    Ⓑ The Chinese were ordered to arrest brigands and thieves on the Silk Road.
    Ⓒ Any robbers that saw the Chinese military immediately fled from them.
    Ⓓ The Chinese military killed any bandits they encountered on the Silk Road.

Actual Test
02

Reading
Section Directions

This section measures your ability to understand academic passages in English.

In this part, you will read 1 passage and answer reading comprehension questions about the passage. Most questions are worth one point, but the last question is worth more than one point. The directions indicate how many points you may receive.

Some passages include a word or phrase that is underlined in blue. Click on the word or phrase to see a definition or an explanation.

When you want to move on to the next question, click on **Next**. You may skip questions and go back to them later. If you want to return to previous questions, click on **Back**. You can click on **Review** at any time and the review screen will show you which questions you have answered and which you have not answered. From this review screen, you may go directly to any question you have already seen in the Reading section.

You may now begin the Reading section. You will read 1 reading passage. You will have **20 minutes** to read the passage and answer the questions.

Click on **Continue** to go on.

Diamond Formation

Diamonds are the hardest substances in the world and also among the most valuable. Their value is due in part to their scarcity since diamonds are only found in certain parts of the world. They are rare since a unique set of circumstances is needed for them to form. On the Earth, there are two ways that diamonds can be created naturally: from the actions of heat and pressure on carbon deep underground and from meteorites striking the planet. These are not the only methods diamonds are formed though. Certain types of diamonds found on the Earth are extraterrestrial in origin and arrived on the planet as parts of meteorites. And scientists have learned how to synthesize diamonds in their labs, which is an artificial way that they can be made.

Billions of years ago, deep within the planet in some places, carbon was subjected to such intense heat and pressure that it formed diamonds. Over a period of time lasting from one to three billion years, the heat and pressure combined to alter the structure of the carbon, giving it a very rigid lattice structure that is known as the diamond lattice. Mineralogists classify diamonds as one of the eight allotropes of carbon, which are types of carbon that are different due to their atomic structure. Part of the diamond lattice is a strong covalent bonding between the carbon atoms, which gives diamonds their unique hardness, thermal conductivity, and luster. The pressure required to create diamonds is between forty-five and sixty kilobars. One kilobar is approximately 1,000 times the atmospheric pressure on the Earth. Additionally, a temperature somewhere between 900 and 1,300 degrees Celsius is necessary for the transformation to take place. These conditions are found approximately 120 to 200 kilometers below the planet's surface. After being formed, most diamonds reach the planet's surface through volcanic action, which explains why most diamonds are found in areas

1. According to paragraph 1, which of the following is true of diamonds?
   Ⓐ They are mined in a number of different countries all around the world.
   Ⓑ They are most valuable when they are created in scientific laboratories.
   Ⓒ The largest ones discovered so far are the results of meteor strikes.
   Ⓓ Some of the ones found on Earth have their origins elsewhere.

2. The word which in the passage refers to
   Ⓐ their atomic structure
   Ⓑ part of the diamond lattice
   Ⓒ a strong covalent bonding
   Ⓓ the carbon atoms

3. According to paragraph 2, why do diamonds form?
   Ⓐ Certain rocks remain subjected to pressure underground for millions of years.
   Ⓑ The element carbon has its structure altered due to both heat and pressure.
   Ⓒ Volcanoes produce the necessary amount of heat instantly to create diamonds.
   Ⓓ Underground heat and pressure make carbon turn into another element.

4. According to paragraph 2, diamonds may rise to the surface because
   Ⓐ they are carried there by underground rivers
   Ⓑ the shifting of the planet's crust pushes them up
   Ⓒ the intense heat underground forces them upward
   Ⓓ volcanic eruptions take them above the ground

5. The word transforming in the passage is closest in meaning to
   Ⓐ changing
   Ⓑ manufacturing
   Ⓒ welding
   Ⓓ appearing

6. In paragraph 3, why does the author mention Siberia?
   Ⓐ To note that it is located within Russia
   Ⓑ To state that microdiamonds have been found there
   Ⓒ To describe an impact crater that is found there
   Ⓓ To claim that more meteorites have struck it than any other area

7. Which of the following can be inferred from paragraph 3 about meteorites?
   Ⓐ They strike Earth at a very regular rate.
   Ⓑ They are responsible for most of the planet's diamonds.
   Ⓒ They can reproduce conditions found deep within the planet.
   Ⓓ They destroy most of the diamonds they are transporting upon impact.

8. The word speculate in the passage is closest in meaning to
   Ⓐ guarantee
   Ⓑ observe
   Ⓒ theorize
   Ⓓ distinguish

9. The word strewn in the passage is closest in meaning to
   Ⓐ scattered
   Ⓑ planted
   Ⓒ buried
   Ⓓ covered

with active, dormant, or extinct volcanoes. In some cases, diamonds are found in alluvial deposits at the mouths of rivers after having been washed downstream from their point of origin.

On rare occasions, diamonds have been found within meteorite impact craters. When a large rock from outer space strikes the Earth, in an instant, the pressure and temperature conditions required to form diamonds occur. The result—the sudden transforming of carbon into diamonds—is called ultrahigh pressure metamorphism, and it creates something called microdiamonds, which are often no bigger than a centimeter across. It has only been in recent years that scientists investigating ancient impact craters have discovered microdiamonds. A site in Siberia in Russia that was impacted around thirty-five million years ago is one example of place that has yielded microdiamonds.

Rarer still are diamonds that were created on distant worlds or asteroids and subsequently arrived on the Earth as parts of meteorites. Scientists speculate that these diamonds formed when dying stars produced intense flashes of radiation. These diamonds are often extremely small and are accordingly known as nanodiamonds. One type of diamond that may be of extraterrestrial origin is the carbonado diamond. These diamonds are found in only two places on Earth: in alluvial deposits of rivers in Brazil in South America and on the west coast of Africa. Mineralogists suspect that these diamonds came from a single major impact at a time when South America and Africa were part of the same landmass. Before the two continents drifted apart, the diamonds in the meteorite were strewn about the land, which explains why they are now found on two continents that are an ocean apart.

Man's desire for diamonds has led to their creation in laboratories. Since the 1950s, scientists have been able to produce synthetic diamonds through a variety of methods. However,

TOEFL iBT Reading

10. The author uses carbonado diamonds as an example of

    Ⓐ the most desired type of diamonds on the planet
    Ⓑ diamonds that take billions of years to form
    Ⓒ perfectly flawless diamonds in composition
    Ⓓ diamonds that did not originate on Earth

11. The word they in the passage refers to

    Ⓐ the world's diamond mining companies
    Ⓑ diamond buyers
    Ⓒ real stones
    Ⓓ diamonds

12. According to paragraph 5, which of the following is NOT true of synthetic diamonds?

    Ⓐ Their use as gemstones has caused problems for diamond mining companies.
    Ⓑ They are formed in a way that mimics their creation within the planet.
    Ⓒ The majority of them are sold for the purpose of being used as jewelry.
    Ⓓ Scientists have been making them for more than half a century.

13. Look at the four squares [■] that indicate where the following sentence could be added to the passage.

    One reason for this is that synthetic diamonds are virtually identical to natural ones but cost much less than real diamonds.

    Where would the sentence best fit?

    Click on a square [■] to add the sentence to the passage.

the main process is similar to that which occurs deep within the planet to produce them naturally. ■ Scientists must subject carbon to extremely high pressure and temperatures in machines. ■ The result of this process is small diamonds that are mostly used for industrial purposes. ■ Some, however, are turned into gemstones, which has raised the ire of the world's diamond mining companies. ■ They insist that diamond buyers want real stones and should therefore not be sold diamonds unless they can be guaranteed of getting the real thing: stones produced deep within the Earth over billions of years.

Glossary
lattice: a regular pattern of crystals
allotrope: one of the different forms that an element may take
alluvial: relating to the silt, sand, and other small particles found in flowing water

Actual Test 02

TOEFL iBT Reading

14. **Directions:** An introductory sentence for a brief summary of the passage is provided below. Complete the summary by selecting the THREE answer choices that express the most important ideas of the passage. Some sentences do not belong because they express ideas that are not presented in the passage or are minor ideas in the passage. *This question is worth 2 points.*

Diamonds may be formed underground over the course of billions of years, or they may also be created by the actions of meteorites as well as in scientific laboratories.

-
-
-

Answer Choices

(A) When carbon is subjected to enough heat and pressure over a long period of time, it can be transformed and turn into a diamond.

(B) There are several different allotropes of carbon, and diamonds are the one that is extremely hard and very lustrous.

(C) When a meteorite strikes the planet, the sudden impact may result in the conditions necessary for diamond creation occurring.

(D) By using modern machines, scientists are able to produce diamonds in their laboratory, and these stones are often then used by industries.

(E) Many diamond hunters look for them around volcanoes since it is often after volcanic eruptions that diamonds are transported from underground to the surface.

(F) Brazil, West Africa, and Siberia are three places on the planet where diamonds of extraterrestrial origin have been found.

Drag your answer choices to the spaces where they belong.
To remove an answer choice, click on it. To review the passage, click on **View Text**.

TOEFL iBT Listening

Listening
Section Directions

This section measures your ability to understand conversations and lectures in English.

In this part, you will listen to 1 conversation and 1 lecture. You will hear the conversation or lecture only **one** time. After the conversation or lecture, you will answer some questions about it. The questions typically ask about the main idea and supporting details. Some questions ask about a speaker's purpose or attitude. Answer the questions based on what is stated or implied by the speakers.

You may take notes while you listen. You may use your notes to help you answer the questions. Your notes will **not** be scored.

If you need to change the volume while you listen, click on the **Volume** icon at the top of the screen.

In some questions, you will see this icon: 🎧 This means that you will hear, but not see, part of the question.

Some of the questions have special directions. These directions appear in a gray box on the screen.

Most questions are worth one point. If a question is worth more than one point, it will have special directions that indicate how many points you can receive.

You must answer each question. After you answer, click on **Next**. Then click on **OK** to confirm your answer and go on to the next question. After you click on **OK**, you cannot return to previous questions.

A clock at the top of the screen will show you how much time is remaining. The clock will not count down while you are listening. The clock will count down only while you are answering the questions.

Now you may begin the Listening section.

Conversation 1~5: Listen to part of a conversation between a student and a professor.

Actual Test 02

TOEFL iBT Listening

1. Why does the student visit the professor?
   - (A) To talk about an upcoming poetry conference
   - (B) To get the professor to interpret a poem for her
   - (C) To find out the schedule for the next school conference
   - (D) To ask about something that has been bothering her

2. What does the professor say about a lot of modern poetry?
   - (A) It is lower in quality than poetry written in the past.
   - (B) It is often very short and written in free verse.
   - (C) It can be difficult for many people to understand.
   - (D) It comes near to equaling the quality of Shakespeare's work.

3. What is the professor's attitude toward the student?
   - (A) She dismisses the student's concerns.
   - (B) She is somewhat aloof of the student.
   - (C) She acts very kindly toward the student.
   - (D) She praises the student's understanding of poetry.

4. What will the student probably do next?
   - (A) She will attend another lecture.
   - (B) She will leave the professor's office.
   - (C) She will show the professor one of the poems.
   - (D) She will go to the conference.

5. Listen again to a part of the conversation. Then answer the question.

   Why does the professor say this?
   - (A) To encourage the student to ask her question
   - (B) To tell the student that she does not have much time
   - (C) To indicate to the student that she shares the same thoughts
   - (D) To let the student know that she should not lie

Lecture 6~11: Listen to part of a lecture in a natural history class.

Natural History

Actual Test 02

TOEFL iBT Listening

6. What is the lecture mainly about?
   - Ⓐ The life and theories of Charles Darwin
   - Ⓑ The voyage of the *Beagle*
   - Ⓒ The theory of evolution
   - Ⓓ How Charles Darwin changed history

7. According to the professor, what resulted from Charles Darwin's trip on the *Beagle*?
   - Ⓐ He became known to people as a great scientist.
   - Ⓑ He completed much of the writing for *The Origin of Species*.
   - Ⓒ He journeyed to many previously undiscovered lands.
   - Ⓓ He discovered seashell fossils on the Galapagos Islands.

8. What is the professor's attitude toward Charles Darwin?
   - Ⓐ He did not fully understand the field he was studying.
   - Ⓑ His work greatly contributed to the history of humanity.
   - Ⓒ He was the most accomplished naturalist in the nineteenth century.
   - Ⓓ Some of his fieldwork was done using improper methodology.

9. How does the professor organize the information about Charles Darwin's life that she presents to the class?
   - Ⓐ By focusing only on the information that pertained to the *Beagle*
   - Ⓑ By highlighting some important aspects of his personal biography
   - Ⓒ By asking questions to the students and then answering them herself
   - Ⓓ By talking about Darwin's life in chronological order

10. What does the professor imply about the new captain of the *Beagle*?
    - Ⓐ He was a childhood friend of Darwin's.
    - Ⓑ He was confident in his abilities as a sailor.
    - Ⓒ He was unaccustomed to sailing in the Pacific Ocean.
    - Ⓓ He stayed alive for the entire five-year trip.

11. Listen again to a part of the lecture. Then answer the question.

    What does the professor imply when she says this?
    - Ⓐ Darwin got some assistance in formulating the theory of evolution.
    - Ⓑ Darwin stole the idea for evolution from a competitor.
    - Ⓒ The theory of evolution should have been published earlier than it was.
    - Ⓓ Darwin's theory of evolution was not unique only to him.

Actual Test
03

TOEFL iBT Reading

Reading
Section Directions

This section measures your ability to understand academic passages in English.

In this part, you will read 1 passage and answer reading comprehension questions about the passage. Most questions are worth one point, but the last question is worth more than one point. The directions indicate how many points you may receive.

Some passages include a word or phrase that is underlined in blue. Click on the word or phrase to see a definition or an explanation.

When you want to move on to the next question, click on **Next**. You may skip questions and go back to them later. If you want to return to previous questions, click on **Back**. You can click on **Review** at any time and the review screen will show you which questions you have answered and which you have not answered. From this review screen, you may go directly to any question you have already seen in the Reading section.

You may now begin the Reading section. You will read 1 reading passage. You will have **20 minutes** to read the passage and answer the questions.

Click on **Continue** to go on.

The New World's Influence on Europe

In 1492, Christopher Columbus discovered the Americas. This set off a wave of exploration that eventually saw the entire New World, as North and South America came to be known, explored and then divided among the European powers. Spain, Portugal, England, and France led the way. The discovery of the New World resulted in a number of changes not only in the Americas but also in the Old World, as Europe was soon called. Some of these changes were fairly minor, yet others were momentous and had far-reaching and long-lasting effects on both continents.

During the sixteenth century, the Spanish, who sent numerous expeditions across the Atlantic Ocean, conquered most of Central and South America. Driven primarily by ambition and greed, Spanish conquistadors defeated the natives and discovered—or seized—massive amounts of gold and silver. The majority of this booty ended up in Spanish coffers. This influx of wealth gave Spain unprecedented power, making it the strongest of all of the European nations for most of the sixteenth century. But the Spanish leaders, particularly King Philip II, did not manage their newfound wealth wisely. Instead, they frequently squandered it, so Spanish monarchs wound up declaring bankruptcy several times in the 1500s. Spain's military adventures were also badly managed, and the English defeat of the Spanish Armada in 1588 was merely the most famous of Spain's military blunders. Eventually, Spain lost its once-dominant position and most of her New World colonies either because of revolutions or wars with other nations.

The discovery of the New World had a dramatic effect on trade in Europe and the economies of its countries. The gold and silver that were exported from the New World, and which the Spanish freely spent, caused a period of inflation that historians have named the "price revolution."

---

1. The word momentous in the passage is closest in meaning to
   - (A) considerate
   - (B) destructive
   - (C) noteworthy
   - (D) effective

2. According to paragraph 1, what did the Europeans do in the New World after Christopher Columbus discovered it?
   - (A) They purchased colonies from its inhabitants.
   - (B) They fought wars against each other there.
   - (C) They changed the geographical shape of the land.
   - (D) They visited the land there and explored it.

3. The word squandered in the passage is closest in meaning to
   - (A) wasted
   - (B) loaned
   - (C) spent
   - (D) invested

4. The word blunders in the passage is closest in meaning to
   - (A) conquests
   - (B) battles
   - (C) escapades
   - (D) errors

5. According to paragraph 2, which of the following is true of the Spanish?
   - (A) They managed to spend most of their wealth in the New World itself.
   - (B) Most of their expeditions to the New World were financed by King Philip II.
   - (C) They became wealthy from the treasure they acquired in the New World.
   - (D) Their economic policies caused a number of European nations to go bankrupt.

6. Why does the author mention Venice and Genoa?
   - (A) To name two places that lost economic power after the discovery of the New World
   - (B) To describe the kind of political system that both were governed by
   - (C) To note their location in Europe as opposed to that of other nations
   - (D) To stress that they remained influential in the Mediterranean region of Europe

7. According to paragraph 3, which of the following is true of trade in Europe after the discovery of the New World?
   - (A) It became based on the exchange of money for goods and services.
   - (B) Trade made the prices of goods decline because so many became available.
   - (C) It continued to rely primarily upon the barter system as a medium of exchange.
   - (D) Trade contributed to the populations of Europe increasing over time.

8. The word They in the passage refers to
   - (A) Many people
   - (B) Many New World imports
   - (C) Staples
   - (D) European's diets

9. In paragraph 4, why does the author mention wheat?
   - (A) To explain why it was a better crop to grow than others were
   - (B) To claim that it was brought to Europe from the New World
   - (C) To make a comparison between it and some other crops
   - (D) To state that it was responsible for improving the health of many Europeans

■ Prices rose five- or six-fold in most of Europe from the middle of the sixteenth century to the end of the seventeenth. ■ This inflation was also a result of rising populations in Europe as well as the demand by people for all kinds of products. ■ There was therefore an increase in trade, and that brought Spanish gold and silver to all corners of the continent. ■ Instead of bartering with products or services, people demanded cash for whatever they were selling. The end result was a shift in Europe's economy. What was once an economy based mostly on the barter system became a cash-based economy instead. At the same time, the center of European trade shifted from the Mediterranean's great city-states, such as Venice and Genoa, to Western Europe. Not only did Spain benefit from the increased trade, but England, France, Portugal, and the Netherlands all saw their power increase as well.

A seemingly smaller—yet more enduring—influence of the New World on the Old World was the importing to Europe of many plants that were common food sources in the New World. Prior to Columbus's voyage, plants such as potatoes, tomatoes, squash, beans, corn, and many types of peppers were unknown in Europe. While many people at first mistrusted some of these plants—particularly tomatoes—and refused to eat them, eventually, many New World imports became staples of Europeans' diets. They proved to be a great benefit for poor European farmers. Potatoes and corn yield higher returns of food energy for the land used and labor expended than wheat does. Thus people managed to improve the quality of their diets with these New World products, which made them much healthier than they had been before.

The exchanges between the New World and the Old World were very one-sided. In return for their gold, silver, and unique crops, the natives of the New World received devastating diseases, the destruction of their cultures, and slavery for

10. In paragraph 4, the author's description of the foods that were imported to Europe from the New World mentions which of the following?

   (A) They were not all universally welcomed by the Europeans.
   (B) They made the Europeans stop planting wheat in their fields.
   (C) They encouraged people to plant their fields with several crops.
   (D) They helped Europeans live longer and healthier lives.

11. Which of the sentences below best expresses the essential information in the highlighted sentence in the passage? *Incorrect* answer choices change the meaning in important ways or leave out essential information.

   (A) There was a strong European presence all throughout the New World for a period that lasted more than four hundred years.
   (B) For four centuries, the Europeans gained wealth and power from the colonies that they had established in the New World.
   (C) Thanks to their exploitation of the New World, Western European countries dominated the world for almost half a millennium.
   (D) It took the countries of the New World almost four centuries to recover from the rapacious actions of the Western Europeans.

12. According to paragraph 5, which of the following is NOT true of the exchanges between Europe and the New World?

   (A) They had an effect on countries in other places in the world.
   (B) They caused much harm to the people in the New World.
   (C) They enabled the New World to become stronger than Asia.
   (D) They strongly benefitted the Europeans.

those few who survived this period of upheaval. As for the nations of Western Europe, the wealth and power they accumulated from their New World colonies permitted them to become the masters of the world for the next four centuries. Over time, their people, languages, and cultures would come to dominate not only the New World but also much of Africa, Asia, and Oceania. They remained the world's supreme powers until the twentieth century, when two destructive world wars saw Europe decline while a former New World colony—the United States—ascended to become a superpower.

Glossary

booty: treasure; loot

inflation: a period of time when prices in an economy increase

staple: a type of food, such as wheat, corn, or rice, that is frequently consumed by people

13. Look at the four squares [■] that indicate where the following sentence could be added to the passage.

Never before had prices risen at such a dramatic rate and over that short a period of time.

Where would the sentence best fit?

Click on a square [■] to add the sentence to the passage.

14. Directions: An introductory sentence for a brief summary of the passage is provided below. Complete the summary by selecting the THREE answer choices that express the most important ideas of the passage. Some sentences do not belong because they express ideas that are not presented in the passage or are minor ideas in the passage. *This question is worth 2 points.*

The discovery of the New World by Christopher Columbus had mostly positive effects for the Europeans yet negative effects for those living in the New World.

-
-
-

Answer Choices

(A) The Spaniards, particularly under King Philip II, had trouble managing their money, so they frequently declared bankruptcy.

(B) Many people in the New World died from diseases introduced by the Europeans while others were enslaved by them.

(C) The traditional economy of Europe was one that utilized barter rather than a money-based system of trade.

(D) New World crops such as corn and potatoes were planted in the Old World and served to improve the health of many Europeans.

(E) Venice, Genoa, and the entire Mediterranean region declined in economic importance after the New World was discovered.

(F) There was a tremendous influx of gold and other treasure into Europe, mostly because of Spain's dealings with the New World.

Drag your answer choices to the spaces where they belong.
To remove an answer choice, click on it. To review the passage, click on **View Text**.

TOEFL iBT Listening

Listening
Section Directions

This section measures your ability to understand conversations and lectures in English.

In this part, you will listen to 1 conversation and 1 lecture. You will hear the conversation or lecture only **one** time. After the conversation or lecture, you will answer some questions about it. The questions typically ask about the main idea and supporting details. Some questions ask about a speaker's purpose or attitude. Answer the questions based on what is stated or implied by the speakers.

You may take notes while you listen. You may use your notes to help you answer the questions. Your notes will **not** be scored.

If you need to change the volume while you listen, click on the **Volume** icon at the top of the screen.

In some questions, you will see this icon: 🎧 This means that you will hear, but not see, part of the question.

Some of the questions have special directions. These directions appear in a gray box on the screen.

Most questions are worth one point. If a question is worth more than one point, it will have special directions that indicate how many points you can receive.

You must answer each question. After you answer, click on **Next**. Then click on **OK** to confirm your answer and go on to the next question. After you click on **OK**, you cannot return to previous questions.

A clock at the top of the screen will show you how much time is remaining. The clock will not count down while you are listening. The clock will count down only while you are answering the questions.

Now you may begin the Listening section.

TOEFL iBT Listening

Conversation 1~5: Listen to part of a conversation between a student and a student center employee. 03-02

Actual Test 03

TOEFL iBT Listening

1. What problem does the student have?

   Ⓐ He cannot find his student ID card.
   Ⓑ He has lost his way around campus.
   Ⓒ He found something that belongs to another person.
   Ⓓ He does not know where his next class is.

2. Why does the woman explain the location of the student services building?

   Ⓐ It is the location of the student's next class.
   Ⓑ The student can apply for a new job there.
   Ⓒ The student needs to go there next.
   Ⓓ It is where the student's missing item may be located.

3. According to the student, where was he when he lost his item?

   Ⓐ He was in the student services building.
   Ⓑ He was somewhere in the library.
   Ⓒ He was in a classroom.
   Ⓓ He was in a nearby café.

4. What can be inferred about the school that the student attends?

   Ⓐ It has a large number of buildings.
   Ⓑ It is located in a large metropolitan area.
   Ⓒ Many of the students there are unfriendly.
   Ⓓ It covers a fairly small area of land.

5. Listen again to a part of the conversation. Then answer the question.

   What does the student mean when he says this?

   Ⓐ The woman needs to provide a better explanation.
   Ⓑ He wants the woman to repeat herself.
   Ⓒ He agrees with what the woman says.
   Ⓓ There is nothing she can do to change his mind.

Lecture 6~11: Listen to part of a lecture in a zoology class.

Actual Test 03

6. What is the main topic of the lecture?
   - Ⓐ How some animals attack others as a means of defense
   - Ⓑ The use of poison and camouflage by some animals
   - Ⓒ Some methods animals use to defend themselves
   - Ⓓ The favored defense mechanisms of predators

7. According to the professor, how do crustaceans protect themselves from predators?
   - Ⓐ They use camouflage to blend in with their surroundings.
   - Ⓑ They have hard shells that can offer them protection.
   - Ⓒ They use their speed to escape from any attackers.
   - Ⓓ They fight predators with their sharp claws and teeth.

8. How is the discussion organized?
   - Ⓐ By listing examples of defense mechanisms and then describing animals that use them
   - Ⓑ By discussing animal defense methods in order of their effectiveness against predators
   - Ⓒ By naming several animals and then describing the types of defenses that they use
   - Ⓓ By asking the students to give some defense methods and then explaining how they work

9. Based on the information in the lecture, do the following sentences refer to collective action or camouflage?

   Click in the correct box for each sentence.

	Collective Action	Camouflage
Ⓐ Animals use it to blend in with their surroundings.		
Ⓑ It involves animals traveling in herds.		
Ⓒ It may require the use of pheromones.		
Ⓓ It is a defense method used by the stonefish.		

10. Listen again to a part of the lecture. Then answer the question.

    What is the purpose of the student's response?
    - Ⓐ To disregard the professor's comments
    - Ⓑ To offer a countering viewpoint
    - Ⓒ To verify some information
    - Ⓓ To express surprise

11. Listen again to a part of the lecture. Then answer the question.

    What can be inferred about the professor when he says this?
    - Ⓐ He believes the students need to consider this information.
    - Ⓑ He feels that he has explained his point sufficiently.
    - Ⓒ He wants the students to consider what he has just said.
    - Ⓓ He would like the students to respond to his question.

Actual Test 04

TOEFL iBT Reading

Reading
Section Directions

This section measures your ability to understand academic passages in English.

In this part, you will read 1 passage and answer reading comprehension questions about the passage. Most questions are worth one point, but the last question is worth more than one point. The directions indicate how many points you may receive.

Some passages include a word or phrase that is underlined in blue. Click on the word or phrase to see a definition or an explanation.

When you want to move on to the next question, click on **Next**. You may skip questions and go back to them later. If you want to return to previous questions, click on **Back**. You can click on **Review** at any time and the review screen will show you which questions you have answered and which you have not answered. From this review screen, you may go directly to any question you have already seen in the Reading section.

You may now begin the Reading section. You will read 1 reading passage. You will have **20 minutes** to read the passage and answer the questions.

Click on **Continue** to go on.

1. The word rectify in the passage is closest in meaning to
   - (A) abandon
   - (B) solve
   - (C) analyze
   - (D) determine

2. According to paragraph 1, which of the following is NOT true of the causes of acid rain?
   - (A) Most of the acid rain on Earth is created by the actions of man.
   - (B) Volcanoes are the leading cause of acid rain in some places.
   - (C) It may often be caused by sulfur dioxide in the atmosphere.
   - (D) It may occur due to the actions of forces within nature itself.

3. Which of the following can be inferred from paragraph 2 about the pH scale?
   - (A) Numbers higher than 7 on it are not acidic in nature.
   - (B) It can be used to detect the presence of sulfur dioxide in an object.
   - (C) It is the most commonly used scale by scientists.
   - (D) Scientists have reported some problems with it concerning accuracy.

4. The word dramatically in the passage is closest in meaning to
   - (A) instantly
   - (B) subsequently
   - (C) considerably
   - (D) subconsciously

5. The word culprit in the passage is closest in meaning to
   - (A) bandit
   - (B) perpetrator
   - (C) accuser
   - (D) victim

Acid Rain

Acid rain is any form of precipitation containing higher than normal amounts of acid. This acid is the result of high levels of sulfur dioxide and nitrogen dioxide, both of which react with the atmosphere to produce sulfuric acid and nitric acid, respectively. The sources of sulfur dioxide and nitrogen dioxide can be either natural or manmade. Among the natural sources are volcanoes and decaying vegetation, yet the vast majority of manmade sources come from the burning of fossil fuels, particularly coal. Acid rain has harmful effects on the flora and fauna of a region as well as manmade structures. While more common in developed countries, it knows no boundaries, so acid-laden clouds formed over one nation may move and drop acid rain on another. Attempts to rectify the problem are growing, but, until humans learn to survive without burning fossil fuels, acid rain will never truly disappear.

Acid is measured using the pH scale, upon which a low number is an indication of a high level of acid. Pure water has a pH of 7—the midpoint on the scale—while precipitation is considered acidic when its pH level is less than 6. The sources of the acidic compounds can influence water's pH level. Two primary sources of sulfur dioxide and nitrogen dioxide are volcanic eruptions and decaying plant matter, both of which have been occurring since the planet's earliest days. Yet studies of glacier ice cores indicate that past rainfall—even in regions with volcanic activity—was only slightly acidic, making it virtually pure.

However, since the world began industrializing more than two centuries ago, the incidence of acid rain has increased dramatically. Burning coal is the biggest problem. The United States Environmental Protection Agency estimates that up to two-thirds of the sulfur dioxide and one quarter of the nitrogen dioxide emissions in the U.S. are a direct result of burning coal to produce

6. According to paragraph 3, there has been an increase in the amount of acid rain because

   Ⓐ coal is being mined in greater amounts than ever before
   Ⓑ people are not very concerned about protecting the environment
   Ⓒ the using of gas and oil as energy sources has released too many noxious toxins
   Ⓓ there has been a long period of industrialization around the planet

7. Which of the sentences below best expresses the essential information in the highlighted sentence in the passage? *Incorrect* answer choices change the meaning in important ways or leave out essential information.

   Ⓐ The acid and aluminum levels in the water cause the fish to suffer by becoming smaller and living shorter lives.
   Ⓑ When there is too much acid in the water, fish are unable to live, so they simply die in very high numbers.
   Ⓒ The amount of food in the body of water becomes much smaller because the water is contaminated by the acid and aluminum.
   Ⓓ Either fish grow smaller and live for a shorter amount of time, or else they are simply killed by the poisons.

8. According to paragraph 4, which of the following is true of the conditions in water when acid rain falls on it?

   Ⓐ It makes lakes and streams unsafe for humans to drink from.
   Ⓑ It causes many bodies of water to become devoid of life forms.
   Ⓒ It increases the pH levels of all of the areas it comes into contact with.
   Ⓓ It releases aluminum from the soil that is found underneath the water.

electricity. The second biggest culprit is gas-burning motor vehicles. This is a global issue since coal-fired electric plants and gas-burning cars contribute significantly to the acid rain problem everywhere.

When acid rain falls, it enters the water system and immediately begins causing problems. Lakes, ponds, and marshes can all become acid and see pH levels of between 4 and 6. These levels of acidity result in the release of toxic aluminum from nearby soil. Fish and other aquatic creatures in the area are either killed by the combination of high levels of acid and aluminum, or they suffer from reduced sizes and longevity because they cannot compete for food and living space. Additionally, the next generation of aquatic life suffers since most fish eggs will not hatch in water with a pH level of 5 or lower. The end result is that tens of thousands of bodies of water around the world have no life in them.

It is not just animals that suffer; acid rain negatively affects plants, too. Many trees have a coating on their bark that protects them from the elements and helps them retain water and nutrients. Acid rain eats away at this protective coating, thereby exposing the trees to the elements. Without protection, the trees are less able to retain moisture, so many die. Trees growing at higher elevations suffer greatly because they are more frequently exposed to acid rain and acid fog than trees at lower levels. The soil where acid rain falls can also be harmed. As the soil becomes more acidic, certain microbes in it die, which reduces the soil's ability to sustain plant life.

One of the most visible signs of acid rain is its effect on manmade structures. Many buildings, bridges, statues, and other monuments show increased wear due to acid rain eroding them. Stone is particularly affected, so buildings constructed of limestone and marble may suffer considerable amounts of damage. ■ Worldwide,

TOEFL iBT Reading

9. The word them in the passage refers to

    (A) animals
    (B) plants
    (C) many trees
    (D) the elements

10. According to paragraph 5, acid rain kills many trees because

    (A) they are unable to grow more bark once the rain causes it to rot
    (B) the trees can no longer absorb nutrients from the ground
    (C) moisture from the ground cannot be captured by the trees' roots
    (D) the acid strips the trees of some valuable protection

11. The word restoring in the passage is closest in meaning to

    (A) resolving
    (B) revolving
    (C) removing
    (D) renovating

12. Why does the author mention limestone and marble?

    (A) To note that they are common materials people use to construct buildings
    (B) To emphasize that buildings made with them may suffer greatly from acid rain
    (C) To say that it costs a lot of money to repair the damage that is caused to them
    (D) To criticize people for constructing buildings made completely out of them

13. Look at the four squares [■] that indicate where the following sentence could be added to the passage.

    Some of this damage may be of a structural nature, which makes the buildings dangerous for their occupants to be in.

    Where would the sentence best fit?

    Click on a square [■] to add the sentence to the passage.

huge sums of money have been spent restoring these buildings and monuments. ■ Cognizant of the harm caused by acid rain, some governments have passed laws restricting the emitting of sulfur dioxide and nitrogen dioxide, and many people are making an effort to reduce their usage of electricity and motor transportation. ■ Yet they are fighting an uphill battle since more coal-fired electric plants and automobiles are constantly being built. ■ Perhaps only when acid rain is definitively linked to human health problems will more people take an interest in it.

Glossary
pH scale: a scale that determines how acidic or how much of a base a substance is
core: a center
marsh: a bog; a swamp-like area

14. **Directions:** An introductory sentence for a brief summary of the passage is provided below. Complete the summary by selecting the THREE answer choices that express the most important ideas of the passage. Some sentences do not belong because they express ideas that are not presented in the passage or are minor ideas in the passage. *This question is worth 2 points.*

Acid rain may occur for both natural and manmade reasons, but, no matter what its cause, it results in a great amount of damage wherever it falls.

-
-
-

Answer Choices

(A) Scientists are able to use modern methods to determine how acidic the rain that fell in the past used to be.

(B) Acid rain that falls on bodies of water such as lakes often kills the fish and other animal life that are living in them.

(C) Some people have reported suffering from ill health when they have been exposed to acid rain falling from the sky.

(D) Scientists use the pH scale to measure how acidic or base something is so that they can determine how contaminated the substance is.

(E) Two hundred years of industrialization has caused an increase in the amount of acid rain, especially because of the burning of coal.

(F) It is possible for erupting volcanoes to spew enough sulfur dioxide into the air to cause acid rain to fall.

Drag your answer choices to the spaces where they belong.
To remove an answer choice, click on it. To review the passage, click on **View Text**.

Listening
Section Directions

This section measures your ability to understand conversations and lectures in English.

In this part, you will listen to 1 conversation and 1 lecture. You will hear the conversation or lecture only **one** time. After the conversation or lecture, you will answer some questions about it. The questions typically ask about the main idea and supporting details. Some questions ask about a speaker's purpose or attitude. Answer the questions based on what is stated or implied by the speakers.

You may take notes while you listen. You may use your notes to help you answer the questions. Your notes will **not** be scored.

If you need to change the volume while you listen, click on the **Volume** icon at the top of the screen.

In some questions, you will see this icon: 🎧 This means that you will hear, but not see, part of the question.

Some of the questions have special directions. These directions appear in a gray box on the screen.

Most questions are worth one point. If a question is worth more than one point, it will have special directions that indicate how many points you can receive.

You must answer each question. After you answer, click on **Next**. Then click on **OK** to confirm your answer and go on to the next question. After you click on **OK**, you cannot return to previous questions.

A clock at the top of the screen will show you how much time is remaining. The clock will not count down while you are listening. The clock will count down only while you are answering the questions.

Now you may begin the Listening section.

TOEFL iBT Listening

Conversation 1~5: Listen to part of a conversation between a student and a professor.

Actual Test 04

TOEFL iBT Listening

1. Why does the student visit the professor?
   - Ⓐ To request some more time to finish a project
   - Ⓑ To submit the paper that she has been writing
   - Ⓒ To propose a new topic for her research paper
   - Ⓓ To describe an interview that she just conducted

2. Who is the man that the student would like to interview?
   - Ⓐ Her professor
   - Ⓑ One of her family friends
   - Ⓒ A relative of her roommate
   - Ⓓ A person she met on a field trip

3. What is the professor's attitude toward the student?
   - Ⓐ He is considerate of her request.
   - Ⓑ He fails to understand her concerns.
   - Ⓒ He dismisses the request she makes.
   - Ⓓ He assists her in developing her plan.

4. Why does the student mention the Freedom Riders?
   - Ⓐ She is interested in conducting more research on them.
   - Ⓑ She wants to interview one of them for her paper.
   - Ⓒ She feels that they had an important role in history.
   - Ⓓ She mentions that she is related to one of them.

5. Listen again to a part of the conversation. Then answer the question.

   What does the professor imply when he says this?
   - Ⓐ He feels like the student has already let him down.
   - Ⓑ The student is going to receive the highest grade in the class.
   - Ⓒ The student's paper should be better than most other students'.
   - Ⓓ He does not appreciate the student making a request so late.

Lecture 6~11: Listen to part of a lecture in a history class.

6. Who was von Tirpitz?
   - Ⓐ The leader of Germany
   - Ⓑ The head of the German navy
   - Ⓒ The German ambassador to England
   - Ⓓ A German shipbuilder

7. How is the discussion organized?
   - Ⓐ By listing some theories on German naval expansion and then considering them
   - Ⓑ By analyzing historical events solely from the point of view of the English
   - Ⓒ By discussing the events leading to World War I in chronological order
   - Ⓓ By considering the postwar aspects of the tremendous naval buildup

8. Based on the information in the lecture, do the following sentences refer to the Germans or the English?

   Click in the correct box for each sentence.

	Germans	English
Ⓐ They sank their own ships at the end of World War I.		
Ⓑ They had Europe's most dominant navy.		
Ⓒ Originally, they had a navy primarily for coastal defense.		
Ⓓ They introduced a new class of naval ship.		

9. Listen again to a part of the lecture. Then answer the question.

   Why does the professor say this?
   - Ⓐ To indicate that he will answer his own question
   - Ⓑ To ask the students for some suggestions
   - Ⓒ To imply that the answer to his question is obvious
   - Ⓓ To let the students know they need to take notes

10. Listen again to a part of the lecture. Then answer the question.

    What does the professor mean when he says this?
    - Ⓐ The English had no choice but to fight the Germans.
    - Ⓑ He wants the student to ask him another question.
    - Ⓒ The Germans had numerous problems at that time.
    - Ⓓ The student should understand what he means.

11. Listen again to a part of the lecture. Then answer the question.

    What does the professor imply when he says this?
    - Ⓐ The English frequently lost naval battles.
    - Ⓑ The English had an inferior army.
    - Ⓒ The skills of English admirals were lacking.
    - Ⓓ The English felt they could defeat the German navy.

Actual Test
05

TOEFL iBT Reading

Reading
Section Directions

This section measures your ability to understand academic passages in English.

In this part, you will read 1 passage and answer reading comprehension questions about the passage. Most questions are worth one point, but the last question is worth more than one point. The directions indicate how many points you may receive.

Some passages include a word or phrase that is underlined in blue. Click on the word or phrase to see a definition or an explanation.

When you want to move on to the next question, click on **Next**. You may skip questions and go back to them later. If you want to return to previous questions, click on **Back**. You can click on **Review** at any time and the review screen will show you which questions you have answered and which you have not answered. From this review screen, you may go directly to any question you have already seen in the Reading section.

You may now begin the Reading section. You will read 1 reading passage. You will have **20 minutes** to read the passage and answer the questions.

Click on **Continue** to go on.

TOEFL iBT Reading

1. The word premise in the passage is closest in meaning to
   - Ⓐ experiment
   - Ⓑ notion
   - Ⓒ sensation
   - Ⓓ phenomenon

2. Which of the sentences below best expresses the essential information in the highlighted sentence in the passage? *Incorrect* answer choices change the meaning in important ways or leave out essential information.
   - Ⓐ Most astronomers believe that the universe had a beginning so will also end in the future.
   - Ⓑ When the universe finally ends, it will have lasted for a finite, yet very long, period of time.
   - Ⓒ While the universe is known to have begun, no one knows if it will ever come to an end.
   - Ⓓ Because all things have a beginning, logic dictates that they must also have an ending.

3. The word ascertained in the passage is closest in meaning to
   - Ⓐ estimated
   - Ⓑ forecast
   - Ⓒ determined
   - Ⓓ questioned

4. Why does the author mention Edwin Hubble?
   - Ⓐ To claim that he was the first person to propose the Big Bang theory
   - Ⓑ To compare his work with that done on cosmic microwave background radiation
   - Ⓒ To explain his contribution to confirming the Big Bang theory
   - Ⓓ To describe him as an important astronomer from the twentieth century

The Creation and Destruction of the Universe

The universe has numerous mysteries, one of which is the nature of its creation. Astronomers have proposed several theories, with the Big Bang theory being the most accepted. It is based on the premise that the universe was created by the explosion of matter from a central point. The belief that the universe had a beginning suggests that it will also have an end, so many scientists think that the universe will cease to exist sometime in the distant future. Astronomers have proposed two major theories concerning this: the Big Crunch theory and the Big Freeze theory.

The Big Bang theory claims that, approximately fifteen billion years ago, a small, infinitely dense point of matter exploded and expanded, which created the universe. Why and how this matter came into existence and exploded, and what existed prior to the Big Bang, are unknown. The theory merely explains the reason for the existence of the universe as well as its history since its creation and subsequent expansion. Evidence for the Big Bang comes from several sources. In the 1920s, American astronomer Edwin Hubble ascertained that faraway galaxies are moving away from Earth. His observations also showed that the more distant galaxies were moving at faster rates. This suggested that the universe itself was expanding from a central point. Years later, in the 1960s, measurements of cosmic microwave background radiation proved that the universe was once hotter than it was at the present and that this cooling was one result of its expansion. Further evidence, which was discovered by powerful modern telescopes, has helped solidify the Big Bang theory as the most widely accepted one concerning the formation of the universe.

It is unknown how large the universe currently is or how big it will ultimately become. Yet there are several competing theories concerning how

5. The author's description of the Big Bang theory mentions all of the following EXCEPT:
   Ⓐ It is widely believed by most astronomers to be correct.
   Ⓑ Telescopes have been used to provide information concerning its validity.
   Ⓒ It has determined precisely when the universe was created.
   Ⓓ Some of the earliest evidence for it was provided by Edwin Hubble.

6. According to paragraph 3, few astronomers believe in the Big Crunch theory today because
   Ⓐ the evidence for the Big Bang theory directly contradicts it
   Ⓑ it is known that the universe's rate of expansion is accelerating
   Ⓒ there is no way to prove that this theory has any basis in reality
   Ⓓ astronomers know that the universe does not oscillate

7. The word exhaust in the passage is closest in meaning to
   Ⓐ recycle
   Ⓑ expend
   Ⓒ expel
   Ⓓ amplify

8. The word infinite in the passage is closest in meaning to
   Ⓐ legendary
   Ⓑ requisite
   Ⓒ profuse
   Ⓓ eternal

it will end. The Big Crunch theory is based on the idea that gravity is so powerful that it is slowing the expansion of the universe. Eventually, the universe will cease expanding and will then begin contracting toward the central point from which it began. Then, every bit of matter will "crunch" back together, thereby destroying the universe. Some believers in this theory suggest that perhaps another Big Bang would create a new universe following the Big Crunch, which would, in effect, result in an oscillating universe. However, there have been few adherents to the Big Crunch theory ever since the discovery in the 1990s that the universe is accelerating away from Earth at increasingly faster rates.

That fact led to astronomers proposing what is a more likely scenario for the end of the universe: the Big Freeze theory. According to it, as the universe expands, it will eventually cool to the point where temperatures will be too low to sustain any kind of life. Galaxies will merge in collisions and form galaxy clusters. As the universe continues expanding, these clusters will become so distant that it will become impossible to observe other clusters. Over billions of years, stars will exhaust their fuel and die. As that happens, the planets around the stars will die, too, and this matter will all subsequently be sucked into the black holes that are found at the center of every galaxy. Approximately 100 trillion years from now, new star formation will cease, and the light from the stars will disappear. After hundreds of trillions of more years, the black holes themselves will vanish, and the basic building blocks of the universe—atoms and their protons, neutrons, and electrons—will fall apart and never join together again. Astronomers call this the Dark Era, and they speculate that it will last for an infinite amount of time.

Some astronomers, however, theorize that the universe could possibly recover from the Dark Era. Perhaps, they claim, there might be a new

TOEFL iBT Reading

9. Why does the author mention protons, neutrons, and electrons?

   Ⓐ To describe what the universe is ultimately made up of
   Ⓑ To name the basic components of an atom
   Ⓒ To state that they comprise all forms of matter
   Ⓓ To explain why they sometimes do not combine with one another

10. The author's description of the Big Freeze theory mentions which of the following?

    Ⓐ It will ultimately result in there being a single galaxy in the universe.
    Ⓑ It is a plausible explanation for how the universe will cease to exist.
    Ⓒ It states that the universe will disappear after 100 trillion years.
    Ⓓ By the time the universe ends, only black holes will exist.

11. According to paragraph 4, which of the following is true of the Dark Era?

    Ⓐ Astronomers predict it will begin in a few billion years.
    Ⓑ It is a major component of the Big Crush theory.
    Ⓒ Its occurrence will mark the end of the universe.
    Ⓓ Galaxy clusters will be formed during this time.

12. The word them in the passage refers to

    Ⓐ the scientists
    Ⓑ any theories
    Ⓒ dark energy and dark matter
    Ⓓ their theories

Big Bang. As of yet, the scientists involved in this research are careful not to commit themselves to any theories until further research has been conducted. Much remains unknown about the universe, and more research into two areas—dark energy and dark matter—may cause them to rethink their theories at some point in time. What astronomers do agree on, for the most part, is that, no matter how it happens, the universe will have an end.

Glossary
cosmic: relating to the cosmos or the universe
contract: to become smaller; to shorten
oscillate: to move back and forth

13. In paragraph 5, the author of the passage implies that astronomers

    Ⓐ are wasting their time thinking about the end of the universe
    Ⓑ need to learn more about the solar system before they discuss the universe's end
    Ⓒ should look to the center of the Milky Way Galaxy to find answers to their questions
    Ⓓ are not confident in the validity of their theories on the end of the universe

14. **Directions:** An introductory sentence for a brief summary of the passage is provided below. Complete the summary by selecting the THREE answer choices that express the most important ideas of the passage. Some sentences do not belong because they express ideas that are not presented in the passage or are minor ideas in the passage. *This question is worth 2 points.*

    Astronomers have come up with one legitimate theory that explains the beginning of the universe and widely accept another theory that explains how it will possibly end.

    -
    -
    -

    Answer Choices

    Ⓐ The majority of astronomers believe that the Big Freeze theory is a plausible explanation for the end of the universe.

    Ⓑ There are black holes in the center of every galaxy in the universe, and they act to keep galaxies from becoming too big.

    Ⓒ In all likelihood, the end of the universe will take place billions or trillions of years in the future.

    Ⓓ There is much evidence that supports the Big Bang theory as being the manner in which the universe was formed.

    Ⓔ The Big Crunch theory is no longer considered possible because astronomers know the universe is still expanding.

    Ⓕ According to the Big Freeze theory, the time when the universe will come to its end will be known as the Dark Era.

    Drag your answer choices to the spaces where they belong.
    To remove an answer choice, click on it. To review the passage, click on **View Text**.

Listening
Section Directions

This section measures your ability to understand conversations and lectures in English.

In this part, you will listen to 1 conversation and 1 lecture. You will hear the conversation or lecture only **one** time. After the conversation or lecture, you will answer some questions about it. The questions typically ask about the main idea and supporting details. Some questions ask about a speaker's purpose or attitude. Answer the questions based on what is stated or implied by the speakers.

You may take notes while you listen. You may use your notes to help you answer the questions. Your notes will **not** be scored.

If you need to change the volume while you listen, click on the **Volume** icon at the top of the screen.

In some questions, you will see this icon: 🎧 This means that you will hear, but not see, part of the question.

Some of the questions have special directions. These directions appear in a gray box on the screen.

Most questions are worth one point. If a question is worth more than one point, it will have special directions that indicate how many points you can receive.

You must answer each question. After you answer, click on **Next**. Then click on **OK** to confirm your answer and go on to the next question. After you click on **OK**, you cannot return to previous questions.

A clock at the top of the screen will show you how much time is remaining. The clock will not count down while you are listening. The clock will count down only while you are answering the questions.

Now you may begin the Listening section.

TOEFL iBT Listening

Conversation 1~5: Listen to part of a conversation between a student and a librarian.

Actual Test 05

TOEFL iBT Listening

1. What are the speakers mainly discussing?
   - (A) Some library fines the student has not paid
   - (B) The due date on some books the student has checked out
   - (C) Some reserve books that the student is using
   - (D) The library's policy on renewing books

2. Why does the librarian visit the student?
   - (A) To get some books back from him
   - (B) To collect the money that he owes
   - (C) To ask him to be more quiet
   - (D) To tell him some students are looking for him

3. According to the librarian, how can the student manage to borrow reserve books overnight?
   - (A) He needs to have written permission from his professor.
   - (B) He must request a special form and then fill it out completely.
   - (C) His professor must accompany him to the reserve desk.
   - (D) Reserve books may not be borrowed overnight under any circumstances.

4. What will the student probably do next?
   - (A) Check out some other books
   - (B) Continue asking questions
   - (C) Give the woman the books
   - (D) Depart the library

5. Listen again to a part of the conversation. Then answer the question.

   What does the student imply when he says this?
   - (A) He often borrows books from the school library.
   - (B) He dislikes some of the library's policies.
   - (C) He has had to pay some library fines recently.
   - (D) He wants the library to stop sending him notices.

Lecture 6~11: Listen to part of a lecture in a health and nutrition class.

Health and Nutrition

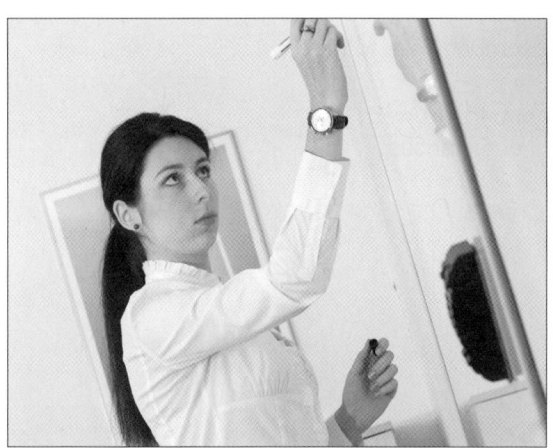

Actual Test 05

TOEFL iBT Listening

6. What is the main topic of the lecture?
   - (A) The work that Louis Pasteur did in his lifetime
   - (B) The various methods of pasteurization
   - (C) The products that need to have bacteria eliminated
   - (D) The costs involved in pasteurizing food products

7. Why does the professor explain the batch method?
   - (A) To compare it with another pasteurization method
   - (B) To name the ideal method of pasteurizing milk
   - (C) To explain how it is different from cold pasteurization
   - (D) To note that it makes use of the HTST method

8. According to the professor, what did Louis Pasteur do in his lifetime?
   - (A) He discovered the source of rabies.
   - (B) He became the first person to kill bacteria in milk.
   - (C) He collaborated with German scientists on experiments.
   - (D) He learned how to keep wine from spoiling.

9. What is UHT pasteurization?
   - (A) A method that uses extreme heat to purify milk
   - (B) A method that gives milk a shelf life of three weeks
   - (C) A method that was invented by the Germans
   - (D) A method that exposes milk to heat for around half a minute

10. Based on the information in the lecture, do the following sentences refer to the batch method or the continuous method?

    Click in the correct box for each sentence.

	The Batch Method	The Continuous Method
(A) It subjects milk to constant temperatures.		
(B) It is the more commonly used method today.		
(C) It puts milk in a vat surrounded by pipes.		
(D) It requires the constant shaking of the milk.		

11. Listen again to a part of the lecture. Then answer the question.

    What does the professor mean when she says this?
    - (A) She wants to take a break.
    - (B) What she is discussing is uninteresting.
    - (C) The class is almost over.
    - (D) She enjoys this particular topic.

Actual Test 06

TOEFL iBT Reading

Reading
Section Directions

This section measures your ability to understand academic passages in English.

In this part, you will read 1 passage and answer reading comprehension questions about the passage. Most questions are worth one point, but the last question is worth more than one point. The directions indicate how many points you may receive.

Some passages include a word or phrase that is underlined in blue. Click on the word or phrase to see a definition or an explanation.

When you want to move on to the next question, click on **Next**. You may skip questions and go back to them later. If you want to return to previous questions, click on **Back**. You can click on **Review** at any time and the review screen will show you which questions you have answered and which you have not answered. From this review screen, you may go directly to any question you have already seen in the Reading section.

You may now begin the Reading section. You will read 1 reading passage. You will have **20 minutes** to read the passage and answer the questions.

Click on **Continue** to go on.

1. The word them in the passage refers to
    - Ⓐ direct teaching, cooperative learning, and lecturing
    - Ⓑ teachers
    - Ⓒ different methods
    - Ⓓ factors

2. The word virtually in the passage is closest in meaning to
    - Ⓐ realistically
    - Ⓑ considerably
    - Ⓒ completely
    - Ⓓ practically

3. According to paragraph 2, which of the following is true of direct teaching?
    - Ⓐ It requires the teacher to speak during the entire class.
    - Ⓑ It lets students demonstrate whether they understand the teacher's instructions.
    - Ⓒ It is utilized only by teachers in mathematics and the sciences.
    - Ⓓ It makes students go back and review information they have previously learned.

4. The author's description of the disadvantages of direct teaching mentions which of the following?
    - Ⓐ Teachers do not get a lot of personal contact with their students.
    - Ⓑ Instructors must have an advanced amount of knowledge in their subjects.
    - Ⓒ Students get the opportunity to show how creative they can be in class.
    - Ⓓ There is a lot of preparation involved in every one of the teacher's lessons.

5. The word detriment in the passage is closest in meaning to
    - Ⓐ relief
    - Ⓑ harm
    - Ⓒ education
    - Ⓓ benefit

Teaching Methods

The goal of all students attending school is to learn, and the responsibility of imparting knowledge upon them rests with their teachers. They use a variety of methods to ensure that their students understand their lessons. While there are many teaching methods, three of the most common ones are direct teaching, cooperative learning, and lecturing. Teachers often employ different methods depending upon a number of factors. Included among them are the type of school at which they are teaching, the age of their students, and the purposes of the individual lessons they are giving.

Direct teaching involves the instructor explaining things to the students, who follow along as the instructor teaches. The teacher explains something step by step, the students listen, and then the students are given the opportunity to work on their own. This method is typically utilized in science and mathematics classes. For example, an instructor may explain how to solve a certain type of math problem. The teacher explains the method, demonstrates it by solving several problems, answers any questions if the students have difficulty understanding, and then gives the students an assignment to test the skills they have just learned. One advantage of direct teaching is that it is useful for all grade levels. In addition, it is usually taught with a specific objective in mind, it is easy to judge students' progress with this method, and it is a widely accepted way to teach basic skills. As for disadvantages, the teacher must often prepare a lot for the lesson and must have good oral skills, especially the ability to provide clear explanations. And this method offers virtually no room for creativity on the part of the teacher or the students.

Cooperative learning takes place when students work together in groups to do a project or class assignment. The teacher is less involved in this method in comparison to group learning. Typically,

6. The author's description of cooperative learning mentions which of the following?

    Ⓐ There is less of a role for the teacher in comparison to direct teaching.
    Ⓑ Students who enjoy being by themselves thrive with this teaching method.
    Ⓒ Students typically all receive the same grade when doing a group project.
    Ⓓ The teacher selects a group leader to act in a supervisory role.

7. The word augment in the passage is closest in meaning to

    Ⓐ supplement
    Ⓑ organize
    Ⓒ review
    Ⓓ present

8. The word elicit in the passage is closest in meaning to

    Ⓐ demand
    Ⓑ require
    Ⓒ obtain
    Ⓓ ascertain

9. In paragraph 4, why does the author mention audiovisual equipment?

    Ⓐ To note that it can be used in support of a lecture
    Ⓑ To discuss the ways in which teachers utilize it
    Ⓒ To prove that using it in class is uncomplicated
    Ⓓ To show why students like when teachers use it

the teacher provides the basics of the assignment and then organizes the students into groups. The teacher then moves from group to group to offer advice and explanations, to settle disputes, and to act in a supervisory role. This method gives students the opportunity to express their creative sides, and it lets them learn social skills such as interacting within groups. Students in groups have to learn to get along well and to listen to others' points of view in order to accomplish their objective. However, this method is unsuitable for loners or shy individuals, and aggressive or highly intelligent students may wind up dominating their groups to the detriment of the other members.

Lectures are the most common in high schools and universities. For them, the teachers must be well prepared and knowledgeable in their subjects. Lectures usually involve the teachers standing in front of their students and explaining various topics at length. Some teachers may use audiovisual equipment to augment their lectures. The students listen, take notes, and ask questions when the material is unclear. Lectures are more common in the arts and humanities than in the sciences. Still, they may be given in practically any type of class, particularly at the university level. Unfortunately, lectures are mostly one sided as the teachers speak while the students listen. Sometimes, lectures may develop into discussions on a topic during which the teachers asks questions to elicit responses from the students. In more advanced university classes, lectures may be dispensed with entirely in favor of seminars. In these classes, students often present papers, which are then the objects of discussion among the students, and the professor acts as a moderator and final authority on the subject being discussed.

While direct teaching and lectures may be somewhat boring to many students, they are necessary methods. Direct teaching enables teachers at all levels to impart knowledge,

10. The author's description of lectures mentions all of the following EXCEPT:

    A. In some instances, students are expected to contribute to these classes.
    B. They may involve the teachers using AV equipment to enhance their lectures.
    C. They are traditionally used more in the sciences than in the humanities.
    D. They are most commonly utilized at the university level.

11. The author of the passage implies that seminar classes

    A. hardly need to have professors in order to be conducted
    B. require students to have a high amount of knowledge on a topic
    C. are open only to students who are majoring in the subject that the class is on
    D. only permit a small number of students to be enrolled in each class

12. Which of the following can be inferred from paragraph 5 about cooperative learning?

    A. It requires a great amount of effort and preparation by the teacher.
    B. Teachers do not make use of it on the first day of class.
    C. It is the least popular method among students and teachers.
    D. It can be highly effective in large introductory-level university classes.

especially to young students, who have shorter attention spans and need more control and supervision. And lectures are still rather common at universities and are often the only practical teaching method in classes with large numbers of students. As for cooperative learning, it works better when the teacher knows his or her students well enough to make groups that will get along and work well together. Ultimately, no matter which method is used, the goal is always for the students to learn.

Glossary

demonstrate: to show by giving an example
supervisory: managerial; relating to some kind of leadership position
impart: to pass on

Actual Test 06

TOEFL iBT Reading

13. **Directions:** Select the appropriate sentences from the answer choices and match them to the teaching method to which they relate. TWO of the answer choices will NOT be used. *This question is worth 3 points.*

Direct Learning
(Select 3)

-
-
-

Lecture
(Select 2)

-
-

Answer Choices

(A) It typically utilizes group learning methods during class.

(B) It can be used to great benefit in math classes.

(C) It is frequently used in high schools and universities.

(D) It may require students to ask questions to get clear explanations.

(E) It is best when the students and teacher are comfortable with one another.

(F) It involves step-by-step explanations of various processes.

(G) It has an objective to be met in each class.

Drag your answer choices to the spaces where they belong.
To remove an answer choice, click on it. To review the passage, click on **View Text**.

Listening
Section Directions

This section measures your ability to understand conversations and lectures in English.

In this part, you will listen to 1 conversation and 1 lecture. You will hear the conversation or lecture only **one** time. After the conversation or lecture, you will answer some questions about it. The questions typically ask about the main idea and supporting details. Some questions ask about a speaker's purpose or attitude. Answer the questions based on what is stated or implied by the speakers.

You may take notes while you listen. You may use your notes to help you answer the questions. Your notes will **not** be scored.

If you need to change the volume while you listen, click on the **Volume** icon at the top of the screen.

In some questions, you will see this icon: 🎧 This means that you will hear, but not see, part of the question.

Some of the questions have special directions. These directions appear in a gray box on the screen.

Most questions are worth one point. If a question is worth more than one point, it will have special directions that indicate how many points you can receive.

You must answer each question. After you answer, click on **Next**. Then click on **OK** to confirm your answer and go on to the next question. After you click on **OK**, you cannot return to previous questions.

A clock at the top of the screen will show you how much time is remaining. The clock will not count down while you are listening. The clock will count down only while you are answering the questions.

Now you may begin the Listening section.

TOEFL iBT Listening

Conversation 1~5: Listen to part of a conversation between a student and a professor.

Actual Test 06

TOEFL iBT Listening

1. What problem does the student have?
   - Ⓐ He is doing poorly in the professor's class.
   - Ⓑ He is having trouble writing a paper.
   - Ⓒ He cannot come up with a topic for his term paper.
   - Ⓓ He does not understand some of the class material.

2. Why does the professor explain about the class assignment?
   - Ⓐ To explain why the student needs to try harder in class
   - Ⓑ To compliment the student for the topic that he has selected
   - Ⓒ To tell the student that he is taking the wrong approach
   - Ⓓ To recommend that the student conduct more research for it

3. What is the student's attitude toward the professor?
   - Ⓐ He is polite and respectful.
   - Ⓑ He is a little overbearing.
   - Ⓒ He interrupts the professor at times.
   - Ⓓ He disregards some of the professor's comments.

4. Listen again to a part of the conversation. Then answer the question.

   What does the professor imply when he says this?
   - Ⓐ Students need to work hard to get good grades in his class.
   - Ⓑ The student will probably not be able to get a passing grade.
   - Ⓒ The student's study habits are not conducive to him getting a good grade.
   - Ⓓ He only gives a small percentage of A's to his students.

5. Listen again to a part of the conversation. Then answer the question.

   What does the professor imply when he says this?
   - Ⓐ He is willing to let the student turn in the first assignment a little late.
   - Ⓑ He thinks that his students are unable to come up with topics of their own.
   - Ⓒ He expects some of his students to come to him for assistance.
   - Ⓓ He wants the student to conduct a large amount of independent research.

Lecture 6~11: Listen to part of a lecture in a physics class.

Physics

Actual Test 06

TOEFL iBT Listening

6. What aspect of sound does the professor mainly discuss?

   A. Chuck Yeager's relationship with it
   B. Its speed in relation with that of light
   C. The sound barrier
   D. The speed at which it travels

7. Why does the professor explain the history of breaking the sound barrier?

   A. To credit Chuck Yeager for accomplishing that feat
   B. To show that it was possible for humans to do
   C. To describe the technical aspects of the Bell X-1
   D. To explain a turning point in human history

8. What is mach?

   A. The altitude at which an object is moving
   B. Slightly more than 1,000 kilometers per hour
   C. How fast an object moves in a fluid
   D. The noise sound makes as it moves

9. What does the professor imply about airplanes?

   A. They will continue to increase the speed at which they can travel.
   B. It is difficult to make them fast enough to exceed the speed of sound.
   C. Only the most technologically advanced ones can break the sound barrier.
   D. Special materials are required to make planes that can go faster than sound.

10. Listen again to a part of the lecture. Then answer the question.

    Why does the professor say this?

    A. To make a humorous comment
    B. To recommend the students read science fiction
    C. To compliment the genre on its realism
    D. To answer a student's inquiry

11. Listen again to a part of the lecture. Then answer the question.

    What does the professor mean when she says this?

    A. The students should already know that information.
    B. She cannot remember all of the details.
    C. She has just made an important point.
    D. They will continue discussing Mach throughout the class.

Actual Test 07

TOEFL iBT Reading

Reading
Section Directions

This section measures your ability to understand academic passages in English.

In this part, you will read 1 passage and answer reading comprehension questions about the passage. Most questions are worth one point, but the last question is worth more than one point. The directions indicate how many points you may receive.

Some passages include a word or phrase that is underlined in blue. Click on the word or phrase to see a definition or an explanation.

When you want to move on to the next question, click on **Next**. You may skip questions and go back to them later. If you want to return to previous questions, click on **Back**. You can click on **Review** at any time and the review screen will show you which questions you have answered and which you have not answered. From this review screen, you may go directly to any question you have already seen in the Reading section.

You may now begin the Reading section. You will read 1 reading passage. You will have **20 minutes** to read the passage and answer the questions.

Click on **Continue** to go on.

1. The word them in the passage refers to
   - (A) these groups
   - (B) a dozen members
   - (C) mammals
   - (D) practical and social reasons

2. The word propagation in the passage is closest in meaning to
   - (A) evolution
   - (B) response
   - (C) safety
   - (D) reproduction

3. According to paragraph 1, which of the following is true of mammals?
   - (A) They always engage in pack behavior whenever they travel.
   - (B) Their tendency to travel in groups helps protect some of them.
   - (C) Small herds of animals are more common than large groups of thousands.
   - (D) By grouping together, prey animals can avoid being hunted by predators.

4. The author discusses prairie dogs in paragraph 2 in order to
   - (A) show how they use group behavior to protect themselves
   - (B) describe the geographical areas that they typically inhabit
   - (C) mention some of the animals that they must be wary of
   - (D) compare their method of evading predators with that of other prey animals

5. The author of the passage implies that prairie dogs
   - (A) reproduce at a fairly rapid rate
   - (B) have a large number of predators
   - (C) are found in prairies throughout the world
   - (D) have no innate defenses of their own

Mammal Groups

Many mammals travel together in groups that are called a variety of names, including herds, prides, and packs. These groups may have fewer than a dozen members or may number in the thousands. Mammals engage in group behavior for both practical and social reasons. Among them are the protections afforded to prey animals and the hunting opportunities they present for predators. Additionally, group behavior helps ensure the propagation of the species, which thereby enables animals to pass their genes on to the next generation.

Prey mammals are those animals that predators hunt for food. To increase their chances of survival, many live in large groups. These enable the mammals to have increased warning time when a predator approaches. With more eyes scanning for danger, prey animals in groups have a better opportunity to detect predators before they attack, and thus they are able to escape with their lives intact. Prairie dogs are one such animal that lives in large groups. Individual prairie dogs are constantly scanning the land for foxes, wolves, and other predators and also watch the sky for hawks and eagles. When one of them detects incoming, or even potential, danger, it alerts the others in its group, so they can all make their escape. Large mammals in Africa—wildebeests, zebras, and antelopes, for instance—also travel in large herds to protect themselves. While predators manage to kill some of them, those that fall victim are typically the weakest and slowest members of the herd.

Predators also live in groups, but their associations are typically smaller than those of prey animals. A herd of some prey mammals may consist of thousands of animals, yet most predator groups have fewer than thirty members. ■ Studies on lion prides in Africa have shown that they usually have one to three males, three to six females, and a small number of cubs. ■

6. According to paragraph 2, which of the following is NOT true of large mammals in Africa?
   Ⓐ They migrate to locations throughout Africa in groups of thousands.
   Ⓑ Predators sometimes succeed in killing them when they are in herds.
   Ⓒ They live together with one another to be more protected.
   Ⓓ The weakest members of the group are susceptible to predators.

7. The word territorial in the passage is closest in meaning to
   Ⓐ obstructive
   Ⓑ violent
   Ⓒ protective
   Ⓓ unapproachable

8. The author's description of lion prides in paragraph 3 mentions which of the following?
   Ⓐ Male lions in them take a role in the raising of the cubs.
   Ⓑ There are more males than females in them.
   Ⓒ They may have as many as twenty-five members.
   Ⓓ Both genders are represented within them.

9. According to paragraph 4, wolves combine to attack larger prey because
   Ⓐ it makes killing the animals much easier for them
   Ⓑ the animals they attack usually have horns or sharp claws
   Ⓒ they are trying to feed every member of the pack
   Ⓓ only large prey animals live in their hunting grounds

Research on wolf packs in Yellowstone National Park in the United States has provided evidence that most packs average between four and ten members while the largest pack had twenty-five wolves. ■ The main reason for these small numbers is the food supply. ■ Predator groups mark out a territory in which they hunt. Their territory and the available food supply limit the size of the group. For this reason, most predator groups are fiercely territorial and will attack any rival member of their own species that strays into an area belonging to them.

The principal reason that predators form groups is to increase their odds of a successful hunt. Having larger numbers enables predators more easily to surround, attack, and then bring down a prey animal, particularly if it is a fairly large one. In Africa, it is not uncommon to see lions, hyenas, or leopards working in tandem to kill a large mammal. Likewise, wolves have been observed surrounding buffalo, elk, and deer—all much larger creatures than the average wolf—and nipping at the animals' legs until they are so weakened that the wolves can drag them down and kill them. The most obvious drawback to hunting in groups is that the kill must be shared by all of the hunters. As a result, large groups must constantly hunt and make kills lest some of their members starve.

Mammals also live together for purposes other than defense and hunting. Many mammal groups are family units. Of course, all of the animals in herds of thousands of animals will not be related to one another. However, in small groups of mammals—both predators and prey—the members often share the same genes. As a result, some groups eventually merge with one another to reproduce. In other cases, the urge to reproduce may cause some groups to break up. For instance, many wolf packs begin with a single pair of mating wolves that eventually become large families. After the pack reaches a certain size, some wolves depart, both to find

10. The word merge in the passage is closest in meaning to
    - (A) unite
    - (B) agree
    - (C) coincide
    - (D) collide

11. According to paragraph 5, some wolves leave their pack because
    - (A) there is not enough food for them to eat
    - (B) the leader of the pack drives them away
    - (C) they are in search of other wolves to reproduce with
    - (D) all of the wolves in the pack are related to one another

12. Look at the four squares [■] that indicate where the following sentence could be added to the passage.

    This large group was considered abnormal though since most packs were much smaller in size.

    Where would the sentence best fit?

    Click on a square [■] to add the sentence to the passage.

new territory to hunt in and to find mates of their own. As for lions, the females only ovulate for a short time, so it is imperative that both males and females travel together in groups so that they may eventually bear cubs. So, by living and traveling in groups, both prey animals and predators can increase their chances of reproducing and thus enable their species to survive.

Glossary
scan: to look over something quickly
wildebeest: a gnu; a large mammal that lives on the plains of Africa
ovulate: to produce eggs from the ovary; to be fertile and able to become pregnant

13. **Directions:** Select the appropriate sentences from the answer choices and match them to the reason some animals live together to which they relate. TWO of the answer choices will NOT be used. *This question is worth 3 points.*

Protection
(Select 3)
-
-
-

Reproduction
(Select 2)
-
-

Answer Choices

(A) It enables animals to bring down their victims more easily.

(B) It provides mammals with an opportunity to escape from attackers.

(C) It sometimes obligates wolves to form their own packs.

(D) It is the reason that many elk live together.

(E) It is not always successful at keeping some members alive.

(F) It lets prairie dogs warn one another of imminent danger.

(G) It requires male and female lions to live together.

Drag your answer choices to the spaces where they belong.
To remove an answer choice, click on it. To review the passage, click on **View Text**.

TOEFL iBT Listening

Listening
Section Directions

This section measures your ability to understand conversations and lectures in English.

In this part, you will listen to 1 conversation and 1 lecture. You will hear the conversation or lecture only **one** time. After the conversation or lecture, you will answer some questions about it. The questions typically ask about the main idea and supporting details. Some questions ask about a speaker's purpose or attitude. Answer the questions based on what is stated or implied by the speakers.

You may take notes while you listen. You may use your notes to help you answer the questions. Your notes will **not** be scored.

If you need to change the volume while you listen, click on the **Volume** icon at the top of the screen.

In some questions, you will see this icon: 🎧 This means that you will hear, but not see, part of the question.

Some of the questions have special directions. These directions appear in a gray box on the screen.

Most questions are worth one point. If a question is worth more than one point, it will have special directions that indicate how many points you can receive.

You must answer each question. After you answer, click on **Next**. Then click on **OK** to confirm your answer and go on to the next question. After you click on **OK**, you cannot return to previous questions.

A clock at the top of the screen will show you how much time is remaining. The clock will not count down while you are listening. The clock will count down only while you are answering the questions.

Now you may begin the Listening section.

Conversation 1~5: Listen to part of a conversation between a student and a Registrar's Office employee.

Actual Test 07

TOEFL iBT Listening

1. Why does the student visit the Registrar's Office?
   - Ⓐ To complain about a wrong grade on his transcript
   - Ⓑ To apply to take an extra class for the semester
   - Ⓒ To pay a bill for school so that he can graduate
   - Ⓓ To request some copies of his transcripts

2. According to the woman, what does the man need to do first?
   - Ⓐ Take a number and wait
   - Ⓑ Complete a form
   - Ⓒ Pay some money
   - Ⓓ Show her his ID card

3. What can be inferred about the woman?
   - Ⓐ She recently started working in the Registrar's Office.
   - Ⓑ She has spoken with the man previously.
   - Ⓒ She understands why the man is worried about his problem.
   - Ⓓ She treats people the way they treat her.

4. Why does the woman mention that she can mail the transcripts for the man?
   - Ⓐ To let him know about a possible option
   - Ⓑ To help him complete his request faster
   - Ⓒ To make sure he fills out the form properly
   - Ⓓ To encourage him to learn more about the school's policies

5. Listen again to a part of the conversation. Then answer the question.

   What does the student imply when he says this?
   - Ⓐ He has a generally impatient personality.
   - Ⓑ Many students are there waiting for service.
   - Ⓒ He has already been waiting for over an hour.
   - Ⓓ The woman needs to complete his request quickly.

TOEFL iBT Listening

Lecture 6~11: Listen to part of a lecture in a film studies class.

Film Studies

Actual Test 07

TOEFL iBT Listening

6. What aspect of blockbusters does the professor mainly discuss?
   - (A) When they first came into being
   - (B) The amount of money they cost to produce
   - (C) Which movies may be considered blockbusters
   - (D) How they changed the film industry

7. According to the professor, how did *Jaws* affect the movie industry?
   - (A) It resulted in movies getting bigger budgets.
   - (B) It enabled *Star Wars* to become a tremendous success.
   - (C) It changed the way in which studios regarded movies.
   - (D) It forced studios to make more prints of certain films.

8. What is the professor's opinion of George Lucas?
   - (A) He is an astute businessman.
   - (B) He makes outstanding movies.
   - (C) He is not Hollywood's best director.
   - (D) His movie scripts are often subpar.

9. Why does the professor mention *Star Wars*?
   - (A) To compare its quality as a film with *Jaws*
   - (B) To describe some of its numerous commercial tie-ins
   - (C) To discuss its effects on the movie industry
   - (D) To note how George Lucas became wealthy because of it

10. What will the professor likely do next?
    - (A) Begin speaking about movie studios
    - (B) Discuss some other blockbusters
    - (C) Continue talking about *Star Wars*
    - (D) Go back to talk about *Jaws*

11. Listen again to a part of the lecture. Then answer the question.

    Why does the student say this?
    - (A) To express her surprise over a factual statement
    - (B) To explain why she feels that way
    - (C) To express her disagreement
    - (D) To challenge the professor's claim

Actual Test
08

TOEFL iBT Reading

Reading
Section Directions

This section measures your ability to understand academic passages in English.

In this part, you will read 1 passage and answer reading comprehension questions about the passage. Most questions are worth one point, but the last question is worth more than one point. The directions indicate how many points you may receive.

Some passages include a word or phrase that is underlined in blue. Click on the word or phrase to see a definition or an explanation.

When you want to move on to the next question, click on **Next**. You may skip questions and go back to them later. If you want to return to previous questions, click on **Back**. You can click on **Review** at any time and the review screen will show you which questions you have answered and which you have not answered. From this review screen, you may go directly to any question you have already seen in the Reading section.

You may now begin the Reading section. You will read 1 reading passage. You will have **20 minutes** to read the passage and answer the questions.

Click on **Continue** to go on.

Marsupials

Marsupials are a subclass of mammals that mostly reside in Australia and parts of South America although there are a few species that live in New Guinea, Indonesia, and Central and North America. Among marsupials, kangaroos, wallabies, possums, and koala bears are perhaps the most well known. Marsupials differ from other mammals in two distinct ways. ■ The first is the manner in which they give birth and rear their young, which involves the use of external pouches during the early stages of infancy. ■ The second difference concerns where they live. ■ There is evidence that, in the distant past, marsupials lived on most continents, but they were eventually out-competed by other mammals. ■ However, they have managed to thrive in Australia and South America thanks to the conditions that exist in those two places.

A marsupial begins its life like any other mammal: as a fertilized egg inside its mother's womb. A typical mammal develops inside the womb, where it obtains nourishment from its mother until gestation is complete and it has sufficient strength to survive in the outside world. Mammals that give birth after their babies have developed are known as placental mammals. Unlike most mammals, marsupials are not placental mammals since their babies do not become fully mature by spending their entire period of growth inside the womb. Instead, after a few weeks or months—the exact time varies from species to species—the baby marsupial is born in an immature state. It promptly crawls inside its mother's external pouch, which zoologists call the marsupium. Within the marsupium are breast nipples that the immature baby latches onto to receive nutrition. There, the immature baby marsupial may spend several additional weeks or months as it grows while being shielded from the outside world thanks to its mother's pouch.

1. According to paragraph 1, which of the following is NOT true of marsupials?
   - Ⓐ They are mammals but do not share all of the same characteristics.
   - Ⓑ They give birth to their young by making use of a pouch in their bodies.
   - Ⓒ Australia is one of the places where they appear in significant numbers.
   - Ⓓ They once lived in more places on the planet than they do at the present time.

2. Which of the following can be inferred from paragraph 1 about marsupials?
   - Ⓐ A young one cannot function for several weeks after leaving its mother's pouch.
   - Ⓑ The majority of them are relatively small in size compared to other mammals.
   - Ⓒ They evolved less than other mammals so often could not adapt to their environment.
   - Ⓓ They will likely only exist on two continents sometime in the near future.

3. The word promptly in the passage is closest in meaning to
   - Ⓐ securely
   - Ⓑ respectively
   - Ⓒ hesitantly
   - Ⓓ immediately

4. The word latches in the passage is closest in meaning to
   - Ⓐ nibbles
   - Ⓑ clasps
   - Ⓒ stretches
   - Ⓓ sucks

5. The word There in the passage refers to
   - Ⓐ the womb
   - Ⓑ an immature state
   - Ⓒ the marsupium
   - Ⓓ nutrition

6. According to paragraph 2, which of the following is true of placental mammals?

   Ⓐ They include the majority of mammals, including marsupials.
   Ⓑ They are better adapted to survival than are other kinds of mammals.
   Ⓒ Their babies spend their gestation periods within their mothers' wombs.
   Ⓓ They can give birth to their babies within weeks of becoming pregnant.

7. According to paragraph 2, baby marsupials manage to survive after birth because

   Ⓐ their mothers make an effort to feed them regularly
   Ⓑ they spend a significant amount of time in the marsupium
   Ⓒ they are fully developed at the time of their birth
   Ⓓ they are protected from predators by the other marsupials

8. Which of the sentences below best expresses the essential information in the highlighted sentence in the passage? *Incorrect* answer choices change the meaning in important ways or leave out essential information.

   Ⓐ A marsupial baby cannot become fully developed unless it lives in its mother's pouch, so it will climb into the pouch as soon as it is born.
   Ⓑ Marsupials grow both in their mothers' wombs and in pouches, but they get most of their nourishment from the yolk found in the womb.
   Ⓒ When the marsupial is born, it moves straight into its mother's pouch, and the yolk found there is able to help it grow and become nourished.
   Ⓓ The yolk in a marsupial's womb is beneficial for the first half of the baby's growth, so it must live in the pouch after being born in order to develop.

The primary reason why marsupials give birth so early is that they do not have a placenta womb but instead have a yolk-style womb, which is more akin to a bird's egg. In placental mammals, the placenta provides a steady supply of blood from the mother to the growing baby, which nourishes it. In a marsupial's womb, the yolk only provides nourishment during the initial stages of growth; thus the baby must be born so that the rest of its growth may take place in the pouch. Some zoologists wonder why nature designed marsupials so differently from other mammals. The best explanation is that a short-term pregnancy is less dangerous than a long-term one. By only having its baby inside the womb for a short time, the mother is at less risk of the various dangers associated with pregnancy. However, there are disadvantages, one of which is that a baby marsupial's forearms have a limited amount of motion. The baby is born with grasping forelimbs that are just strong enough for it to crawl out of the womb and into the pouch. Furthermore, in some species, the forelimbs have limited locomotion since they fail to develop much after birth.

Outside of Australia and South America, marsupials are fairly rare. This was not always true though. The fossil record indicates that marsupials once lived in North America and Eurasia in significant numbers. In fact, the oldest marsupial fossils have been unearthed in China, which suggests that marsupials may have originated in Asia and then migrated to other parts of the world. Still, marsupials are mostly found in just two places. Zoologists suggest that marsupials failed to keep up with placental mammals in the fight for food and habitats on the other continents. However, both Australia and South America have relatively hot climates. This has given marsupials an advantage. They are able to go for long periods of time without eating and are also able to survive in the absence of food

9. The word locomotion in the passage is closest in meaning to

   (A) extension
   (B) movement
   (C) ability
   (D) coordination

10. The author's description of the fossil record mentions which of the following?

    (A) Some marsupials have been migrating to China in recent years.
    (B) More marsupials once lived in North America than do currently.
    (C) The bodies of marsupials have changed little over millions of years.
    (D) Marsupials evolved in Europe and then spread out around the world.

11. According to paragraph 4, why do marsupials thrive in Australia?

    (A) There are enough small animals there for them to consume.
    (B) They have few natural predators that hunt and kill them.
    (C) The abundance of water lets them gain their nourishment from it.
    (D) They suffer less than other animals in the hot and dry weather there.

12. In paragraph 4, the author of the passage implies that marsupials

    (A) have fairly low metabolic rates
    (B) can eat both plants and animals
    (C) are effective at foraging for food
    (D) give birth to multiple babies

13. Look at the four squares [■] that indicate where the following sentence could be added to the passage.

    Of all the animals that have pouches, kangaroos are arguably the ones that people are the most familiar with.

    Where would the sentence best fit?

    Click on a square [■] to add the sentence to the passage.

sources. This has been particularly advantageous to marsupials in Australia, which is the driest of all of Earth's continents. In addition, every year, the amount of vegetation—which most marsupials feed on—that will grow is uncertain, so this makes survivability for prey animals difficult at times. Because of these conditions in Australia, many placental species, which have higher metabolic rates, died there long ago while the marsupials survived and even thrived in the continent's harsh environment. Since Australia is so isolated geographically from other landmasses, few new placentals arrived, and thus the marsupials faced very little competition there.

Glossary

gestation: the period of time from conception to giving birth
forearm: one of an animal's front limbs; a forelimb
unearth: to dig up from beneath the ground

14. Directions: An introductory sentence for a brief summary of the passage is provided below. Complete the summary by selecting the THREE answer choices that express the most important ideas of the passage. Some sentences do not belong because they express ideas that are not presented in the passage or are minor ideas in the passage. *This question is worth 2 points.*

Although marsupials are mammals, they differ from most mammals with regard to how they give birth to their young and where on the planet they may be found.

-
-
-

Answer Choices

(A) The yolk-style womb of the marsupial is different from most other mammals' wombs, which are placental in nature.

(B) A marsupial baby is born in an undeveloped state, so it must spend a period of time in its mother's pouch in order to reach maturity.

(C) Kangaroos, wombats, and possums are just three of the many species of marsupials that live in various places around the world.

(D) Scientists believe that the first marsupials may actually have evolved in China and then spread out across the world.

(E) Most marsupials live either in Australia or South America, but there are some species that live on other continents.

(F) Australia has a very harsh climate, but marsupials face fewer problems living there than do many other mammals.

Drag your answer choices to the spaces where they belong.
To remove an answer choice, click on it. To review the passage, click on **View Text**.

TOEFL iBT Listening

Listening
Section Directions

This section measures your ability to understand conversations and lectures in English.

In this part, you will listen to 1 conversation and 1 lecture. You will hear the conversation or lecture only **one** time. After the conversation or lecture, you will answer some questions about it. The questions typically ask about the main idea and supporting details. Some questions ask about a speaker's purpose or attitude. Answer the questions based on what is stated or implied by the speakers.

You may take notes while you listen. You may use your notes to help you answer the questions. Your notes will **not** be scored.

If you need to change the volume while you listen, click on the **Volume** icon at the top of the screen.

In some questions, you will see this icon: 🎧 This means that you will hear, but not see, part of the question.

Some of the questions have special directions. These directions appear in a gray box on the screen.

Most questions are worth one point. If a question is worth more than one point, it will have special directions that indicate how many points you can receive.

You must answer each question. After you answer, click on **Next**. Then click on **OK** to confirm your answer and go on to the next question. After you click on **OK**, you cannot return to previous questions.

A clock at the top of the screen will show you how much time is remaining. The clock will not count down while you are listening. The clock will count down only while you are answering the questions.

Now you may begin the Listening section.

TOEFL iBT Listening

Conversation 1~5: Listen to part of a conversation between a student and a professor.

Actual Test 08

TOEFL iBT Listening

1. What are the speakers mainly discussing?
   - (A) The student's decision to change his major
   - (B) A paper that the student recently submitted
   - (C) A decision the student has made concerning his academic life
   - (D) The course load that the student is taking for that semester

2. According to the student, why is a minor in chemistry important?
   - (A) It will help him improve his overall grades.
   - (B) It will give him more knowledge of the sciences.
   - (C) It will assist him at some time in the future.
   - (D) It will be easier than studying biology.

3. What can be inferred about Professor Adelman?
   - (A) The student is currently studying with him.
   - (B) He is the head of the Chemistry Department.
   - (C) The professor thinks highly of him.
   - (D) He sometimes teaches chemistry classes.

4. Listen again to a part of the conversation. Then answer the question.

   What can be inferred about the professor when she says this?
   - (A) She believes chemistry is harder than history and English.
   - (B) She feels that the student should be able to do the work.
   - (C) She wants the student to transfer to the History Department.
   - (D) The student should drop his history and English classes.

5. Listen again to a part of the conversation. Then answer the question.

   Why does the professor say this?
   - (A) To ask the student to reconsider his decision
   - (B) To find out how determined the student is
   - (C) To challenge the student to work harder
   - (D) To question the student's loyalty to the department

Lecture 6~11: Listen to part of a lecture in a sociology class.

6. What is the lecture mainly about?
   - Ⓐ The decline of urban centers
   - Ⓑ The GI Bill
   - Ⓒ The growth of suburbs
   - Ⓓ The Federal Housing Administration

7. What did the Federal Housing Administration do?
   - Ⓐ It constructed new homes in American suburbs.
   - Ⓑ It provided funds for potential homeowners.
   - Ⓒ It encouraged people to remain in large cities.
   - Ⓓ It loaned money to housing construction companies.

8. What is the professor's attitude toward the GI Bill?
   - Ⓐ It was the best work the FHA ever did.
   - Ⓑ It could have been improved in several ways.
   - Ⓒ Its programs should have been ended decades ago.
   - Ⓓ It was a beneficial piece of legislation.

9. How does the professor organize the information about the GI Bill that he presents to the class?
   - Ⓐ He describes the process through which it went from being a bill to a law.
   - Ⓑ He focuses on how it helped more Americans become educated.
   - Ⓒ He explains its benefits and how it led to development in the suburbs.
   - Ⓓ He compares its effects with those that were made by the FHA.

10. What does the professor imply about Levittown?
    - Ⓐ Its houses resembled those in other suburbs across the United States.
    - Ⓑ It was built too close to New York City to become a big suburb.
    - Ⓒ It became the largest suburb in the entire United States.
    - Ⓓ It was a model of urban planning that many cities based their street design upon.

11. Listen again to a part of the lecture. Then answer the question.

    Why does the professor say this?
    - Ⓐ To express doubt about his own facts
    - Ⓑ To emphasize the information he just gave
    - Ⓒ To question the relevance of his information
    - Ⓓ To see whether the students believe him or not

Actual Test
09

TOEFL iBT Reading

Reading
Section Directions

This section measures your ability to understand academic passages in English.

In this part, you will read 1 passage and answer reading comprehension questions about the passage. Most questions are worth one point, but the last question is worth more than one point. The directions indicate how many points you may receive.

Some passages include a word or phrase that is underlined in blue. Click on the word or phrase to see a definition or an explanation.

When you want to move on to the next question, click on **Next**. You may skip questions and go back to them later. If you want to return to previous questions, click on **Back**. You can click on **Review** at any time and the review screen will show you which questions you have answered and which you have not answered. From this review screen, you may go directly to any question you have already seen in the Reading section.

You may now begin the Reading section. You will read 1 reading passage. You will have **20 minutes** to read the passage and answer the questions.

Click on **Continue** to go on.

TOEFL iBT Reading

1. The word bulk in the passage is closest in meaning to
   Ⓐ majority
   Ⓑ load
   Ⓒ weight
   Ⓓ burden

2. Which of the sentences below best expresses the essential information in the highlighted sentence in the passage? *Incorrect* answer choices change the meaning in important ways or leave out essential information.
   Ⓐ Although most people praise machines for being so advanced, they have caused breakdowns in the environment and society.
   Ⓑ Social and environmental problems that had never previously existed are two results of the mechanization of human society.
   Ⓒ While machines have helped humans develop more quickly, they have also created problems in various aspects of people's lives.
   Ⓓ Because society is advancing so rapidly, most people remain unconcerned about any negative effects, such as environmental and social issues.

3. According to paragraph 1, human culture advanced slowly for much of history because
   Ⓐ few people were involved in research that could improve technology
   Ⓑ the lack of machines made people rely on other sources of power to do work
   Ⓒ most humans were too concerned with living their daily lives to make new inventions
   Ⓓ the low level of technology in most machines caused them to break down with frequency

The Mechanization of Society

For most of human history, progress occurred very slowly. This was mainly on account of the fact that labor was performed either by human or animal power. Over time, the inventing of certain devices, such as the wheel, helped ease this burden. Nevertheless, while the wheel, lever, and other simple machines made work slightly less difficult, they did not change the fact that humans and animals were still relied upon to do the bulk of the work. Then, starting in the eighteenth century, a period of mechanization began during which machines started replacing human and animal power. Thanks to these machines, human progress advanced at a much more rapid rate than ever before; however, mechanization was not without its drawbacks as it resulted in various social and environmental issues that were of a negative nature.

Mechanization is the use of machinery to perform labor in any field of human activity. These fields may include—but are not limited to—agriculture, industry, transportation, communications, medicine, and the military. The first large-scale implementation of mechanization took place in England during the 1700s. Once James Watt perfected the steam engine, the country began to industrialize. The results were phenomenal. In agriculture, the use of machines made it easier for farmers to grow more crops on more land but with fewer workers. Since fewer people were needed on farms, there was a huge labor pool in England that found work in the factories that began springing up all over the country. Soon, many industries were mechanized, which enabled people to create more products faster and more efficiently as well as for less money. It was not only England that was industrializing; many countries throughout Europe and in the Americas reaped the benefits of industrialization as well.

4. The word implementation in the passage is closest in meaning to
   Ⓐ invention
   Ⓑ extraction
   Ⓒ coercion
   Ⓓ execution

5. The word reaped in the passage is closest in meaning to
   Ⓐ planted
   Ⓑ gained
   Ⓒ considered
   Ⓓ admired

6. Why does the author mention James Watt?
   Ⓐ To include his name in the proper historical context
   Ⓑ To credit him for having invented the steam engine
   Ⓒ To acknowledge his contribution to the industrialization of society
   Ⓓ To state that his steam engine was used exclusively in agriculture

7. Which of the following can be inferred from paragraph 2 about industrialization in England during the 1700s?
   Ⓐ It was responsible for England's unemployment issues at that time.
   Ⓑ People began earning more money than they had when they were farmers.
   Ⓒ The number of factories built then was much greater than before.
   Ⓓ The products that England exported to other countries increased.

8. According to paragraph 3, which of the following is true of Henry Ford?
   Ⓐ He came up with the idea for developing the assembly line.
   Ⓑ He founded a company that would build large numbers of cars.
   Ⓒ His manufacturing methods caused other factories to go out of business.
   Ⓓ He helped change the way that some items were manufactured.

At the end of the nineteenth century, mechanization entered a new stage. It was around this time that manufacturers, such as Henry Ford in the United States, devised and perfected the assembly line process. This allowed workers to specialize in the manufacturing process and decreased the time needed to make even large items such as cars or various appliances. Throughout the twentieth century, machines began appearing everywhere—in factories, offices, and homes and on farms.

Despite the fact that machines made many aspects of life much easier for people, not everyone was enamored of them. Ever since the beginning of the Industrial Age, people have been concerned that machines will take jobs away from humans. This fear has been exacerbated in recent times because of the invention of robots. Robots are highly specialized machines that currently perform many jobs around the world. Many of these, including those on assembly lines in factories, are those that humans once did. ■ As of now, most robots do repetitive tasks that may cause stress and boredom in human workers. ■ There are some robots that may do tasks such as assisting with precision surgery, but they are few in number. ■ Still, many people fear that, as robot technology increases, more and more workers will find themselves unemployed. ■

There are some other drawbacks to mechanization. Many factories are noisy, noxious, and dangerous places in which workers can be injured or even killed. Toiling on assembly lines and around machinery can cause a great deal of mental stress on humans, too. Some workers find that the repetitive natures of their jobs are both boring and uninspiring. Mechanization has also caused harm to the environment. Most machines require some sort of power to make them work. Early factories burned coal or wood to create the steam needed to operate the machines. Factories nowadays use electricity that is frequently created

9. The word these in the passage refers to
   - (A) robots
   - (B) highly specialized machines
   - (C) many jobs
   - (D) assembly lines in factories

10. The author's description of robots mentions which of the following?
    - (A) They are used in some countries that have declining populations.
    - (B) There usage is a cause for worry among many laborers.
    - (C) Many workers remain unemployed because their jobs have been filled by robots.
    - (D) Some robots will perform complete surgical operations in the near future.

11. The word depletes in the passage is closest in meaning to
    - (A) reduces
    - (B) wastes
    - (C) exhausts
    - (D) partitions

12. The author's description of the drawbacks of mechanization mentions all of the following EXCEPT:
    - (A) It has caused the natural environment to become dirtier.
    - (B) Some people find their jobs to be quite dull.
    - (C) It has enabled many people to purchase their own cars.
    - (D) It is using up many valuable natural resources.

from the burning of coal, oil, or gas. Thus the use of machines depletes the planet's resources while the burning of fossil fuels causes there to be more pollution. Not only that, but many of the products manufactured in factories—such as automobiles—are also major contributors to pollution. Finally, the mechanization of society has caused many people to move away from rural areas and into urban centers. The large populations of cities have resulted in various social ills, including overcrowding, crime, stress, and the breakdown of the family unit.

Mechanization clearly is a double-edged sword as it has brought both benefits and problems to the world. It is clear, though, that the world will continue industrializing, so the hope is that solutions to the problems it has caused will be both found and implemented.

Glossary
enamored: captivated by; in love with
exacerbate: to make worse or more severe
toil: to work very hard; to labor

13. Look at the four squares [■] that indicate where the following sentence could be added to the passage.

    However, each year, as robots become more advanced, they are able to perform an even greater number of highly specialized jobs.

    Where would the sentence best fit?

    Click on a square [■] to add the sentence to the passage.

14. **Directions:** An introductory sentence for a brief summary of the passage is provided below. Complete the summary by selecting the THREE answer choices that express the most important ideas of the passage. Some sentences do not belong because they express ideas that are not presented in the passage or are minor ideas in the passage. *This question is worth 2 points.*

    While the process of mechanization has brought about many changes in society, not all of them are positive as some have actually been harmful in nature.

    -
    -
    -

    Answer Choices

    (A) Some people are concerned that robots will become too highly developed and will therefore cause problems in society.

    (B) Once machines started being used, human society began to develop at a greater pace than it ever had before.

    (C) Inventors such as James Watt were responsible for many of the advances to machines like the steam engine.

    (D) As factories require the burning of various fossil fuels, the amount of pollution in certain places has increased.

    (E) Some people may lose their lives while working with machines, and others find their jobs to be uninspiring.

    (F) Many people are aware of the social changes that have occurred as much of the world moves from a rural culture to an urban one.

    Drag your answer choices to the spaces where they belong.
    To remove an answer choice, click on it. To review the passage, click on **View Text**.

Listening
Section Directions

This section measures your ability to understand conversations and lectures in English.

In this part, you will listen to 1 conversation and 1 lecture. You will hear the conversation or lecture only **one** time. After the conversation or lecture, you will answer some questions about it. The questions typically ask about the main idea and supporting details. Some questions ask about a speaker's purpose or attitude. Answer the questions based on what is stated or implied by the speakers.

You may take notes while you listen. You may use your notes to help you answer the questions. Your notes will **not** be scored.

If you need to change the volume while you listen, click on the **Volume** icon at the top of the screen.

In some questions, you will see this icon: 🎧 This means that you will hear, but not see, part of the question.

Some of the questions have special directions. These directions appear in a gray box on the screen.

Most questions are worth one point. If a question is worth more than one point, it will have special directions that indicate how many points you can receive.

You must answer each question. After you answer, click on **Next**. Then click on **OK** to confirm your answer and go on to the next question. After you click on **OK**, you cannot return to previous questions.

A clock at the top of the screen will show you how much time is remaining. The clock will not count down while you are listening. The clock will count down only while you are answering the questions.

Now you may begin the Listening section.

TOEFL iBT Listening

Conversation 1~5: Listen to part of a conversation between a student and the dean of students.

Actual Test 09

TOEFL iBT Listening

1. What problem does the student have?
   - Ⓐ She is going to have to drop out of school.
   - Ⓑ She cannot afford the cost of tuition.
   - Ⓒ She is not being allowed to graduate that semester.
   - Ⓓ She cannot register for some classes.

2. Why does the student visit the dean of students?
   - Ⓐ To file a letter of protest against the Registrar's Office
   - Ⓑ To complain about a problem with another department
   - Ⓒ To ask him to let her graduate after four and a half years
   - Ⓓ To find out if she can apply for any scholarships

3. What will the dean of students probably do next?
   - Ⓐ Give the student a form to complete
   - Ⓑ Schedule another time for the student to meet him
   - Ⓒ Ask the student to provide some more information
   - Ⓓ Telephone someone at the Registrar's Office

4. Listen again to a part of the conversation. Then answer the question.

   Why does the dean of students say this?
   - Ⓐ To encourage the student to speak more openly
   - Ⓑ To convince the student her choice was correct
   - Ⓒ To provide a personal anecdote
   - Ⓓ To find out more about the student

5. Listen again to a part of the conversation. Then answer the question.

   What does the dean of students mean when he says this?
   - Ⓐ He appreciates it when people speak openly with him.
   - Ⓑ He does not understand why the student is speaking with him.
   - Ⓒ He believes that the student owes him an apology.
   - Ⓓ He only wants to talk to students that have actual problems.

Lecture 6~11: Listen to part of a lecture in an astronomy class.

Astronomy

Actual Test 09

TOEFL iBT Listening

6. What is the lecture mainly about?
   - Ⓐ Which ancient cultures had excellent sailing skills
   - Ⓑ Modern developments in navigation
   - Ⓒ How people utilized celestial navigation
   - Ⓓ The best means of navigating by the stars

7. According to the professor, what is wayfinding?
   - Ⓐ Another name for the star charts some cultures kept
   - Ⓑ The use of the astrolabe to navigate with
   - Ⓒ A method of navigating used by the Polynesians
   - Ⓓ The preferred method of sailing the Phoenicians utilized

8. What is the professor's opinion of wayfinding?
   - Ⓐ It was not always effective.
   - Ⓑ It was fairly primitive.
   - Ⓒ It should be refined for modern times.
   - Ⓓ Its usage was impressive.

9. Based on the information in the lecture, do the following sentences refer to the Polynesians or the Phoenicians?

   Click in the correct box for each sentence.

	Polynesians	Phoenicians
Ⓐ They were the greatest sailors in ancient times.		
Ⓑ They may have sailed their ships up to England.		
Ⓒ They sailed to numerous islands distant from one another.		
Ⓓ They employed a unique system of navigation passed down to subsequent generations.		

10. What will the professor probably do next?
    - Ⓐ Explain how the astrolabe works
    - Ⓑ Give the students a homework assignment
    - Ⓒ Go into more detail on the Polynesians
    - Ⓓ Conduct a demonstration for the students

11. Listen again to a part of the lecture. Then answer the question.

    What does the professor imply when he says this?
    - Ⓐ There are directional markers in some oceans today.
    - Ⓑ People had difficulty sailing the oceans a century ago.
    - Ⓒ Sailing methods remained constant for thousands of years.
    - Ⓓ Sailors use modern equipment to navigate with today.

Actual Test 10

TOEFL iBT Reading

Reading
Section Directions

This section measures your ability to understand academic passages in English.

In this part, you will read 1 passage and answer reading comprehension questions about the passage. Most questions are worth one point, but the last question is worth more than one point. The directions indicate how many points you may receive.

Some passages include a word or phrase that is underlined in blue. Click on the word or phrase to see a definition or an explanation.

When you want to move on to the next question, click on **Next**. You may skip questions and go back to them later. If you want to return to previous questions, click on **Back**. You can click on **Review** at any time and the review screen will show you which questions you have answered and which you have not answered. From this review screen, you may go directly to any question you have already seen in the Reading section.

You may now begin the Reading section. You will read 1 reading passage. You will have **20 minutes** to read the passage and answer the questions.

Click on **Continue** to go on.

1. The word inundate in the passage is closest in meaning to
   Ⓐ overwhelm
   Ⓑ damage
   Ⓒ blockade
   Ⓓ intermingle

2. The author uses hurricanes, typhoons, and cyclones as examples of
   Ⓐ tropical storms that can cause significant damage
   Ⓑ storms that may have winds that blow at extreme levels
   Ⓒ tropical storms that can cause flooding in coastal areas
   Ⓓ storms that can create the largest waves on the ocean

3. The word colossal in the passage is closest in meaning to
   Ⓐ considerable
   Ⓑ average
   Ⓒ enormous
   Ⓓ overbearing

4. The author's description of the factors involved in determining the height of a wave mentions all of the following EXCEPT:
   Ⓐ the deepness of the water
   Ⓑ the amount of water over which the wind is blowing
   Ⓒ the rapidity that the wind is blowing
   Ⓓ the amount of salinity in the water

5. According to paragraph 2, the highest waves form on oceans because
   Ⓐ the deepest waters in the world are found in the oceans
   Ⓑ it can produce a longer fetch than other bodies of water
   Ⓒ tropical storms only form over large bodies of water such as oceans
   Ⓓ the wind can blow for days in some areas of the ocean

Water Waves

Waves are common sights on bodies of water such as oceans and lakes, and they range in height from just a few centimeters to monster waves on the open ocean that rise over thirty meters in height. Waves are created by the action of the wind on the water, and there are several factors that determine how high they become. The largest waves are typically the result of powerful tropical storm systems such as hurricanes, typhoons, and cyclones, all of which have strong winds that blow across the water for extended periods of time. These storms may also produce powerful waves that wash onshore and inundate coastal regions. In other cases, some large waves may be caused by undersea earthquakes, which can displace so much water that they produce the fastest, largest, and most destructive waves in nature: tsunamis.

When the wind blows across the surface of a body of water, many small interactions occur as the wind's energy is transferred to the water. Small ripples on the water's surface are indicators of the onset of wave creation. How high a wave becomes depends upon fetch, wind speed, the length of time the wind blows, and the depth of the water. Fetch is the length of the water over which the wind blows in a constant direction. Fast winds blowing across vast stretches of water can produce extremely high waves. The ocean, with its huge expanses of empty water, produces higher waves than landlocked lakes because of the greater area of fetch. In addition, the longer the wind blows, the more energy that is transferred to the water, which results in higher waves. Should the wind only blow for a short time, then the resulting waves are smaller. Naturally, winds that last for hours or even days, such as those in a hurricane, can create waves of colossal size. Weather-recording buoys in the North Atlantic Ocean have measured waves over thirty meters in height during severe storms.

TOEFL iBT Reading

6. The author of the passage implies that the North Atlantic Ocean
   Ⓐ sometimes gets storms that can last for several days
   Ⓑ is the area where the greatest number of tropical storms occur
   Ⓒ is dangerous for many ships that sail on the ocean
   Ⓓ produces waves that have sunk countless ships over the years

7. According to paragraph 3, how does the depth of the water affect the height of waves?
   Ⓐ Waves tend to crest to great heights in shallow water.
   Ⓑ The depth of the water is unimportant if the fetch is small.
   Ⓒ Water that has a greater depth can form very high waves.
   Ⓓ Water of average depth can produce some monster waves.

8. The author discusses ocean swells in paragraph 3 in order to
   Ⓐ explain how a wave can exist in the absence of wind
   Ⓑ note that they can cause problems for some sailors
   Ⓒ compare them with waves that are in shallow water
   Ⓓ describe the manner in which they crest and break apart

9. The word those in the passage refers to
   Ⓐ winds
   Ⓑ thirty knots
   Ⓒ waves
   Ⓓ three meters

    The depth of the water is also instrumental in determining the size of a wave. Larger waves are formed in deeper water; however, as waves reach shallower water, they break apart. The reason for this is their internal structures. The water particles in a wave move in a circular motion, so they continuously roll along underwater as part of the wave once it is formed. Even if the wind dies, a wave may continue as an ocean swell, which is a wave found in an area with no wind action. These waves roll along until their energy is depleted and the water calms. Once waves reach shallow water near the coast, friction with the seafloor causes them to become unstable, so they break apart as the wave particles and wave energy are disturbed. This is the reason why waves crest, curl, and then crash ashore on coastlines around the world.

    The most significant of all of the factors in determining wave size is wind speed. On average, for each increase of ten knots per hour in wind speed, there is a doubling of wave height. ■ Winds blowing thirty knots per hour create waves with an average height of about three meters while those blowing forty knots an hour can produce waves around six meters high. ■ Additionally, the gale force winds of hurricanes can result in monster waves. ■ Waves reach their maximum possible height when they travel as fast as the winds that produce them. ■ It is therefore unsurprising that the biggest waves are found in those areas with the strongest winds. The powerful winds of the North Atlantic Ocean and the South Indian Ocean can produce waves that average over six meters in height. In contrast, the calm winds near the equator create the smallest waves.

    One exception to wind-produced waves is tsunamis. They form after an earthquake occurs beneath the ocean floor, which results in the displacement of water and then a tsunami. On the open ocean, tsunamis may appear very small or not even be noticeable, but they are powerful

TOEFL iBT Reading

10. The author's description of wind speed mentions which of the following?

    Ⓐ Fast winds can force some large waves to crest before reaching shore.
    Ⓑ Some winds have created waves that are over forty meters in height.
    Ⓒ The wind blows the fastest in the North Atlantic Ocean.
    Ⓓ It is the most important of all factors involved in wave height.

11. The word they in the passage refers to

    Ⓐ tsunamis
    Ⓑ thousands of kilometers
    Ⓒ a few hours
    Ⓓ the coast

12. The word slammed in the passage is closest in meaning to

    Ⓐ waded
    Ⓑ crashed
    Ⓒ proceeded
    Ⓓ washed

13. Look at the four squares [■] that indicate where the following sentence could be added to the passage.

    Some of these gigantic waves are so immense that they have damaged large ships such as luxury liners and even naval ships.

    Where would the sentence best fit?

    Click on a square [■] to add the sentence to the passage.

and fast moving. They can travel thousands of kilometers in a few hours, and, as they near the coast, they actually grow in height. Upon making landfall, tsunamis can be several meters high. On December 26, 2004, a series of tsunamis following a major earthquake slammed ashore throughout Southeast Asia and killed at least a quarter of a million people.

Glossary
landlocked: surrounded completely by land and having no access to open water
crest: to reach the highest level
gale: a very strong wind

14. **Directions:** An introductory sentence for a brief summary of the passage is provided below. Complete the summary by selecting the THREE answer choices that express the most important ideas of the passage. Some sentences do not belong because they express ideas that are not presented in the passage or are minor ideas in the passage. *This question is worth 2 points.*

There are several different factors that are involved in the creation of waves on all of the world's bodies of water.

-
-
-

Answer Choices

(A) Tsunamis like the one that hit Southeast Asia in 2004 can cause a great deal of death and destruction when they reach land.

(B) The speed of the wind is a major factor in determining how high the waves on a body of water can become.

(C) Fetch is the amount of open space over water that the wind can blow on, and the greater it is, the higher the waves become.

(D) The South Indian Ocean is one place that has incredibly powerful winds that blow almost constantly.

(E) Monster waves, or rogue waves as some call them, can suddenly appear on the ocean and thus damage ships that encounter them.

(F) When waves form over deep water, they tend to be higher than those waves that form over shallow water.

Drag your answer choices to the spaces where they belong.
To remove an answer choice, click on it. To review the passage, click on **View Text**.

Listening
Section Directions

This section measures your ability to understand conversations and lectures in English.

In this part, you will listen to 1 conversation and 1 lecture. You will hear the conversation or lecture only **one** time. After the conversation or lecture, you will answer some questions about it. The questions typically ask about the main idea and supporting details. Some questions ask about a speaker's purpose or attitude. Answer the questions based on what is stated or implied by the speakers.

You may take notes while you listen. You may use your notes to help you answer the questions. Your notes will **not** be scored.

If you need to change the volume while you listen, click on the **Volume** icon at the top of the screen.

In some questions, you will see this icon: 🎧 This means that you will hear, but not see, part of the question.

Some of the questions have special directions. These directions appear in a gray box on the screen.

Most questions are worth one point. If a question is worth more than one point, it will have special directions that indicate how many points you can receive.

You must answer each question. After you answer, click on **Next**. Then click on **OK** to confirm your answer and go on to the next question. After you click on **OK**, you cannot return to previous questions.

A clock at the top of the screen will show you how much time is remaining. The clock will not count down while you are listening. The clock will count down only while you are answering the questions.

Now you may begin the Listening section.

TOEFL iBT Listening

Conversation 1~5: Listen to part of a conversation between a student and a professor.

Actual Test 10

TOEFL iBT Listening

1. Why does the student visit the professor?
   - Ⓐ To ask him to sign a form so that she can drop the class
   - Ⓑ To tell him she is thinking of quitting his class
   - Ⓒ To ask him about their upcoming midterm exam
   - Ⓓ To request that he give her some extra assistance

2. Who is Professor Sanderson?
   - Ⓐ The student's advanced film studies professor
   - Ⓑ The student's advisor
   - Ⓒ The head of the Film Studies Department
   - Ⓓ The professor the student is speaking with

3. Why does the professor discuss staying in his class with the student?
   - Ⓐ He is trying to provide her with some options.
   - Ⓑ He believes she needs his class to graduate.
   - Ⓒ He wants her to get an A in his class.
   - Ⓓ He feels that she can handle the extra homework.

4. What can be inferred about the professor?
   - Ⓐ He wants the student to remain in his class.
   - Ⓑ He typically lectures to the students during class.
   - Ⓒ He frequently shows videos in his classes.
   - Ⓓ He is not concerned about the welfare of his students.

5. Listen again to a part of the conversation. Then answer the question.

   Why does the professor say this?
   - Ⓐ To refute a point the student makes
   - Ⓑ To agree with the student
   - Ⓒ To make a suggestion
   - Ⓓ To consider the student's request

Lecture 6~11: Listen to part of a lecture in a geology class.

Actual Test 10

TOEFL iBT Listening

6. What aspect of permafrost does the professor mainly discuss?

   (A) The places where it most commonly occurs
   (B) The type of weather it needs to form
   (C) The characteristics of each type of it
   (D) The ability of people to erect buildings on it

7. Why does the professor explain about the existence of natural resources in Canada, Russia, and Alaska?

   (A) To explain why some people would want to live there
   (B) To note that the Eskimos, Inuits, and Lapps have exploited them
   (C) To express his hope that they will not be mined
   (D) To complain about the amount of pollution caused when they are extracted

8. What is the treeline?

   (A) The area above which no trees can grow
   (B) The parts of mountains that have no trees
   (C) The necessary conditions for trees to grow in soil
   (D) The closeness to water sources trees must be to live

9. How is the discussion organized?

   (A) By discussing permafrost and its effects on the plants and animals living on it
   (B) By showing slides of areas of permafrost and noting the differences between them
   (C) By telling personal stories connected with the time he spent living on permafrost
   (D) By focusing on the places where the existence of permafrost is most prevalent

10. Based on the information in the lecture, do the following sentences refer to continuous permafrost or isolated permafrost?

    Click in the correct box for each sentence.

	Continuous Permafrost	Isolated Permafrost
(A) It is often found in Scandinavia.		
(B) It may have trees growing on it.		
(C) It may have frozen ground thousands of feet thick.		
(D) It can support the growth of mosses.		

11. Listen again to a part of the lecture. Then answer the question.

    What does the professor mean when he says this?

    (A) The student should consider the effects of what the professor said.
    (B) He wants the student to develop his answer more.
    (C) The answer is not the one that he was expecting.
    (D) The student's answer is correct yet simplistic.

Compact
Actual iBT

10 mini TOEFL® Tests

Reading & Listening

3

Answer Book

Compact Actual iBT 3
Reading & Listening

Answer Book

Actual Test 01

Reading Section   p.9

Answers

1. Ⓐ [Vocabulary Question]
2. Ⓒ [Rhetorical Purpose Question]
3. Ⓓ [Factual Question]
4. Ⓒ [Vocabulary Question]
5. Ⓑ [Negative Factual Question]
6. Ⓑ [Reference Question]
7. Ⓓ [Vocabulary Question]
8. Ⓒ [Factual Question]
9. Ⓐ [Inference Question]
10. Ⓐ [Negative Factual Question]
11. Ⓓ [Sentence Simplification Question]
12. Ⓒ [Factual Question]
13.

	TYPE OF CLOUD
High Level Clouds	Ⓑ, Ⓕ, Ⓖ
Middle Level Clouds	Ⓐ, Ⓘ
Low Level Clouds	Ⓒ, Ⓔ

[Fill in a Table Question]

Translation

구름

구름은 대기에 축적되어 있는 수증기가 눈에 보이는 것이다. 본질적으로, 공기 중의 수증기가 포화 단계에 이르면, 액화되어 물방울을 형성하게 되고, 이것들이 먼지나 염 입자에 달라붙어서 구름의 모습으로 보이게 된다. 하지만, 수증기는 따뜻한 조건에서보다 차가운 공기에서 더 빠르게 액화되기 때문에 그 포화단계는 기온에 따라 다양해진다. 여러 가지 유형의 구름이 있지만, 기상학자들은 일반적으로 4가지 유형으로 구름을 분류한다: 상층운, 중층운, 하층운, 그리고 수직운이 그것이다. 구름의 모양에 따라 분류를 하는 부차적인 분류법도 있다. 적운은 부푼 모습을 하고 있으며 일반적으로 높이와 넓이가 동일하지만, 층운은 보다 평평하며 여러 개의 층을 이룬다.

상층운은 해발 약 3,000~12,000미터의 고도에서 형성된다. 이 구층은 높은 대기의 차가운 온도 때문에 얼음 결정들로 이루어져 있으며, 하얗고, 얇은, 들쭉날쭉한 줄기처럼 보인다. 고고도 상의 기본적인 구름 형태는 단순히 권운이라고 불리며, 부차적인 유형에는 권적운과 권층운이 있다. 권적운은 약간의 수분을 함유하고 있지만, 주로 얼음 결정들로 이루어져 있다. 이 구름은 약간 부푼 모습을 띠고 있으며, 넓은 띠를 형성하고, 얼음 결정들이 거의 없는 물방울들을 냉각시키기 때문에 금방 사라져버린다. 이러한 냉각 현상으로 인하여, 너무 얇아서 관측하기 힘든 권층운이 형성된다. 해무리가 있다는 것은 종종 권층운의 징후가 된다.

기상 학자들은 중고도에서 형성되는 구름을 나타내기 위해 "alto"라는 접두사를 사용하는데, 이러한 구름은 해발 2,000~6,000미터의 범위에 걸쳐져 있다. 이 구름들은 거의 물방울들로 이루어져 있다; 하지만, 더 높은 고도에서는, 약간의 얼음 결정들을 포함하기도 한다. 두 가지 주요한 유형으로는 고층운과 고적운이 있다. 대부분 얼음 결정들로 이루어진 고층운은, 일반적으로 하늘 전체를 덮고 있으며 회백색이나 청회색을 띤다. 고층운을 통해 보면 태양은 보통 어둑어둑하게 보인다. 반면, 고적운은 회색보다는 흰색을 띠고 있으며 고층운에 비해서는 더 부푼 모습을 보인다. 이 구름은 물방울들로 이루어져 있고 서로 조화를 이루며 이동한다. 일반적으로, 이 구름들은 장마 전선이나 뇌우가 다가온다는 전조가 된다.

다양한 유형을 가지고 있는 하층운은, 지표면에서부터 해발 2,000미터까지의 범위에서 나타난다. 가장 낮은 높이에서 형성되는 안개는 대양이나 바닷가 근처에서 흔히 볼 수 있는 것인데, 이곳에서는 수증기가 염 입자에 붙어서 액화된다. 지상에서는, 4가지의 주요한 하층운 유형이 있다: 적운, 난층운, 층적운, 그리고 층운이 그것이다. 적운은 따뜻한 상승 기류의 결과로서 만들어진다. 더운 날, 지표면의 공기가 가열되어 상승할 때 이 구름들이 흔하게 나타난다. 공기가 상승하면서, 냉각되고, 액화되어, 적운을 형성하게 되는데, 이것은 솜털 조각을 쌓아 올려 놓은 듯한 모습을 띠게 된다. 난층운은 극도로 낮은 높이에서 하늘 전체를 덮고 있으며 회색 빛을 띠고 부드러운 겉모습을 가진다. 이 구름들은 거의 항상 비를 뿌린다. 층적운은 대규모로 형성되며 어두운 색을 띠고 부푼 모습을 보인다. 이것들은 그 위의 대기층이 안정적이기 때문에 특별히 높은 곳에 위치하고 있지는 않다. 층적운은 종종 아열대 지역의 수역에서 나타나며 거의 비를 뿌리지 않는다. 하층운의 마지막 유형인 층운은 낮은 높이에서 하늘을 덮고 있으며 흰색을 띤다. 이러한 구름은 하늘을 흐릿하게 보이게 하며, 지표면보다 높은 곳에 위치하고 있다는 점을 제외하면, 안개와 유사하다.

마지막 유형의 구름이 아마도 가장 위험할 것이다: 수직운으로, 뇌운이 그 주된 유형이다. 이 구름들은 불안정한 대기 상태에서 형성되는데, 이러한 대기 상태는 상승 기류로 하여금 수증기를 위로 올려 보내도록 만들어, 그 결과 기저부분은 낮지만 23,000미터 높이에 이를 수도 있는 구름이 형성된다. 수직운은 격렬한 날씨와 관련이 있는데, 이 구름들이 갑작스런 폭우, 강한 돌풍, 그리고 번갯불의 섬광을 일으키기 때문이다.

Listening Section   p.15

Answers

1. Ⓑ [Gist-Content Question]
2. Ⓓ [Detail Question]
3. Ⓑ [Understanding Organization Question]
4. Ⓐ [Understanding Attitude Question]

5. Ⓒ [Understanding Function Question]
6. Ⓑ [Gist-Content Question]
7. Ⓓ [Gist-Purpose Question]
8. Ⓐ [Detail Question]
9. Ⓒ [Understanding Organization Question]
10. Ⓒ [Making Inferences Question]
11. Ⓓ [Understanding Function Question]

Script

| 01-02 |

W Student: Good afternoon. Uh, I was told that I need to come here to get a, uh, replacement key for my dorm room.

M Student Services Employee: That's right. Lost your key, huh?

W: Yeah, and I have absolutely no clue what happened to it. One minute it was in my bag, and the next minute . . . Well, it was nowhere to be found.

M: ⁴These things happen. Don't worry about it.

W: I know, but I'm just not used to losing things. It's not my style. Anyway . . . So, uh, what exactly do I need to do in order to get a new key?

M: It's pretty simple. You need to fill out this form here . . . You know, just write down your name, address, and all of the other stuff it asks for. Oh, and I need to see a copy of your student ID to verify that you are who you say you are.

W: Sure. That makes sense to me. Anything else?

M: Yeah, it'll cost you twenty dollars to get the new key made up.

W: Twenty dollars? But, but I didn't have to pay anything when I got my key the first time.

M: Sure. Everyone gets their key for free on the first day of school. But if you lose your key, you have to pay the replacement fee to get a new one made up. And the replacement fee comes to twenty dollars.

W: ⁵Okay. What you say makes sense. I guess I can come up with the money. After all, it's my fault that it's missing anyway.

M: That's the spirit. You know, most students whine and complain about the cost. It's nice to see someone like you take a little bit of personal responsibility. I don't get to see that too often.

W: Thanks, but I'm still not happy about having to pay the fee. Oh well . . . Like you said, I ought to be personally responsible for it . . . And it's not your fault I lost it either. So, uh, when will I be able to pick up my key? Later today?

M: Uh, no. Sorry. Er, your key will be ready by Monday morning.

W: Monday morning? Surely you must be joking. Today's Friday. What am I supposed to do over the weekend? How am I going to get in and out of my room for the next three days?

M: I don't know. Borrow your roommate's key?

W: Hmm . . . I suppose I could do that, but she's going away for the weekend.

M: That sounds perfect then. Just borrow her key while she's gone and then give it back to her when she comes back on Sunday night.

W: Actually, that's, uh, that's kind of a problem. You see . . . She won't be coming back until Monday afternoon, and I've got class all day long. She might be locked out of the room for a while. Are you sure there isn't any possible way you could get me the key before you close today?

M: Well . . . Okay, I could put a rush order on it, but that will cost you an extra ten dollars. That would bring the amount you owe to thirty dollars. Is that all right?

W: I guess I don't really have much of a choice. Should I pay you now, or can I wait until I come back later this afternoon?

M: Just pay me when you get the key. Be here by five thirty, and I'll have everything ready for you.

Translation

W Student: 안녕하세요. 음, 기숙사의 대체 키를 받아가야 해서요, 음, 저, 여기로 와야 한다고 이야기를 들었거든요.

M Student Services Employee: 맞아요. 열쇠를 잃어버리셨군요, 그렇죠?

W: 네, 어떻게 그런 일이 일어났는지 정말 알 수가 없어요. 한 순간엔 제 가방에 있었다가, 바로 다음 순간에… 아, 찾을 수가 없는 거예요.

M: 흔히 일어나는 일인걸요. 신경 쓰지 마세요.

W: 알아요, 하지만 저는 물건을 잘 잃어버리지 않는 편이거든요. 저랑은 어울리지 않아요. 어쨌든… 저, 음, 새 열쇠를 받으려면 정확히 제가 어떻게 해야 하나요?

M: 아주 간단해요. 여기 양식의 빈 칸에 기입을 해주셔야 하는데… 그러니까, 단지 이름, 주소, 그리고 다른 사항들을 기입해주시면 돼요. 아, 그리고 당신의 신분을 증명할 수 있는 학생증 사본을 제가 확인해야 해요.

W: 물론이죠. 당연히 그러셔야죠. 다른 것은요?

M: 네, 새 열쇠를 제작하는 데는 20달러가 들 거예요.

W: 20달러라고요? 하지만, 하지만 제가 처음에 열쇠를 받았을 때는 돈을 내지 않았는데요.

M: 물론이죠. 모두가 개강 첫날에는 무료로 열쇠를 받죠. 하지만 열쇠를 잃어버리면, 새로 제작하는 교체 비용을 지불하셔야 해요. 그리고 대체 키는 20달러의 비용이 들고요.

W: 네, 일리가 있네요. 돈을 낼 수 있을 것 같아요. 결국, 어쨌든 잃어버린 것은 제 잘못이니까요.

M: 바로 그거예요. 아시다시피, 대부분의 학생들은 비용에 대해 우는 소리를 하거나 불평을 털어놓죠. 학생같이 개인적인 책임을

어느 정도 받아들이는 사람을 만나서 반갑네요. 그런 사람을 볼 기회는 많지가 않거든요.

W: 고마워요. 하지만 역시 비용을 지불해야 한다니 기분이 좋지는 않네요. 아 그러니까… 선생님이 말씀하시는 것처럼, 저는 제 개인적인 책임을 느끼고 있어요… 그리고 제가 잃어버린 것이 선생님의 잘못도 아니고요. 그러면, 음, 언제 제 열쇠를 받으러 오면 될까요? 오늘 늦게 정도?

M: 음, 아니오. 죄송해요. 음, 열쇠는 월요일 아침에 준비가 될 거예요.

W: 월요일 아침이요? 말도 안돼요. 오늘이 금요일인데. 주말에는 어떻게 하라고요? 앞으로 3일 동안 제 방에는 어떻게 출입을 하라는 건가요?

M: 잘 모르겠군요. 룸메이트의 열쇠를 빌려보는 것은 어떨까요?

W: 흠… 그렇게 해도 되겠네요. 그녀가 주말에 어디를 다녀오거든요.

M: 그럼 잘 되었네요. 그녀가 떠나 있는 동안만 열쇠를 빌리고 일요일 밤에 돌아오면 열쇠를 돌려주면 되잖아요.

W: 사실은, 음, 문제가 하나 있어요. 그러니까… 그녀는 월요일 오후까지는 돌아오지 않을 예정이고, 저는 그날 하루 종일 수업이 있어요. 그녀는 문이 잠겨서 한동안 밖에 있어야 할 거예요. 정말 오늘 문 닫기 전에 제가 열쇠를 받을 수 있는 방법은 없을까요?

M: 음… 좋아요. 제가 속달로 주문을 할 수는 있는데요, 그러면 10달러의 추가비용이 들어요. 그러면 총 30달러의 비용이 드는 것이죠. 괜찮겠어요?

W: 제 생각에는 선택의 여지가 없는 것 같네요. 지금 돈을 드려야 하나요, 아니면 오후에 다시 와서 드려도 되나요?

M: 열쇠를 받을 때 주세요. 5시 30분까지 여기로 오시면, 제가 다 준비를 해놓고 있을게요.

Script

| 01-03 |

M Professor: Okay, so let's move on to the Silk Road trade routes and their impact on the history of the regions that they covered. First, to clear up a couple of points, look at this map here . . . As you can see, the Silk Road's two ends were in China here . . . and the Mediterranean area right here . . . Note that there was no single road planned and built as there would be today. Instead, over a long period of time, people in cities and towns developed connections with their neighbors. These connections led to the establishing of trade routes, so, eventually, the entire way from the Mediterranean to China could be traversed by land. Don't be mistaken though. These routes weren't standardized. Sometimes there was a single track. Other times, there was an actual road. And, at times, like in deserts or on the steppes, there were simply markers pointing the way.

W Student: Professor Cameron, how old is the Silk Road?

M: Hmm . . . It depends on where you are. The archaeological evidence points to some parts of it being thousands of years old. Additionally, artifacts thousands of miles from their points of origin have been found along it. For instance, what's believed to be Chinese silk has been found in ancient Egyptian tombs.

Now, what permitted the Silk Road to stretch for more than 5,000 miles? Without a doubt, it was the domestication of animals, particularly pack animals such as donkeys, camels, and horses, which enabled trade to flourish. These animals could carry heavy loads over great distances. Also, the grasslands on the Central Asian steppes provided food for the animals, so their masters could carry less fodder and more items to trade. Of course, the journey was long . . . It could take a year or more to cover . . . and it was perilous, with brigands suddenly attacking, fierce storms springing up, and, uh, high mountains that needed to be passed.

So, the connections people made while on the Silk Road led to a great deal of, well, a great deal of cultural interaction. Interestingly enough, the actions of some cultures let other cultures expand along it. Let me explain . . . The great Persian Empire, which covered the lands occupied by modern-day Iran and Iraq built many roads along the Silk Road. These eased transportation problems throughout the empire. Yet it was the forces of Alexander the Great, in the fourth century B.C., which made use of those roads to invade the Persians and conquer them. Thus Hellenism, which is the spread of Greek culture, language, and ideals, moved along the Silk Road. Centuries later, Islamic forces traveled on the Silk Road to spread Islam to Central Asia. Even today, there are Muslim enclaves in the far western region of China. Yet another example is that Buddhism traveled along the Silk Road from India to China, and, um, elsewhere in East Asia, where it remains a powerful influence today.

[11]By the first century A.D., the Silk Road was well established. The Chinese in particular made tremendous efforts, both of a diplomatic and military nature, to ensure that its links to the West remained open. For some time, they even had military forces patrolling sections of the route. **These forces dealt, er, shall we say, mercilessly with brigands and other thieves.** The Chinese also sent ambassadors to the lands of Central Asia to make treaties that would guarantee the free passage of traders. These efforts were quite effective, as evidenced by the transfer of Chinese technology to the West. While the matter is still subject to debate, the developments of paper, gunpowder, printing, and even large oceangoing ships in the West were all, to some extent, influenced by the Chinese.

In the late thirteenth century, the Mongols managed to conquer much of Northern and Central Asia. Ironically, despite all of the warfare, the Mongols brought stability to the Silk Road. You see, the Mongols, for all their terrifying ability on the battlefield, were wise administrators who were keen for trade with the West to continue. It was around that time that Marco Polo made his famous journey along the Silk Road to the Mongol court of Kublai Khan. Also, while the Mongols kept the central and eastern parts of the road open, the Byzantine Empire did the same in the western part for many centuries. However, in 1453, the Ottoman Turks conquered the Byzantines and took their capital, Constantinople. This put the western terminus of the Silk Road in peril.

With the Ottoman Turks in control, the people of Western Europe started looking for alternative routes to the Far East. They sent ships around the southern tip of Africa and pushed into the Indian Ocean. Later, they sailed across the Atlantic in search of what they had hoped would be a shorter route to Asia. Naturally, that didn't happen since North and South America stood in their way. But that's a topic for another day, so let's get into some more specific aspects of the Silk Road right now.

Translation

M Professor: 좋아요, 그럼 이제 실크로드 무역 루트와 그것이 해당 지역에 미친 역사적인 영향에 대해 알아봅시다. 첫째로, 몇 가지 사항을 명확히 하기 위해, 여기 있는 지도를 보세요… 보시다시피, 실크로드의 양쪽 끝은 여기 중국과… 바로 여기 지중해 지역입니다… 오늘날과 같이 계획해서 건설되었던 길은 없었다는 점에 주목해 주세요. 대신, 오랜 기간 동안, 도시와 마을의 사람들이 이웃 지역과의 연결 망을 발전시켰던 것입니다. 이 연결 망이 무역 루트로 자리잡게 되었고, 그래서, 결과적으로 지중해로부터 중국에 이르기까지 전체적인 경로가 육로로 횡단될 수 있게 된 것입니다. 하지만 오해하지는 마세요. 이 경로들이 표준화되어 있지는 않았습니다. 때로는 좁은 길이 있는 경우도 있었고, 실제 도로가 있는 경우도 있었습니다. 그리고, 때로는, 사막 지역 혹은 대초원 지대와 같은 곳에, 방향을 가리키는 단순한 표식만 있는 경우도 있었습니다.

W Student: *Cameron* 교수님, 실크로드는 얼마나 오래되었죠?

M: 음… 위치에 따라 다릅니다. 고고학적 증거에 따르면, 몇몇 지역에서는 수천 년이 되었다는 것을 알 수가 있어요. 게다가 몇몇 유물들은 원래 그것들이 있던 지역으로부터 수천 마일 떨어진 곳에서 발견되기도 합니다. 예를 들면, 중국산 비단이 고대 이집트의 무덤에서 발견되기도 했죠.

그러면, 실크로드가 5,000마일 이상 뻗어나갈 수 있었던 이유는 무엇이었을까요? 의심할 바 없이, 가축화 때문이었는데, 특히 당나귀, 낙타, 그리고 말과 같이 짐을 나르는 동물들을 가축으로 기르게 되었기 때문에 무역이 번성하게 된 것입니다. 이 동물들은 무거운 짐을 싣고 매우 먼 거리를 이동할 수 있었습니다. 또한, 동물들이 중앙 아시아 대초원 지대의 목초지에서 먹이를 먹을 수가 있었기 때문에, 동물의 주인들은 사료를 덜 싣고, 더 많은 무역 물품들을 실어 나를 수가 있었죠. 물론 여정은 길었습니다… 1년 혹은 그 이상 걸릴 수도 있었죠… 그리고 이는 위험한 것이기도 했는데, 도적들이 갑자기 공격해온다거나, 맹렬한 폭풍이 일어난다거나, 그리고 넘어가야 할 높은 산들이 있었기 때문입니다.

그리고, 실크로드에서 만들어졌던 연결 망 덕분에 정말이지 엄청나게 많은 문화적 상호 작용이 일어났습니다. 매우 흥미롭게도, 몇몇 문화적 활동 덕분에, 다른 문화의 확장이 이루어지기도 했습니다. 설명을 해 보자면… 지금의 이란과 이라크의 영토를 차지하고 있던 페르시아 제국은 실크로드를 따라 많은 도로를 건설했습니다. 이 도로들로 인해 페르시아 제국의 수송 문제가 완화되었습니다. 하지만 이 도로는 기원전 4세기경 알렉산더 대왕의 군대가 페르시아를 침범해서 그들을 정복했을 때 사용되었던 바로 그 도로였습니다. 이런 식으로 그리스의 문화, 언어, 그리고 사상을 전파한 헬레니즘 문명이 실크로드를 따라 이동하게 되었습니다. 수세기 후에는, 이슬람 군대가 실크로드를 통해서 이슬람 문명을 중앙아시아 지역으로 확산시켰습니다. 심지어 오늘날까지, 중국 서쪽의 멀리 떨어져 있는 곳에는 소수의 이슬람 집단들이 있습니다. 또 다른 사례는 불교가 실크로드를 따라 인도로부터 중국으로, 그리고 동아시아의 다른 지역들로 전파된 것인데, 불교는 오늘날에도 강한 영향력을 발휘하고 있습니다.

A.D. 1세기경, 실크로드는 기반이 잡혀있었습니다. 특히 중국인들이 서양과의 관계를 계속 유지하기 위해, 외교적, 군사적 측면에서 막대한 노력을 기울였습니다. 한동안, 그들은 자신들의 군대로 이 루트 상의 구역들을 순찰하기까지 했습니다. 이 군대는, 음… 뭐랄까요, 도적들과 다른 강도들을 무자비하게 대했습니다. 또한 중국인들은 무역상인들의 무료 통행을 보장하는 조약을 만들기 위하여 중앙아시아 지역에 특사를 파견하기도 했습니다. 이 노력들은 상당히 효과가 있었는데, 이는 중국의 기술이 서양으로 전파된 사실에서 입증될 수 있을 것입니다. 여전히 논쟁거리가 되고는 있지만, 서양은 종이, 화약, 인쇄술, 그리고 심지어 대형 외항선의 발명에 있어서, 전적으로, 혹은 부분적으로 중국의 영향을 받았습니다.

13세기 후반, 몽골인들은 북아시아와 중앙아시아를 점령했습니다. 모순적이게도, 이 모든 전쟁에도 불구하고, 몽골은 실크로드에 안정을 가져다 주었습니다. 여러분도 아시다시피, 몽골인들은 무서운 전투 능력도 가지고 있었지만, 서양과 계속해서 무역을 열심히 했던, 현명한 관리인들이었습니다. 이 때가 바로 그 유명한 마르코 폴로가 실크로드를 따라서 몽골의 쿠빌라이 황제의 궁전에 갔던 시기였습니다. 또한, 몽골이 이 루트의 중부와 동부 지역을 계속 개방해 두는 동안, 비잔틴 제국은 수 세기에 걸쳐 서쪽 지역에서 같은 역할을 수행했습니다. 하지만 1453년에 오스만 투르크가 비잔틴 제국과 그 수도인 콘스탄티노플을 정복했습니다. 이로 인하여 실크로드의 서쪽 끝은 위험에 처하게 되었죠.

오스만 투르크의 지배로 인해, 서유럽인들은 극동 지역으로의 대체 루트를 찾기 시작했습니다. 아프리카 남단으로 선박을 보내서, 인도양에 다다르도록 했습니다. 그 후, 그들은 아시아로 가는 더 가까운 경로를 찾기 위하여, 대서양을 가로질러 항해를 했습니다. 당연하게도, 남아메리카와 북아메리카가 길을 막고 있었기 때문에 그들의 목적은 달성되지 않았습니다. 하지만 이는 차후에 논의할 문제이며, 지금은 실크로드의 더 상세한 측면들을 다루어보기로 하겠습니다.

Actual Test 02

Reading Section   p.21

Answers

1. D [Factual Question]
2. C [Reference Question]
3. B [Factual Question]
4. D [Factual Question]
5. A [Vocabulary Question]
6. B [Rhetorical Purpose Question]
7. C [Inference Question]
8. C [Vocabulary Question]
9. A [Vocabulary Question]
10. D [Rhetorical Purpose Question]
11. B [Reference Question]
12. C [Negative Factual Question]
13. 4th [Insert Text Question]
14. A, C, D [Prose Summary Question]

Translation

다이아몬드의 형성

다이아몬드는 세상에서 가장 단단한 물질이며 가장 값비싼 것이기도 하다. 다이아몬드의 가치는 부분적으로 그 희소성에 기인하고 있는데, 이는 다이아몬드가 전 세계의 특정 지역에서만 발견되기 때문이다. 다이아몬드가 형성되기 위해서는 특별한 환경이 요구되므로 다이아몬드는 희귀하다. 지구상에는, 자연적으로 다이아몬드가 형성될 수 있는 두 가지 방법이 존재한다: 열과 압력이 땅 속 깊은 곳의 탄소에 영향을 미치는 경우와 운석이 지구에 충돌하는 경우가 그것이다. 하지만 이것이 다이아몬드가 형성되는 유일한 방법은 아니다. 지구상에 존재하는 특정 종류의 다이아몬드에는 우주에서 생성되어 운석의 조각으로서 지구에 도달한 것도 있다. 그리고 과학자들은 실험실에서 다이아몬드를 합성해 내는 법을 알게 되었는데, 이는 다이아몬드가 만들어질 수 있는 인공적인 방법이 된다.

수십억 년 전, 지구의 일부 지역의 깊은 곳에서, 탄소는 엄청난 열과 압력을 받아 다이아몬드를 형성시켰다. 10억에서 30억 년간에 걸쳐, 열과 압력이 합쳐져 탄소의 구조가 변형되었고, 다이아몬드 격자라고 알려진 매우 단단한 격자 구조가 만들어졌다. 광물학자들은 다이아몬드를 제8탄소 동소체 중의 하나로 분류하고 있는데, 이는 그 원자 구조로 말미암아 종류가 다른 탄소이다. 다이아몬드 격자의 일부분은 탄소 원자들의 강력한 공유 결합으로 이루어져 있는데, 이것에 의해 다이아몬드는 독특한 경도, 열전도성, 그리고 광도를 가지게 된다. 다이아몬드의 생성에 필요한 압력은 45~60킬로바 정도이다. 1킬로바는 대략 지구 기압의 1,000배이다. 또한, 그러한 변형이 발생하기 위해서는 섭씨 900~1,300° 정도의 온도가 필요하다. 이러한 조건은 지구 표면에서 대략 120~200킬로미터 정도 아래에서 발견될 수 있다. 일단 다이아몬드가 형성되면, 대부분은 화산 활동에 의하여 지표면에 도달하게 되는데, 이는 다이아몬드가 왜 활화산, 휴화산, 그리고 사화산 지역에서 발견되는지를 설명해 준다. 몇몇 경우, 다이아몬드는 생성되었던 지점에서 물에 의해 하류로 쓸려 내려온 후, 강 하구의 충적토에서 발견되기도 한다.

드문 경우이긴 하지만, 운석구에서 다이아몬드가 발견되기도 한다. 우주에서 날아 온 커다란 암석이 지구에 충돌할 때, 순간적으로, 다이아몬드가 생성되기 위해 필요한 압력 및 온도 상의 조건이 형성된다. 그 결과 – 즉 순식간에 탄소가 다이아몬드로 변형되는 현상은 – 초고온 변성 작용이라고 불리며, 이로써 마이크로 다이아몬드가 생성된다. 마이크로 다이아몬드의 크기는 대개 1센티미터를 넘지 않는다. 오래된 충돌 분화구를 조사하던 학자들이 마이크로 다이아몬드를 발견해낸 것은 최근의 일이었다. 3천 5백만 년 전에 운석의 충돌이 있었던 러시아 시베리아의 한 장소는 마이크로 다이아몬드가 생성되었던 지역 중의 하나이다.

외계 혹은 소행성에서 생성되어 운석의 일부분으로서 지구에 도달하게 된 다이아몬드는 훨씬 더 희귀하다. 과학자들은 수명을 다한 별이 강력한 방사선 섬광을 만들어낼 때, 이러한 다이아몬드가 생성된다고 추측하고 있다. 이 다이아몬드들은 종종 크기가 상당히 작기 때문에 나노 다이아몬드라고 알려져 있다. 우주에서 생성될 수 있는 다이아몬드 중의 하나는 탄소 나노 다이아몬드이다. 이 다이아몬드들은 지구상에서 오직 두 곳에서만 발견되고 있다: 남아메리카 브라질의 충적토와 아프리카의 서쪽 해안이다. 광물학자들은 남아메리카와 아프리카가 하나의 대륙을 이루고 있었을 때 한 번의 큰 충돌로 이러한 다이아몬드가 만들어졌다고 추측하고 있다. 두 대륙이 분리되기 전, 운석에 포함되어 있던 다이아몬드가 땅에 흩어졌다는 것인데, 이는 바다에 의해 갈라져 있는 두 대륙에서 현재 나노 다이아몬드가 발견되고 있는 원인을 설명해 준다.

다이아몬드에 대한 인간의 욕망으로 인하여 다이아몬드는 실험실에서도 만들어지고 있다. 1950년대 이후, 과학자들은 여러 가지 방법을 통해서 합성 다이아몬드를 만들 수 있었다. 하지만, 그 과정은 지구상 깊은 곳에서 다이아몬드가 자연적으로 만들어지는 과정과 유사하다. 과학자들은 다이아몬드에 엄청난 고온과 고압을 가해야 한다. 이러한 과정의 결과로서 주로 산업용 목적으로 사용되는 작은 다이아몬드가 생성된다. 그러나, 일부는 다이아몬드 원석으로 변하기도 하는데, 이는 전세계 다이아몬드 채광 기업들의 노여움을 사고 있다. (그러한 이유 중 하나는 합성 다이아몬드가 사실상 천연 다이아몬드와 동일하지만 비용은 진짜 다이아몬드보다 훨씬 더 저렴하다는 사실에 있다.) 이들은 다이아몬드 구매자들이 진짜 다이아몬드를 원하고 있기 때문에 그들이 진짜 다이아몬드를 얻었다고 확신하지 않는 한, 즉 수억 년에 걸쳐서 지구 깊은 곳에서 만들어진 진짜 다이아몬드라는 점이 보장되지 않는 한, 다이아몬드가 판매되어서는 안 된다고 주장하고 있다.

Listening Section   p.27

Answers

1. D [Gist-Purpose Question]
2. C [Detail Question]
3. C [Understanding Attitude Question]
4. B [Making Inferences Question]
5. A [Understanding Function Question]
6. A [Gist-Content Question]
7. A [Detail Question]
8. B [Understanding Attitude Question]
9. B [Understanding Organization Question]
10. D [Connecting Content Question]
11. D [Making Inferences Question]

Script

| 02-02 |

W1 Student: Hi, Professor Sanderson. Do you happen to have a moment to talk to me?

W2 Professor: Of course, Lisa. Oh, uh, before I forget, I'd really like to thank you for all of the help that you gave me at the poetry conference last weekend. Your assistance, and that of all of the other student volunteers, of course, was invaluable to us pulling off a successful conference.

W1: Oh, it was nothing. I was just glad to be able to attend the conference and get to meet a lot of writers. I found it was a totally . . . uh, well, a totally amazing experience. I can't wait to attend the next conference.

W2: Well, hopefully you won't have to do so much work the next time, and, instead, you'll get to listen to some of the authors read their poetry or their critiques on other writers' poems. That would probably be more fun than setting up chairs and putting out refreshments.

W1: Yeah, that would really be ideal.

W2: Okay, so, what did you want to see me about?

W1: Oh, right. I almost forgot. Actually, er, it's connected to the poetry conference. You see, I was wondering . . .

W2: ⁵Yes? Wondering what?

W1: Well, okay . . . This is a little embarrassing, but I want to be totally honest with you.

W2: Go ahead and spit it out. It's all right.

W1: You see, I had no idea what most of those poems were about. Okay, some were pretty easy to understand. Like, uh, like the ones by Professor Michelson and Gene Emerson. They were easy for me to figure out what they were talking about, but, uh . . .

W2: Yeah, some of the others were a little, uh, shall we say . . . obscure.

W1: Yes. That's the word I'm looking for.

W2: Let me guess . . . So now you're feeling like you, uh, shouldn't be majoring in English literature if you can't figure out what a few short poems mean, right?

W1: Exactly. It's been bothering me for the past week. I don't know what to do.

W2: Okay, well, the first thing you should do is relax. You see, a lot of modern poetry can be . . . hmm . . . I suppose you'd say it can be incomprehensible.

W1: Then how do we know if it's any good?

W2: That's a good question. It's also something I'm going to focus on in tomorrow's lecture.

W1: Really? That's a relief. I mean, it seemed to me that some of those poets just wrote down whatever words popped into their heads at times.

W2: I wouldn't go that far, but I see your point. Anyway, if you can be patient and wait until tomorrow, I'll go over some of the poems that were presented and explain how we can tell quality poems from ones that aren't so good.

W1: Is it really possible to tell that?

W2: Sure. I mean, don't get quality confused with personal taste. I think most people would agree that William Shakespeare wrote quality work, but not everyone likes his plays or poems. See what I mean?

W1: Ah, I think so. So, some of those poems might have seemed silly or boring to me, but that doesn't detract from their value as literature. Am I right?

W2: Bingo. That's exactly what I'm talking about.

W1: Okay. I can hardly wait until tomorrow's lecture then. I'll see you then.

Translation

W1 Student: Sanderson 교수님, 안녕하세요. 저와 잠시 이야기를 나눌 수 있는 시간이 되시나요?

W2 Professor: 물론이죠, Lisa. 아, 음, 잊어버리기 전에, 지난 주 시 토론회에서 도와줘서 정말 고마워요. 학생의 도움이, 물론, 다른 지원자들도 그랬지만, 성공적인 토론회를 이끌어내는 데 매우 중요했어요.

W1: 아, 아닙니다. 저는 토론회에 참여해서 많은 작가들을 만난 것만으로도 기뻤어요. 저에게는 정말… 아, 그러니까, 정말 놀라운 경험이었어요. 다음 토론회에도 꼭 참석하고 싶어요.

W2: 음, 아마도 다음 번에는 그렇게 많은 것을 하지는 않아도 되고, 대신, 작가들이 자신들의 시를 읽고 다른 작가들의 시를 비평하는 것을 듣게 될 거예요. 의자를 준비하고 다과를 내놓는 것보다는 더 재미있겠죠.

W1: 네, 그러면 정말 좋을 것 같아요.

W2: 좋아요, 그럼, 나를 만나고자 한 이유가 무엇인가요?

W1: 아, 맞아요. 잊어버릴 뻔 했어요. 사실은, 음, 시 토론회와 관계가 있는 거예요. 그러니까, 제가 궁금해서…

W2: 네? 무엇이 궁금한가요?

W1: 음, 좋아요… 좀 부끄럽긴 하지만, 정말 솔직하게 말씀 드릴게

요.

W2: 계속 말해봐요. 괜찮아요.

W1: 그러니까, 저는 이 시들이 대부분 무엇에 관한 것인지 잘 모르겠어요. 그래요, 몇몇 시들은 이해하기가 꽤 쉬워요. 마치, 음, 마치 *Michelson* 교수님과 *Gene Emerson* 교수님이 쓰신 것처럼요. 그 시들은 무엇에 대해 말하고 있는지를 이해하기가 쉬운데요, 하지만, 음…

W2: 네, 다른 작품들은 약간, 음, 말하자면… 모호하죠.

W1: 네, 제가 찾던 표현이 그거예요.

W2: 제가 맞춰 볼게요… 그러니까 학생은 자신이, 음, 자신이 몇몇 짧은 시를 이해하지 못한다면 영문학을 전공해서는 안 된다고 생각하는 거죠, 그렇죠?

W1: 맞아요. 지난 주에 계속 고민했어요. 어떻게 해야 좋을지 모르겠어요.

W2: 좋아요, 음, 우선 좀 진정할 필요가 있겠네요. 알다시피, 많은 현대 시는… 음… 이해하기 힘든 것일 수도 있다고 생각해요.

W1: 그러면 그 시가 좋은 것인지를 어떻게 알 수 있나요?

W2: 좋은 질문이에요. 내일 강의에서 초점을 맞춰 볼 문제이기도 하고요.

W1: 정말인가요? 안심이 되네요. 제 생각에, 일부 시인들은 그때 그때 자신들의 머릿속에서 떠오르는 말들을 적어놓는 것 같이 보였거든요.

W2: 그렇게까지는 생각하지 않지만, 학생이 말하고 있는 바는 알겠군요. 어쨌든, 내일까지 기다릴 수 있다면, 제시된 시들을 검토해보고 좋지 않은 시들과 뛰어난 시들을 구분할 수 있는 방법을 설명해 줄게요.

W1: 그것들을 구분하는 것이 가능한가요?

W2: 물론이죠. 내 말은, 우수성과 개인적인 취향을 혼동해서는 안 된다는 거예요. 내 생각에, 대부분의 사람들은 윌리엄 셰익스피어가 우수한 작품들을 썼다는데 동의하겠지만, 모든 사람들이 그의 희곡과 시를 좋아하지는 않을 거예요. 내 말이 무슨 뜻인지 알겠어요?

W1: 아, 그런 것 같아요. 그렇다면, 몇몇 시들이 저에게 우스워 보이거나 지루해 보일 수도 있지만, 그것이 문학으로서의 가치를 떨어뜨리는 것은 아니라는 것이죠, 맞나요?

W2: 그래요. 제 말이 바로 그거예요.

W1: 좋아요. 내일 강의가 정말 기다려져요. 내일 뵙겠습니다.

Script

| 02-03 |

W Professor: There's no argument that Charles Darwin is among the greatest of all naturalists in history. His fame rests on the works published late in his life, most especially *The Origin of Species*, which laid the groundwork for his theories on evolution and natural selection. Many of the ideas for his theories came to him during his five-year voyage aboard a ship called the *Beagle*, which was engaged in a British scientific expedition from, uh, I believe it was 1831 to 1836. It made a voyage around the world during that time. So, first, let's talk a bit about Charles Darwin, and then we'll concentrate on his voyage on the *Beagle*.

Darwin was British and was born in, ah, 1809. He married his cousin Emma when he was almost thirty, and they had ten children, seven of whom survived to adulthood. Darwin's father was a wealthy doctor and wanted Charles to enter the same profession, but Charles was far more interested in geology and natural history. His father's wealth enabled him to indulge in his passions, and he had become well known in scientific circles by the time he traveled on the *Beagle*. Darwin was only twenty-two at the time of the voyage. The captain of the *Beagle* had wanted a gentleman companion for the long voyage, and, after much searching, Darwin was selected. The previous captain of the *Beagle* had committed suicide while on a scientific expedition, and the new captain feared that the loneliness of command might get to him as well. So he wanted someone around his age . . . oh, the captain was only twenty-five . . . You know, he wanted someone to be his friend. In a fortuitous event, for himself and for human history, Darwin was chosen.

The *Beagle* was on a scientific expedition, so, to that end, its crew was entrusted to map the coast of South America, to engage in astronomical and chronological timekeeping experiments, to examine the geological features of the South American coast, and to examine the flora and fauna of the lands the ship visited. Interestingly enough, on the voyage, Darwin spent more time on land than at sea. His observations and collections of specimens were periodically sent back to England by whatever ship the *Beagle* encountered. As the voyage continued and Darwin sent back more plant and animal specimens—many of which were previously unknown—his fame grew. By the time he returned to his homeland, he was treated as a great scientific mind.

Now, the *Beagle* made many stops on its voyage and went completely around the world, but it is most famous for its visits to the Galapagos Islands to the west of South America. Much has been made of Darwin's observations there and how they influenced his later theories, which he published in *The Origin of Species*. The reality is that, well, the entire voyage had a profound influence on his ideas and many other theories as well. For example, his observations of seashell fossils high in the Andes Mountains gave credence to the notion that mountains rise from lowlands to highlands. Yet, it was on the Galapagos Islands that he made one of his most profound observations. A group of finches—a type of bird—were observed and discovered to be unlike any other finches found elsewhere in the world. Fossils of the same birds found on the island also showed distinctive differences. So, well, Darwin put two and two together and theorized that the birds had somehow transformed from the earlier fossilized species into their current form. The birds transmuted, or, as we prefer to say now, they evolved.

Initially, Darwin kept his theories on evolution to himself and a select circle of friends and colleagues. He did this mostly because of his fear of being persecuted. Nowadays, we may laugh at this notion, but, in Darwin's time, the ideas that man descended from apes and that animals actually evolved contradicted most religious, by which I mean Christian, sentiment. Most Europeans' religious beliefs held that all species were as God created them and that they couldn't change. Darwin and many others, however, believed in transmutation. According to them, a species could adapt itself to its environment and to other changes over time. Hand in hand with this belief went the idea that natural selection was at play here. Natural selection was the theory that a species changes to make itself better, faster, and stronger and that the best and strongest members of a species survive while the others fail to reproduce and die.

[11]Darwin worked on his theory of evolution for around twenty years and didn't dare to publish it until he was absolutely certain of his thoughts. **Then, in 1858, a fellow scientist sent him a letter explaining his own ideas, which were remarkably similar to Darwin's.** Almost immediately, Darwin presented his theory at a scientific gathering, and, in November 1859, *The Origin of Species* was published. So . . . what happened after he announced his findings? Let's take a look at that now.

Translation

W Professor: 찰스 다윈이 역사상 가장 위대한 동식물학자들 중의 한 명이라는 점에 대해서는 이견이 없습니다. 그의 명성은 그가 노년에 펴낸 저서들, 특히 진화와 자연 선택의 이론에 근거를 둔 종의 기원과 같은 책에서 얻은 것입니다. 그의 이론상 많은 견해들은 그가 비글이라는 배로 5년간 해외여행을 하면서 얻은 것인데, 음… 제 생각엔 아마도 이 배가 1831년에서 1836년까지 영국의 과학 탐험에 참여한 것 같습니다. 이 배는 이 시기에 세계를 항해했습니다. 그래서 우선, 찰스 다윈에 대한 이야기를 좀 하고, 비글호에서의 그의 항해에 집중해 보도록 하겠습니다.

다윈은 영국 태생으로, 어, 1809년에 태어났습니다. 그는 거의 30세가 다 되어서야 사촌 엠마와 결혼을 했고, 10명의 아이를 두었는데, 그 중 7명이 생존해서 성인이 되었습니다. 다윈의 아버지는 부유한 의사였으며, 아들도 같은 직업을 갖기를 원했지만, 찰스는 지질학과 자연 과학에 더 많은 관심을 가지고 있었습니다. 아버지의 부유함 덕분에 그는 자신의 열정에 빠져들 수 있었고, 비글호를 타고 여행할 당시에는 과학계에서도 잘 알려져 있었습니다. 항해를 할 당시 그는 겨우 22세였습니다. 비글호 선장은 기나긴 항해를 같이 할 점잖은 동료를 원하고 있었는데, 물색 끝에 다윈을 선택했습니다. 비글호의 전 선장은 과학 탐험 도중 자살을 했고, 새로운 선장은 지휘에 따르는 외로움 때문에 자신 역시 영향을 받게 될지도 모른다는 두려움을 갖고 있었습니다. 그래서 그는 자기와 나이가 비슷한 사람을 원했는데… 음, 그 선장은 겨우 25세였습니다. 여러분도 아시다시피, 그는 자신의 친구가 될만한 사람을 원했던 것입니다. 뜻밖의 사건으로 인하여, 그 스스로를 위해 그리고 인류 역사를 위해 다윈이 선택되었습니다.

비글호는 과학 탐험 중이었는데, 그렇기 때문에, 탑승자들은 남아메리카 해안의 지도를 완성하는 임무와, 천문 및 연대 측정 실험, 남아메리카 해안의 지질학적 특징에 대한 조사, 그리고 배가 방문하게 되는 지역들의 동식물들에 관한 조사 임무를 맡고 있었습니다. 매우 흥미롭게도, 항해하는 도중, 다윈은 바다에서 보다 육지에서 더 많은 시간을 보내게 되었습니다. 그가 관찰한 것들과 수집한 표본들은 비글호가 만났던 배를 통해 정기적으로 영국에 보내졌습니다. 항해가 계속되고 다윈이 더 많은 동식물의 표본들을 보냄에 따라, - 이 표본들 중 다수는 이전에는 알려지지 않았던 것들이었는데 - 그의 명성은 높아졌습니다. 그가 고국으로 돌아왔을 때, 사람들은 그를 위대한 과학자로 대했습니다.

음, 비글호는 항해도중 여러 곳에 들렀으며 전 세계를 돌아다녔는데, 그 중 가장 유명한 것은 남아메리카 서쪽의 갈라파고스 군도를 방문한 것이었습니다. 다윈이 그곳에서 관찰한 것들과 그것들이 그의 차후 이론에 영향을 미치게 된 방법에 대해서는 많은 이야기들이 있어왔는데, 그는 종의 기원에서 자신의 이론을 발표하였습니다. 실제로는, 음, 전체적인 항해가 그의 생각과 다른 여러 이론들에도 심오한 영향을 주었습니다. 예를 들면, 안데스 산맥의 고원 지대에서 발견한 바닷조개 화석은 이 산맥이 저지대에서 고지대로 융기했다는 믿음을 심어주었습니다. 그러나 그가 가장 심오한 관찰을 하게 되었던 곳은 바로 갈라파고스 군도였습니다. 핀치라는 - 새의 종류입니다 - 무리가 관찰되었는데, 이는 전세계 어느 곳에서 발견되는 핀치와는 다른 종류였습니다. 이 섬에서 발견되는 같은 종류의 새들도 화석들간에는 확연한 차이점이 보였습니다. 그래서, 음, 다윈은 이러한 정보를 활용해서 그 새가 이전에 화석화된 종에서 현재의 형태로, 어떤 식으로든 변형되었다는 이론을 세웠습니다. 이 새는 변형된 것이었습니다. 즉, 우리가 오늘날 말하는 바대로, 그들은 진화한 것이었습니다.

처음에, 진화에 대한 이론은 다윈 자신과 친구들, 그리고 동료들끼리만 알고 있었습니다. 이렇게 했던 주요한 이유는 종교적 박해에 대한 두려움 때문이었습니다. 지금은 이와 같은 생각이 우스워 보일지는 몰라도, 다윈이 살던 시대에는, 인간이 유인원으로부터 유래되었고 동물들이 실제로 진화했다는 생각은 대부분의 종교, 즉, 기독교적인 정서와 배치되는 것이었습니다. 대부분 유럽인들의 종교적인 믿음에 따르면 모든 종들은 신이 창조했고 그들은 변할 수 없는 존재였습니다. 하지만, 다윈과 다른 많은 이들은 변화에 대해 믿고 있었습니다. 그들에 따르면, 종은 환경에 적응할 수 있으며 시간이 흐르면서 다른 변화에도 적응할 수 있었습니다. 이러한 믿음에서 자연 선택이 작용하고 있다는 점이 도출되었습니다. 자연 선택이란 한 종이 더 뛰어나고, 더 빠르고, 더 강한 종으로 변화해서, 가장 뛰어나고 가장 강한 종의 일부만 살아남고 그렇지 못한 것들은 번식에 실패한 채 죽는다는 이론입니다.

다윈은 진화론 연구를 20년 정도 계속했지만, 자신의 생각에 대해 절대적으로 확신하기 전까지는 감히 그것을 발표하지 못했습니다. 그리고 나서 1858년에, 한 동료 과학자가 자신의 생각을 설명하는 편지를 그에게 보냈는데, 이는 다윈의 생각과 상당히 비슷한 것이었습니다. 곧바로, 다윈은 자신의 이론을 과학 모임에서 발표하게 되고, 1859년 11월에 종의 기원을 출판합니다. 그래서… 그가 자신이 발견한 것들을 발표한 후에 무슨 일이 일어났을까요? 이제 그것에 대해서 알아보도록 합시다.

Actual Test 03

Reading Section   p.33

Answers

1. C   [Vocabulary Question]
2. D   [Factual Question]
3. A   [Vocabulary Question]
4. D   [Vocabulary Question]
5. C   [Factual Question]
6. A   [Rhetorical Purpose Question]
7. A   [Factual Question]
8. B   [Reference Question]
9. C   [Rhetorical Purpose Question]
10. A   [Factual Question]
11. C   [Sentence Simplification Question]
12. C   [Factual Question]
13. 2nd   [Insert Text Question]
14. B, D, F   [Prose Summary Question]

Translation

신세계가 유럽에 미친 영향

1492년, 크리스토퍼 콜럼버스가 미대륙을 발견했다. 이러한 발견은, 남아메리카와 북아메리카가 알려지게 되면서, 결국 신세계 전체가 탐사되어 유럽의 열강들에게 분할되는 결과로 이어졌다. 스페인, 포르투갈, 영국, 그리고 프랑스가 가장 앞서나갔다. 신세계의 발견은 미대륙뿐만 아니라, 구대륙에도, 유럽은 곧 이렇게 불리게 되었는데, 많은 변화를 가져왔다. 이러한 변화 중 몇 가지는 매우 사소한 것들이었지만, 중대한 변화들도 있었으며, 이는 광범위하고 장기적인 영향을 두 대륙 모두에 끼치게 되었다.

16세기 동안, 대서양으로 수많은 탐험대를 보냈던 스페인 인들은, 중앙아메리카와 남아메리카를 정복했다. 주로 야망과 탐욕에 이끌려, 스페인 정복자들은 원주민들을 패배시키고 막대한 양의 금과 은을 찾아내거나 - 혹은 빼앗았다. 이 노획물의 대부분은 결국 스페인의 국고로 들어갔다. 이와 같은 부의 유입으로 인해 스페인은 전례 없던 힘을 가지게 되었고, 이로써 16세기 대부분 동안 스페인은 유럽에서 최강국이 되었다. 하지만 스페인의 지도자들은, 특히 필립 2세는 새로 발견된 부를 현명하게 관리하지 못했다. 대신, 종종 낭비를 일삼아서, 1500년대 스페인 군주들은 수 차례의 파산을 선언하게 되었다. 스페인의 군사적 활동 역시 방만하게 운영되었고, 1588년 스페인의 무적함대가 영국군에게 패배한 사건은 스페인 군의 가장 유명한 실책이 되었다. 결국, 스페인은 혁명과 다른 나라와의 전쟁으로 인하여, 한때 지배적이었던 지위와 신세계 식민지의 대부분을 잃게 되었다.

신세계의 발견은 유럽에서의 무역과 유럽 국가들의 경제에 극적인 영향을 미쳤다. 신세계에서 유입되고 스페인에 의해 방탕하게 사용된 금과 은은, 역사학자들이 "가격혁명"이라고 부르게 된, 인플레이션의 시기를 이끌어냈다. 16세기 중반에서 17세기 후반까지, 유럽 대부분의 지역에서 물가는 5배, 혹은 6배 정도 상승했다. (이전에는 그와 같이 급격한 비율로 그리고 그렇게 짧은 기간 동안 물가가 상승한 적이 없었다.) 이러한 인플레이션은 모든 제품에 대한 수요의 증가뿐만이 아니라, 유럽의 인구가 증가한 결과이기도 했다. 따라서 무역량이 증가하게 되었고, 스페인의 금과 은은 유럽 대륙의 각지로 퍼져나갔다. 상품이나 서비스를 물물 교환하는 대신, 사람들은 판매되는 모든 것에 대해 현금을 요구했다. 그러한 결과, 유럽 경제는 변화했다. 한때는 주로 물물 교환에 기반을 두고 있었던 경제가 이제는 현금에 기반을 둔 경제로 바뀌게 된 것이다. 이와 동시에, 유럽 무역의 중심지는 베니스나 제노아와 같은 지중해의 거대한 도시 국가에서 서유럽쪽으로 이동했다. 무역의 증가로 인해 스페인이 혜택을 받았을 뿐만 아니라, 영국, 프랑스, 포르투갈, 그리고 네덜란드 또한 자신들의 국력이 상승하는 현상을 목격하게 되었다.

신세계가 구세계에 미친, 겉으로 보기에는 보다 미미하지만 - 더 지속적이었던 영향은 신세계에서 흔한 식량 자원이었던 식물들이 유럽으로 수입된 점이다. 콜럼버스의 항해 이전, 감자, 토마토, 호박, 콩, 옥수수, 그리고 많은 종류의 후추들이 유럽에서는 알려져 있지 않았다. 많은 사람들이 처음에는 이러한 일부 식물들 - 특히 토마토에 대해 - 불신을 나타냈고 먹지 않으려 했지만, 결국, 신세계로부터의 여러 수입품들은 유럽 식단의 주요 식품이 되었다. 이것들은 가난한 유럽의 농부들에게 막대한 혜택을 가져다 주었다. 밀과 비교해 보면 감자와 옥수수는 토지 및 노동 사용량에 비해 보다 높은 음식 에너지를 생산해 냈다. 따라서 사람들은 이와 같은 신세계의 생산물들로 식단의 질을 향상시킬 수 있었는데, 이로 인해 사람들은 예전보다 훨씬 더 건강해 질 수 있었다.

신세계와 구세계의 무역은 매우 일방적인 것이었다. 금, 은, 그리고 특별한 곡물들에 대한 보답으로, 신세계의 원주민들은 끔찍한 질병, 문화의 파괴, 그리고 그와 같은 격변기에 거의 살아남을 수 없었던 노예라는 지위를 얻었다. 서유럽 국가들에 대해 말하자면, 그들은 신세계 식민지들에서 축적한 부와 권력 덕분에 이후 4세기 동안 세계의 지배자가 될 수 있었다. 시간이 흐르면서, 이들의 국민들, 언어, 그리고 문화는 신세계에서뿐만 아니라 아프리카, 아시아, 그리고 오세아니아에서도 지배적인 지위를 누리게 되었다. 이와 같은 국가들은 20세기까지 전세계적인 강대국들로 남아있었는데, 20세기의 두 차례 파멸적인 전쟁으로 유럽은 쇠락하게 되었고, 반면 신세계 식민지였던 미국은 초 강대국으로 부상하게 되었다.

Listening Section   p.39

Answers

1. A   [Gist-Content Question]
2. C   [Gist-Purpose Question]

3. Ⓓ [Detail Question]
4. Ⓐ [Connecting Content Question]
5. Ⓒ [Understanding Attitude Question]
6. Ⓒ [Gist-Content Question]
7. Ⓑ [Detail Question]
8. Ⓐ [Understanding Organization Question]
9.

	Collective Action	Camouflage
Ⓐ		X
Ⓑ	X	
Ⓒ	X	
Ⓓ		X

[Connecting Content Question]

10. Ⓓ [Understanding Function Question]
11. Ⓑ [Understanding Attitude Question]

Script

| 03-02 |

M Student: Excuse me. I'm sorry to disturb you, but I have a really important question, and I'm not exactly sure with whom I should be speaking.

W Student Center Employee: Oh, sure. What can I help you with then?

M: Well, um, you see, I lost my student ID the other day, and, um, I'm not sure what I'm, um, supposed to do about it.

W: Okay, you've definitely come to the right place in that case. Uh, I'm assuming that you believe that you lost your ID card here in the student center, right?

M: Yeah, I'm pretty sure that's what happened. You see, I think I left it on one of the tables in the café over there. And, yeah, before you ask, I already went and spoke with the manager, but she said no one had turned a card in to her.

W: All right. That was going to be the first thing I was planning to suggest for you to do.

M: Yeah, strike one I guess. So, uh, what else can I do?

W: Well, a lot of times, people turn lost items . . . uh, books, ID cards, wallets, and other stuff . . . in to me. So let me see if I've got your ID card here.

M: Wow. That would be awesome.

W: Oh, I need your name and student ID number, please. All of the cards are organized alphabetically.

M: Sure. My name is Scott Johnson, and my ID number is 24034-2999.

W: Okay. Hold on a second . . .

M: Any luck? Is it there?

W: No, sorry. There's a David Johnson, but there's no Scott Johnson. Sorry to disappoint you. But it was a long shot that anyone would have turned in your ID anyway. In all likelihood, it got thrown out and is in the trash somewhere.

M: Out of curiosity, do you really have that many cards? Why don't you mail them to the students or call them when they lose their cards?

W: ⁵Well, first of all, we don't have access to the students' phone numbers, so we don't have any way of calling them.

M: Oh, uh, yeah. I suppose that makes sense.

W: And the second reason is the suggestion that I'm going to give you right now.

M: Oh? What's that?

W: It's that you're probably going to have to go and get yourself a new ID card. Most students do that as soon as they realize that their ID cards are missing, so that's why we don't bother trying to return them. They get a new one, and their old one is immediately deactivated so that no one can use it.

M: Oh . . . Um, okay, so what do I do to get a card?

W: You need to go to the student services building that's . . . Ah, you're a freshman here, aren't you?

M: Yeah, so I've got no clue where that building is. Sorry. Actually, er, to be honest, this campus is so big that I still have trouble finding my classrooms some of the time.

W: Don't apologize. It's no problem, and I totally understand. This is a big campus. Anyway . . . Go out this door here, turn right, and walk to the second building on your right. That's where you should go. The woman at the front desk—her name's Marcy—will tell you everything you need to do to get a new ID.

M: Wow, you've been a big help. Thanks so much.

Translation

M Student: 실례합니다. 방해해서 죄송하지만, 정말 중요한 질문이 하나 있는데요, 제가 누구와 이야기를 해야 될지 잘 모르겠어요.

W Student Center Employee: 아, 좋아요. 무엇을 도와드릴까요?

M: 음, 어, 그러니까, 제가 며칠 전에 학생증을 잃어버렸는데, 그래서, 음, 제가, 음, 어떻게 해야 할지 몰라서요.

W: 네, 그런 경우라면 잘 찾아 오셨네요. 그러니까, 학생은 여기 학생회관에서 학생증을 분실한 것 같다는 말씀이죠, 그렇죠?

M: 네, 분명히 그런 것 같아요. 그러니까, 제 생각에는 저기 카페 테이블 위에 놓아두었던 것 같은데요. 그리고, 아, 물어보시기 전에, 제가 이미 카페 매니저에게 가서 얘기해 봤지만, 그녀는 자신에게 학생증을 가져온 사람이 없었다고 했어요.

W: 좋아요. 제가 제안하려고 했던 첫 번째 일이 바로 그것이었어요.

M: 네, 제 추측이 맞았네요. 그러면, 음, 제가 무엇을 해야 하나요?

W: 음, 종종, 사람들이 분실물들을… 음, 책이나, 학생증, 지갑, 그리고 다른 것들도… 저에게 가져다 주죠. 그러니 학생의 학생증

이 여기 있는지 제가 확인해볼게요.

M: 오. 좋아요.

W: 아, 성함이랑 학번을 알려주세요. 모든 학생증이 알파벳 순으로 정리되어 있거든요.

M: 물론이죠. 제 이름은 *Scott Johnson*이고, 제 학번은 24034-2999에요.

W: 네, 잠시 기다려 주세요…

M: 찾으셨나요? 거기 있나요?

W: 아니요, 안됐네요. *David Johnson*은 있는데, *Scott Johnson*은 없군요. 실망시켜드려서 유감이네요. 하지만 누군가 당신의 학생증을 가져갈 것 같지는 않아요. 아마도, 버려져서 어딘가의 쓰레기 더미 속에 있을 것 같아요.

M: 궁금해서 여쭤보는 건데, 정말로 많은 학생증이 있다고 하셨죠? 학생증을 잃어버린 학생들에게 메일이나 전화를 해주는 것이 어떨까요?

W: 음, 우선, 우리는 학생들의 전화번호를 입수할 수 있는 권한이 없기 때문에, 연락을 할 수 있는 방법이 없어요.

M: 아, 음, 네. 이해할 수 있겠네요.

W: 그리고 두 번째 이유는 제가 지금 학생에게 제안하려는 것인데요.

M: 어? 무엇인가요?

W: 아마 직접 가서 새 학생증을 만들어야 할 거예요. 대부분의 학생들은 학생증을 잃어버렸다는 것을 알게 되자마자 그렇게 하죠. 새로운 학생증을 발급받으면, 기존의 학생증은 즉시 효력을 잃게 되어 다른 사람이 쓸 수 없게 되어요.

M: 아… 음, 알겠어요. 그러면 학생증을 받으려면 어떻게 해야 하나요?

W: 학생 복지 회관으로 가야 하는데… 아, 신입생이죠, 그렇죠?

M: 네, 그래서 그 건물이 어디에 있는지 잘 모르겠어요. 죄송해요. 사실은, 음, 솔직히 말하면, 이 캠퍼스가 너무 커서 아직 가끔씩 강의실 찾는데도 어려움이 있거든요.

W: 미안해할 필요는 없어요. 괜찮아요, 충분히 이해할 수 있어요. 이곳 캠퍼스는 정말 크죠. 어쨌든… 이 문을 나가서, 우회전하고, 우측의 두 번째 건물까지 걸어가세요. 그곳이 학생이 가야 될 장소에요. 프론트 데스크에 있는 여직원이 – 그녀의 이름은 *Marcy*인데 – 새 학생증을 발급받기 위해 해야 할 모든 것들을 알려줄 거에요.

M: 와, 큰 도움이 되었네요. 정말 고마워요.

Script

| 03-03 |

M Professor: Most animals, whether wild or domesticated, have defensive mechanisms that help them survive. These range from the most obvious—sharp teeth and claws, speed, and muscular strength—to some more, er, unusual defensive mechanisms, such as camouflage, venom, and, uh, shells. Above all else are the animals' instincts. These are the animals' natural abilities to sense danger and to take action in response to that danger. Even the tamest animal has retained some instincts from when it was wild despite the fact that domesticated animals aren't as suited to surviving in the wild as are their untamed cousins.

We'll focus on instincts another time. Right now, however, I want to explore the basics of animal defense systems. Animals' sight and hearing, which are typically sharp and keen, allow them to recognize an approaching enemy or potential danger. Most animals' eyes aren't forward looking but are instead situated on the sides of their heads. This enables them to see approaching danger from the side and behind them. Some animals are also quite sensitive to changes in their surroundings. Let's see . . . Snakes, for instance, can detect vibrations from approaching animals. As for hearing, well, bears have sharp hearing, so hikers often carry small bells on their backpacks to warn bears of their presence. This isn't just for the benefit of the bears though. It's also to help the, uh, the hikers since bears are among nature's most aggressive animals when surprised. I remember how I was once in Alaska on a field exhibition . . . Well, we surprised a grizzly and her cub . . . Phew. Let me just say that we were all fortunate that no one got hurt . . . or worse. Anyway, bears' strength, combined with their teeth and claws, makes them killing machines. So too are lions and tigers. They're built for battle. Sharks in the oceans and crocodiles and alligators in rivers are other examples of animals that prove that the best defense is a good offense.

The vast majority of animals, including creatures such as insects . . . well, they lack features that let them defend themselves by attacking. So they compensate in other ways. Collective action is one such defense method. Basically, animals act in concert to defend each other. For example, while some animals are feeding, others may stand guard. Some breeds of African wild dogs have a scout dog that patrols the outskirts of the pack while looking for danger and sending warnings to the others. Many species use pheromones to signal incoming danger. Oh, yeah, right . . . Pheromones. What are they . . . ? They're chemical signals that are often scents unique to each species. Depending on their scents, they can have different meanings. One example is field mice, which use a pheromone that can signal other mice that danger is approaching. This lets all the mice flee together. A third collective method of protection is traveling in herds. Many mammals do this, so a protective group can sometimes stand its ground . . . and even assault predators. There is a remarkable video from South Africa that shows a herd of water buffaloes rescuing a baby from a group of lions that had run it down. The buffaloes fought back against multiple lions. They formed a group and charged the lions. One lion even got gored and sent airborne by a water buffalo. It was simply incredible to watch. Yes?

W Student: [10]Are those the only defensive methods animals use?

M: Not at all. Many animals use poison to defend themselves.

W: Seriously? Like what?

M: Let's see . . . Bees' stingers often have venom. Snakes, spiders, jellyfish, lizards, and even toads, among others, may employ some form of poison. Of course, sometimes the poison is a hunting tool used to weaken an opponent before killing and consuming it. But these venoms can be used defensively as well. And, in other animals, like the jellyfish, poison is primarily a defense measure.

Camouflage is yet another defensive mechanism. The ability to hide from one's enemies is highly desired in warfare, and it's not much of a stretch of the imagination to suggest that soldiers got the idea for camouflage from the animal world. Let's see. Military uniforms and vehicle paint schemes are designed to hide both men and machines into the background. [11]Similarly, many mammals have brown fur, which allows them to remain well hidden on land. In the Arctic region, polar bears and other animals are white to blend in with the snow. Many species in jungles are green . . . They're brown in the desert, blue in the oceans, and so on. **You get the point, right?** Some animals can even look like other objects. The walking stick looks like a stick, hence the name, while the stonefish looks like, uh, what else? A stone.

Hmm . . . Protective shells are another defensive measure some animals use. Turtles are the most well-known example. A turtle can withdraw its limbs inside its protective covering during times of danger. Crustaceans, such as lobsters, crabs, and seashells, all have hard outer shells, or carapaces, to provide protection from predators.

Translation

M Professor: 대부분의 동물들은, 야생 동물이건 사육되는 동물이건, 생존에 도움을 주는 방어 기제를 지니고 있습니다. 방어 기제에는 가장 손쉽게 알 수 있는 것들 – 이를테면, 날카로운 이빨과 발톱, 빠른 속도와 근육의 강도 – 도 있고, 더 나아가, 음, 예를 들면 위장, 독, 그리고… 음… 껍질과 같은 보다 특별한 방어 기제들도 있습니다. 무엇보다 중요한 것은 동물의 본능입니다. 본능이란 위험을 감지하고 그에 대응하여 행동을 취할 수 있는 동물의 능력을 말합니다. 심지어 가장 잘 길들여진 동물일지라도, 야생에 놓이게 되면, 비록 길들여지지 않은 같은 종류의 동물만큼 야생에서의 생존에는 적합하지 않을지 몰라도, 어느 정도의 본능은 가지고 있습니다.

본능에 대해서는 다음에 자세히 다루어 보기로 하겠습니다. 지금은 기본적인 동물의 방어 시스템에 대해서 알아 보도록 하죠. 동물의 시각과 청각은 매우 날카롭고 예민한데, 이로 인해 동물들은 접근하는 적이나 잠재적인 위험을 감지해낼 수 있습니다. 대부분 동물의 눈은 앞을 향해있지 않고, 대신 머리의 양 옆에 달려있습니다. 그렇기 때문에 옆이나 뒤에서 다가오는 위험을 알아차릴 수 있습니다. 몇몇 동물들은 또한 주변 환경의 변화에도 상당히 민감합니다. 그러니까… 예를 들면 뱀은 다가오는 동물의 진동을 감지할 수 있습니다. 청각에 대해 말하자면, 음, 곰은 예민한 청각을 지니고 있어서, 등산객들이 종종 자기들의 존재를 곰에게 경고하기 위해 배낭에 작은 종을 달고 다닙니다. 하지만 이것은 곰의 경우에만 꼭 도움이 되는 것은 아닙니다. 이는 등산객들에게도 도움이 되는데, 음, 곰은 놀라면 가장 공격적인 동물이 되기 때문입니다. 제가 알래스카의 야외 전시회에 갔었던 때가 기억나네요. 음, 우리는 회색 곰과 그것의 새끼 때문에 놀랐습니다. 휴, 한 말씀만 드리자면, 우리 모두가 운이 좋아서 그 누구도 다치거나… 더 나쁜 일을 당하지는 않았습니다. 어쨌든, 곰의 힘은, 이빨과 발톱이 합쳐지면, 곰을 살인 기계로 만들어 놓습니다. 사자와 호랑이 역시 마찬가지입니다. 이들은 싸움을 위해 만들어졌습니다. 바다의 상어와 강에서 서식하는 악어들은 가장 좋은 방어가 바로 효과적인 공격이라는 점을 나타내주는 또 다른 동물들입니다.

곤충 같은 생물들을 포함해서… 음, 대다수의 동물들은 공격을 통해 스스로를 방어하는 특성을 지니고 있지는 않습니다. 그래서 이들은 다른 방법으로 보완을 합니다. 집단 행동은 이러한 하나의 방법이 됩니다. 기본적으로, 동물들은 서로를 방어해주기 위해 협력하여 행동을 합니다. 예를 들면, 몇몇 동물들이 먹이를 먹는 동안, 다른 동물들은 망을 보게 됩니다. 아프리카 들개의 몇몇 종에는 정찰견이 따로 있는데, 이들은 위험 요소를 찾아내고 다른 개들에게 경고를 보내면서 무리의 외곽 지역을 정찰합니다. 많은 종들은 다가오는 위험을 알리기 위해 페로몬을 사용하기도 합니다. 오, 그래요, 맞습니다… 페로몬. 이것은 무엇일까요…? 페로몬은 각각의 종이 지니고 있는 고유한 냄새를 나타내는 화학적 신호입니다. 냄새에 따라, 페로몬은 각기 다른 의미를 나타냅니다. 하나의 예로서 들쥐를 들 수 있는데, 이들은 페로몬을 사용해서 곧 위험에 처하게 될 다른 쥐들에게 신호를 보낼 수 있습니다. 이로써 모든 쥐들이 함께 달아납니다. 세 번째 방어적인 집단 행동은 무리를 지어 다니는 것입니다. 많은 포유류들이 이렇게 하는데, 이러한 보호 집단은 때때로 공격도 버텨냅니다… 그리고 심지어는 포식자를 공격하기도 하지요. 여기 남아프리카에서 온, 사자들을 들이받고 새끼를 구해내는 물소 떼에 관한 놀라운 비디오가 있습니다. 물소들이 여러 마리의 사자들과 맞서 싸웠습니다. 이들은 무리를 지어 사자를 공격했습니다. 사자 한 마리는 물소에게 받쳐 공중으로 떠올랐습니다. 정말 믿을 수 없는 장면입니다. 그렇죠?

W Student: 동물들이 사용하는 방어 수단에는 그것들밖에 없나요?

M: 그렇지는 않아요. 많은 동물들이 스스로를 방어하기 위해 독을 사용하기도 합니다.

W: 정말인가요? 어떤 것들이 있나요?

M: 봅시다… 흔히 벌의 침에는 독이 들어있죠. 뱀, 거미, 해파리, 도마뱀, 그리고 심지어 두꺼비도, 그리고 여타 동물들도 일정 형태의 독을 사용할 수 있습니다. 물론, 때로는 독이 상대를 죽여서 먹기 전에 그것을 약화시키는데 쓰이는 사냥 도구가 되기도 합니다. 하지만 독은 또한 방어용으로도 쓰이기도 하죠. 그리고, 해파리와 같은, 다른 동물들의 경우에는, 독이 주로 방어의 수단으로 사용됩니다.

위장은 또 다른 방어 기제입니다. 적으로부터 몸을 숨기는 능력은 전투에서 필수적인 것이고, 따라서 군인들이 동물의 세계에서 위장에 대한 생각을 가져왔을 것이라는 점은 너무 지나친 생각이 아닐 것입니다. 봅시다. 군복과 수송 수단에 색칠되어있는 문양은 사람과 기계를 모두 주변 환경에 숨길 수 있도록 고안된 것입니다. 이와 비슷하게, 많은 포유류들이 갈색 털을 지니고 있는데, 이러한 사실로 인하여 이들은 땅에서 잘 숨어있을 수 있습니다. 북극 지방에서는, 북극곰과 다른 동물들이 눈과 잘 섞일 수 있도록 흰 색을 띠고 있습니다. 밀림의 많은 종들은 녹색입니다… 사막에서는 갈색을 띠고, 바다에서는 파란색을 띠고, 그런 식입니다. 여러분들은 요점을 알 수 있을 것입니다, 그렇죠? 몇몇 동물들은 심지어 다른 물체처럼 보일 수도 있습니다. 대벌레는 막대기처럼 생겨서, 그렇게 이름이 붙여졌고, 반면 스톤피쉬는 마치, 음, 뭘까요? 돌처럼 생겼습니다.

흠… 방어용 껍질은 몇몇 동물들이 사용하는 또 다른 방어 수단입니다. 거북이가 가장 잘 알려진 사례가 되겠네요. 거북이는 위험에 처했을 때 팔다리를 방어 껍질 속으로 집어넣을 수가 있습니다. 갑각류들은, 예를 들어 바닷가재, 게, 그리고 조가비들은 모두 다 포식자들로부터 방어하기 위한 단단한 겉 껍질, 즉 갑각을 지니고 있습니다.

Actual Test 04

Reading Section p.45

Answers

1. Ⓑ [Vocabulary Question]
2. Ⓑ [Negative Factual Question]
3. Ⓐ [Inference Question]
4. Ⓒ [Vocabulary Question]
5. Ⓑ [Vocabulary Question]
6. Ⓓ [Factual Question]
7. Ⓓ [Sentence Simplification Question]
8. Ⓑ [Factual Question]
9. Ⓒ [Reference Question]
10. Ⓓ [Factual Question]
11. Ⓓ [Vocabulary Question]
12. Ⓑ [Rhetorical Purpose Question]
13. 1st [Insert Text Question]
14. Ⓑ, Ⓔ, Ⓕ [Prose Summary Question]

Translation

산성비

산성비는 정상치 보다 더 많은 양의 산을 포함하고 있는 강수의 형태이다. 이 산은 높은 수치의 이산화 황과 이산화 질소의 결과물인데, 두 물질 모두 대기와 반응하여 각각 황산과 질산을 만들어낸다. 이산화황과 이산화질소의 공급원은 자연적인 것이거나 인공적인 것이다. 자연적인 공급원으로는 화산 및 부패중인 식물 등이 있지만, 인공적인 공급원은 대부분은 화석 연료, 특히 석탄의 연소로부터 비롯된다. 산성비는 인간이 만들어낸 구조물뿐만 아니라 특정 지역의 식물군과 동물군에도 해로운 영향을 끼친다. 산성비는 선진국에서 보다 흔하긴 하지만, 이는 국경을 가리는 것이 아니므로, 한 나라에서 형성된 산성비 구름은 다른 나라로 이동하여 산성비를 내리게 할 수 있다. 이러한 문제를 개선하려는 시도가 증가하고는 있지만, 인간이 화석 연료 없이도 살아갈 수 있는 방법을 배우기전까지는 산성비가 결코 사라지지 않을 것이다.

산성도는 pH 척도를 사용하여 측정되는데, 이 수치가 낮으면 산성도가 높다는 점을 알 수 있다. 순수한 물의 경우, pH 수치는 7이며 – 이는 중간 수치이다 – 반면 pH 수치가 6이하면 산성비로 간주된다. 산성 물질을 포함한 화합물은 물의 pH 수치에 영향을 미칠 수 있다. 이산화 황과 이산화 질소의 두 가지 주요한 공급원은 화산분출과 부패 중인 식물인데, 이 두 가지 모두는 지구가 처음 형성되었을 때부터 존재해왔던 것들이다. 그러나 빙하의 중심부를 연구한 결과에 따르면, 과거의 강우는 – 화산 활동이 있었던 지역에서 조차도 – 매우 약한 산성을 띠고 있어서, 사실상 순수한 물이었다.

하지만, 200년 이전부터 전세계가 산업화되기 시작한 이후, 산성비의 발생률은 급격히 증가해왔다. 석탄의 연소가 가장 큰 문제이다. 미 환경 보호국은 미국 내 이산화황 배출량의 2/3와 이산화질소 배출량의 1/4이 전력 생산을 위해 석탄을 연소시킨 직접적인 결과로서 나타난 것이라고 추정하고 있다. 두 번째로 가장 큰 원인은 휘발유를 연료로 사용하는 차량들이다. 그 어디에서나 화력 발전소와 휘발유 차량들은 산성비 문제에 악영향을 끼치고 있기 때문에, 이는 국제적인 문제가 되고 있다.

산성비가 내리면, 이는 하천의 수계에 흘러 들어가서 즉각적으로 문제를 일으킨다. 호수, 연못, 그리고 습지 모두는 산성을 띠게 될 수 있으며 pH 수치는 4에서 6정도가 될 수 있다. 이와 같은 산성도는 인근 토양으로부터 독성 알루미늄이 흘러나오는 결과를 초래한다. 해당 지역의 물고기나 기타 수중 생물들은 높은 수치의 산성도와 알루미늄이 합쳐진 결과 죽음을 맞이하거나, 혹은 먹이와 서식지에 대한 경쟁을 할 수 없게 되어 그 크기가 감소되거나 수명이 줄어들게 된다. 또한, 대부분의 물고기 알들이 pH 수치가 5, 혹은 더 낮은 수역에서는 부화하지 않기 때문에, 다음 세대의 수중 생물들 또한 고통을 겪게 된다. 그 결과 전세계의 수많은 수역에서 생명체가 사라져버릴 수도 있다.

고통을 받는 것은 동물뿐만이 아니다; 산성비는 식물에게도 부정적인 영향을 끼친다. 많은 나무들의 나무껍질에는 코팅이 되어 있는데, 나무껍질은 환경으로부터 스스로를 보호하고 수분과 양분을 함유하는데 도움을 준다. 산성비는 이러한 보호막을 부식시켜서, 나무를 환경에 노출시킨다. 보호막이 없어지면, 나무의 수분 함유 능력은 저하되고, 따라서 많은 나무들이 죽게 된다. 보다 높은 고도에서 자라는 나무들은 낮은 지대의 나무들에 비해서 산성비나 산성 안개에 더 많이 노출되므로 막대한 고통을 겪게 된다. 산성비가 내리는 지역의 토양 또한 피해를 입는다. 토양의 산성도가 증가함에 따라, 그 안에 있는 특정 미생물들이 죽게 되어, 식물을 자라게 할 수 있는 토양의 능력이 감소하게 되는 것이다.

가장 눈에 띄는 산성비의 영향은 인간이 만든 구조물에 대한 것이다. 많은 건물, 교량, 조각상, 그리고 기타 기념비들이 산성비로 인해 부식되어 심하게 마모된 모습을 보여준다. 석재가 특히 영향을 많이 받기 때문에, 석회암이나 대리석으로 만들어진 건물들은 막대한 피해를 입을 수도 있다. (이러한 피해 중 몇몇은 건물 구조에 미칠 수도 있는 것인데, 이로써 건물이 입주하기에 위험한 곳이 되기도 한다.) 전세계적으로, 건물이나 기념물들을 복구하는데 엄청난 양의 금액이 사용되고 있다. 산성비의 피해를 인식하고 있는 몇몇 정부들은 이산화황과 이산화질소의 배출을 제한하는 법안을 통과시켰으며, 많은 사람들이 전기 사용량과 차량 수송량을 감소시키기 위해 노력하고 있다. 그러나 보다 많은 화력 발전소와 자동차들이 계속 만들어지고 있기 때문에 그러한 노력은 힘든 싸움이 되고 있다. 아마도 산성비가 인간의 건강 문제와 명확한 연관성을 가지게 된 후에야, 보다 많은 사람들이 이러한 문제에 대해 관심을 가지게 될 것이다.

Listening Section
p.51

Answers

1. Ⓐ [Gist-Content Question]
2. Ⓒ [Detail Question]
3. Ⓐ [Understanding Attitude Question]
4. Ⓑ [Understanding Organization Question]
5. Ⓒ [Making Inferences Question]
6. Ⓑ [Detail Question]
7. Ⓒ [Understanding Organization Question]
8.

	Germans	English
Ⓐ	X	
Ⓑ		X
Ⓒ	X	
Ⓓ		X

[Connecting Content Question]

9. Ⓐ [Understanding Function Question]
10. Ⓓ [Understanding Attitude Question]
11. Ⓑ [Making Inferences Question]

Script

| 04-02 |

M Professor: Good afternoon, Stephanie. I received your email about you wanting to meet with me today. So, tell me, uh, what's on your mind?

W Student: Well, first, thanks for seeing me today, Professor Baker. I know that you don't have any office hours scheduled for Wednesday, so I really appreciate it that you made the time to let me come in.

M: Oh, don't mention it. I'm here in my office just about every day. Just because I don't have office hours posted doesn't mean that I can't talk to my students. Besides, that's what I'm paid to do, so I might as well do my job, huh? So, uh . . .

W: Ah, right. Sorry. Anyway, I wanted to talk to you about the report that we're doing.

M: That would be the report due this Friday two days from now, yes?

W: Er, right.

M: And may I assume that you're going to ask for an extension for some reason?

W: Er, uh, yes . . . But . . .

M: Okay, go ahead and try me.

W: Actually, sir, I've almost got my entire paper written.

M: Then what do you need an extension for?

W: Well, I'm writing my paper on the Civil Rights Movement . . .

M: A good topic. Yes, yes, go ahead.

W: Well, just the other night, I started talking to my roommate about the paper that I'm writing. And, uh, you'll never guess who my roommate's grandfather is.

M: I give up.

W: Well, uh, he was one of the Freedom Riders that rode on the buses down in the South during the Civil Rights Movement. I mean, he was actually there when history was being made.

M: Well, that's, uh, shall we say, fascinating.

W: Yeah, so, uh, you can see where I'm going with this, can't you?

M: You'd like to conduct an interview with him and use the information that he gives you in your paper.

W: Yes. That's exactly what I'd like to do. The only problem is that he lives about an hour away from school, so I can't get to his place until the weekend. I've already spoken with him a couple of times on the telephone, and I've gotten some pretty good information from him that way, but I think that having a face-to-face meeting would be even more enlightening. And, I mean, that's kind of what history is all about, isn't it? Uh, you know, talking to the people who actually helped make it.

M: Well, yes, that's definitely an important aspect of history. We can learn a lot from oral history, especially if it's being told by the people who were involved in the events as they happened.

W: So, uh, what do you say to my extension?

M: That depends. Normally, I don't give extensions to students. That's a policy of mine. However . . . I will make an exception in your case simply because you've got such an outstanding opportunity that it would be a waste not to pursue it. Can you get me the paper by class on Monday?

W: Yes, that's exactly what I was going to propose. I'm going to meet him on Saturday and then complete my paper on Sunday.

M: Outstanding. I must say that you've piqued my curiosity, Stephanie. ⁵I'm definitely looking forward to reading your paper now. I hope your interview works out. And I'll be expecting a quality paper from you. **Please don't**

disappoint me.

Translation

M Professor: 좋은 오후에요, Stephanie. 오늘 나를 만나보고 싶다는 학생의 이메일을 받았어요. 자, 말해봐요, 음, 어떤 생각을 하고 있죠?

W Student: 음, 우선, 오늘 만나주셔서 감사합니다, Baker 교수님. 제가 알기로는 교수님께서 수요일에는 수업이 없으신 것으로 알고 있는데요. 저를 위해 시간을 내 주셔서 정말로 감사합니다.

M: 아, 괜찮아요. 나는 매일 내 사무실에 있어요. 내가 수업이 없다고 해서 학생들과 이야기하지 못한다는 것은 아니니까요. 게다가, 그것도 내 일이고, 그리고 난 내 일을 잘 해야 하고, 그렇죠? 그러니, 음…

W: 아, 그렇군요. 죄송해요. 어쨌든, 제가 작성 중인 보고서에 관해서 말씀을 드리고 싶은데요.

M: 이틀 뒤 금요일까지 제출해야 하는 보고서를 말하는군요, 그렇죠?

W: 음, 맞아요.

M: 그리고 아마 학생은 몇 가지 이유로 기한 연장을 요청했던 것으로 기억하는데요?

W: 어, 음, 그래요… 그런데…

M: 괜찮아요. 계속 해봐요.

W: 사실은, 교수님, 보고서는 거의 다 작성해 두었는데요.

M: 그렇다면 왜 연기하려고 하는 거죠?

W: 음, 저는 시민평등권운동에 관한 보고서를 작성하고 있어요.

M: 좋은 주제군요. 예, 예, 계속 하세요.

W: 음, 어느 날 밤, 저는 룸메이트와 제가 쓰고 있는 논문에 대한 이야기를 시작하게 되었어요. 그리고, 음, 교수님께서는 제 룸메이트의 할아버지가 누구인지 짐작도 못하실 것 같아요.

M: 모르겠군요.

W: 그러니까, 음, 그분이 시민평등권운동 당시 남부에서 버스에 타고 있었던 '자유의 여행자들' 중 한 분이셨어요. 제 말은, 그분이 역사의 순간에 그 곳에 계셨던 것이죠.

M: 음, 그게, 아, 무엇이라고 해야 좋을까요. 정말 흥미롭군요.

W: 네, 그래서, 음, 제가 왜 이 말씀을 드리는지 아실 것 같은데요, 그렇죠?

M: 인터뷰를 해서 그분이 주신 정보를 논문에 활용하고 싶은 것이로군요.

W: 네, 제가 하려고 하는 것이 바로 그거예요. 문제는 그분이 학교에서 한 시간쯤 떨어진 곳에 살고 있고, 저는 주말에나 그분을 찾아갈 수 있어요. 이미 전화로 그분과 두어 번 이야기를 나누었고, 그렇게 해서 그분께 정말 좋은 정보를 얻었지만, 제 생각에는 직접 만나 뵙는 것이 훨씬 더 확실할 것 같아요. 그리고, 제 말은, 이것이 바로 역사잖아요, 그렇죠? 어, 그러니까, 실제로 역사를 만드는 데 도움이 된 사람들과 이야기를 나누는 것 말이죠.

M: 음, 그래요, 정말 역사의 중요한 측면이죠. 구술 역사를 통해, 특히 사건이 발생했을 때 관련된 사람들의 말을 통해서라면 많은 것을 배울 수가 있죠.

W: 그러면, 음, 기한 연장에 대해서는 어떻게 되는 것인가요?

M: 글쎄요. 보통은, 학생들에게 연기를 허락하지 않아요. 그게 제 방침이죠. 하지만… 이렇게 놓치기 아까운 놀라운 기회를 얻었으니 이번 경우는 예외로 하죠. 월요일 수업시간까지는 보고서를 가져올 수 있나요?

W: 네, 그렇게 하려고 했어요. 토요일에 그분을 만나고 일요일에 논문을 완성하려고 해요.

M: 좋아요. 내 호기심을 자극했다고 말하고 싶네요, Stephanie. 이제 정말 학생의 보고서를 읽어보고 싶군요. 인터뷰가 잘 되길 바라요. 그리고 훌륭한 보고서를 기대하고 있을게요. 실망시키지 말아요.

Script

| 04-03 |

M1 Professor: Let's turn to another cause of World War I. That would be the pre-war naval rivalry between Germany and England. It was, for the most part, the reason why England sided with France and Russia against Germany and Austria-Hungary in the war. In fact, this combination was, uh, quite unusual in European history. After all, France was England's traditional enemy, and it was English policy for centuries to prevent France from dominating the continent. Historically, the German states were among England's greatest allies at keeping the French in line. [9]**Also, the king of Germany, Kaiser Wilhelm II, and the king of England, George V, were first cousins. So, how did England and Germany find themselves on opposite sides during World War I?** Let's find out, shall we?

By 1871, the German states had united. As a result, Germany, not France, became the continent's strongest power. Why? Well, the newly unified German states had a large population, a strong industrial base, and Europe's most powerful army. This caused the other European powers to scramble to make defensive alliances with each other. England, however, remained neutral. Its citizens felt safe behind their ocean barrier and powerful navy. However, events soon pushed them toward France, Germany's great enemy. By 1905, France and England had entered secret discussions for England to provide military assistance should Germany ever attack the French. While there never was a formal treaty, the agreement they came to was the cornerstone of English aid to France during the war.

Also, in 1888, Wilhelm II came to power in Germany following the death of his father. Wilhelm was young—only twenty-nine then—brash, and arrogant, and he loved all things connected with the military. He almost always appeared in public wearing military uniforms, and he made a great show of parades and military life. Yet Germany lacked one thing . . . a strong navy. His English cousins had the world's strongest navy, and Wilhelm was, uh, well, simply put, he was jealous of this, particularly since he was something of a sailor himself. So he found an advocate for his plans for naval expansion in Admiral von Tirpitz, the head of Germany's navy. At that time, the German navy was mostly small ships used for coastal defense. Wilhelm and Tirpitz decided to change this.

In the 1890s, the expanding German navy caused alarm in England. For almost a century, ever since the Napoleonic Wars, the Royal Navy had ruled the waves unchallenged. The English used their navy to project global power, to protect their colonies, and to guard their merchant fleet and the home islands. When the English inquired as to the nature of the new German fleet, the Germans responded that they needed it to protect their own merchant fleet and overseas colonies in Africa and the Pacific. This was no different than the reasons that English gave for having their own fleet. Yet the English couldn't help but notice that most of the ships the Germans were building were not designed for around-the-world voyages.

M2 Student: Oh? What were they for then?

M1: [10]They appeared to be designed for operations in the cold and stormy North Sea, which forms England's eastern coast . . . **Ah, see the problem now?** England's policy had always been to have a navy stronger than its two largest rivals combined. France had been its main naval opponent, but the English began regarding the Germans as potential enemies. This brought about an arms race as each side began building a plethora of ships.

In 1906, the English constructed the *Dreadnought*. It was a battleship with nothing but big guns. This was a revolutionary design that inspired most of the other navies around the world to build their own dreadnoughts, as that class of ship came to be known. The English easily built more than the Germans, and the government's policy was to have three or four dreadnoughts for every two the Germans built. But dreadnoughts and other classes of ships were expensive, so people in both countries began demanding that their governments cease building warships and instead spend funds on social reforms. Yet construction continued unabated until 1914.

M2: How come?

M1: Well, tensions between the two countries concerning their navies prevented them from viewing things logically. They couldn't arrive at an agreement. [11]The English felt that their way of life depended on protecting the sea lanes and viewed, correctly I'd say, the German navy's mere existence as a threat to them. It was once said that the admiral of an English fleet could lose a war in an afternoon if his fleet were sunk since that would leave England unprotected. On the other hand, a German admiral couldn't do that since Germany had the strongest army in Europe.

So, when war finally broke out, there were battles and losses on both sides, but the English remained the masters of the seas. The great German fleet surrendered following the country's defeat. The ships were sailed into English waters, whereupon the crews, on orders from their admiral, scuttled the ships and sent the proud German fleet to a watery grave.

> **Translation**

M1 Professor: 제1차 세계 대전의 또 다른 원인을 알아 보도록 합시다. 그 원인은 전쟁이 일어나기 전 독일과 영국 사이의 해군력의 경쟁이 될 수 있을 것입니다. 이러한 경쟁은, 독일 및 오스트리아-헝가리 제국과 맞섰던 전쟁에서 영국이 왜 프랑스와 러시아 편에 있었는지에 대한 전반적인 이유가 됩니다. 사실, 이러한 조합은, 음, 유럽의 역사에서 상당히 특이한 일이었습니다. 요컨대, 프랑스는 영국의 전통적인 적국이었고, 프랑스가 대륙을 지배하지 못하도록 하는 것이 수 세기 동안 영국의 정책이었습니다. 역사적으로, 독일의 주들은 프랑스 인들이 영토를 확장하지 못하도록 하는 영국의 최대 동맹국들이었습니다. 또한, 독일의 왕 빌헬름 2세와, 영국의 왕 조지 2세는, 사촌 간이었습니다. 자, 그러면 어떻게 제1차 세계 대전 중에 영국과 독일이 적대 관계를 형성하게 되었을까요? 이제 알아보도록 하죠. 그럴까요?

1871년경, 독일이 통일되었습니다. 그 결과, 프랑스가 아닌 독일이 유럽 대륙에서 가장 강한 국가가 되었습니다. 왜 그랬을까요? 음, 통일된 독일은 많은 인구와, 강력한 산업 기반, 그리고 유럽에서 가장 강력한 군대를 가지고 있었기 때문이었죠. 이는 다른 유럽의 강대국들이 방어 동맹을 형성하기 위해 급히 행동을 하도록 만들었습니다. 그러나, 영국은 중립을 유지했죠. 영국인들은 바다라는 장벽과 강력한 해군 덕분에 스스로 안전하다고 생각했습니다. 하지만, 여러 가지 사건으로 인해 영국인들은 독일의 커다란 적이었던 프랑스 편에 서게 되었습니다. 1905년경, 프랑스와 영국은 독일이 프랑스를 공격하면 영국이 프랑스에게 군사적 도움을 제공해준다는 비밀 회담에 들어갔습니다. 정식 조약은 존재하지 않았지만, 그들이 맺은 협약은 전쟁 도중 프랑스에 대한 영국의 지원의 기반이 되었습니다.

또한, 1888년, 빌헬름 2세는 아버지가 죽고 난 뒤 독일 내 권력을 장악했습니다. 빌헬름은 어렸고 – 그때 고작 29세였죠 – 경솔했고, 오만했으며, 그리고 군대와 관련된 모든 것들을 좋아했습니다. 그는 거의 항상 대중들 앞에 군복을 입고 나타났고, 거대한 퍼레이드와 군대를 과시했습니다. 하지만 독일이 가지지 못한 것이 하나 있었는데… 강력한 해군이었습니다. 그의 영국인 사촌은 세계 최강의 해군을 가지고 있었으며, 빌헬름은, 어, 음, 단순하게 이야기해서, 이것에 관해 질투심을 느꼈는데, 이는 특히 그 자신이 일종의 해군이었기 때문입니다. 그래서 그는 해군 확장에 대한 자신의 계획을 지지해줄 사람을 찾고 있었는데 그가 바로 독일 해군의 수장인 틸피츠 제독이었습니다. 그 당시, 독일의 해군은 거의 모두 연안 방어를 위한 작은 배들로 이루어져 있었습니다. 빌헬름과 틸피츠는 이를 바꾸기로 결심했죠.

1890년대, 독일의 해군 확장은 영국에 경각심을 불러 일으켰습니다. 나폴레옹 전쟁 때부터 거의 1세기 동안, 영국 해군은 그 적수가 없을 정도로 바다를 장악해 왔습니다. 영국인들은 세계적인 강대국의 이미지를 심고, 자신들의 식민지를 방어하고, 그리고 상선단과 본국을 지키는데 해군을 활용해왔습니다. 영국이 새로운 독일 함대의 성격에 대해 물어보면, 독일은 자신들의 상선단과 아프리카 및 태평양의 해외 식민지를 보호하기 위해 필요하다고 응답했습니다. 이것은 영국이 자신들의 함대에

부여한 존재 이유와 다를 바가 없었습니다. 그러나 영국은 독일이 건조한 대부분의 선박들이 전세계를 항해하기 위해 설계된 것이 아니라는 점에 주목하지 않을 수 없었습니다.

M2 Student: 어? 그러면 그것들은 무엇을 위한 것이었나요?

M1: 그것들은 춥고 날씨가 험한 북해에서 운용할 목적으로 설계된 것처럼 보였는데, 이 지역은 영국의 동쪽 해안에 해당되는 곳이었죠… 아, 이제 문제가 무엇인지 아시겠죠? 영국의 정책은 항상 가장 큰 두 경쟁국들을 합한 것 보다 더 강한 해군을 보유하는 것이었습니다. 프랑스가 주요한 해군의 경쟁 상대로 자리잡고 있었지만, 영국은 독일을 잠재적인 적으로 간주하기 시작했습니다. 이 때문에 양국은 과도하게 배를 건조하기 시작하면서 군비경쟁을 하게 되었습니다.

1906년, 영국은 드레드노트 전함을 건조했습니다. 이것은 단지 거대한 포들만이 달려있는 전함이었습니다. 이러한 종류의 배가 알려지게 되면서, 전세계의 다른 해군들도 드레드노트 전함을 만들 생각을 했을 만큼, 이는 혁신적인 설계였습니다. 영국은 독일보다 더 많은 전함을 순조롭게 건조했으며, 독일이 드레드노트 한 척을 건조할 때마다 세 척 혹은 네 척의 드레드노트 전함을 건조하는 것이 정부의 정책이 되었습니다. 그러나 드레드노트 전함과 다른 종류의 함선은 건조 비용이 많이 들었고, 그래서 양국의 국민들은 정부가 전함의 건조를 중단하고 대신 사회 개혁에 그 자금을 쓰도록 요구하기 시작했습니다. 하지만 1914년까지 함선의 건조는 계속되었습니다.

M2: 어째서요?

M1: 음, 양국간의 해군과 관련된 긴장감 때문에 그들은 논리적으로 사태를 파악할 수 없었습니다. 협정을 맺을 수도 없었죠. 영국인들은 자신들의 삶이 항로를 지키는데 달려있다고 생각했고, 아마도 분명, 단지 독일 해군의 존재 자체가 그들에게 위협이 된다고 생각했을 것입니다. 영국 함대의 제독은 만일 자신의 함대가 침몰한다면 영국은 무방비 상태가 되기 때문에 자신이 영국을 하루 아침에 패전으로 몰아넣을 수도 있다고 말한 적이 있습니다. 반면, 독일은 유럽 최강의 육군을 보유하고 있었기 때문에, 독일의 제독에게는 그런 일이 있을 수가 없었죠.

그래서, 마침내 전쟁이 발발하자, 여러 차례의 전투가 일어났고 양측 모두는 피해를 입게 되었습니다. 하지만 영국은 여전히 바다의 지배자였습니다. 위대한 독일의 함대는 자국의 패배와 함께 항복을 했습니다. 선박들은 영국 해안으로 보내졌고, 그 후 선원들이, 제독의 명령으로, 배를 침몰시켜서 자랑스런 독일의 함대는 수중 묘지에 묻히게 되었습니다.

Actual Test 05

Reading Section   p.57

Answers

1. Ⓑ [Vocabulary Question]
2. Ⓐ [Sentence Simplification Question]
3. Ⓒ [Vocabulary Question]
4. Ⓒ [Rhetorical Purpose Question]
5. Ⓒ [Negative Factual Question]
6. Ⓑ [Factual Question]
7. Ⓑ [Vocabulary Question]
8. Ⓓ [Vocabulary Question]
9. Ⓐ [Rhetorical Purpose Question]
10. Ⓑ [Factual Question]
11. Ⓒ [Factual Question]
12. Ⓐ [Reference Question]
13. Ⓓ [Inference Question]
14. Ⓐ, Ⓓ, Ⓕ [Prose Summary Question]

Translation

우주의 생성과 소멸

우주에는 수많은 미스터리가 있는데, 그 중 하나가 우주의 생성에 관한 것이다. 천문학자들은 여러 가지 이론을 제시하고 있으며, 이 중 빅뱅 이론이 가장 널리 받아들여지고 있다. 이 이론은 우주가 중심점으로부터 물질이 폭발함으로써 생성되었다는 전제에 기반을 두고 있다. 우주에 시작이 있다는 믿음은 우주에 끝도 있을 것이라는 사실을 암시해주기 때문에, 많은 과학자들은 우주가 먼 미래의 언젠가는 종말을 맞이하게 될 것이라고 생각하고 있다. 천문학자들은 이러한 점과 관련된 두 가지 주요한 이론을 제시하고 있다: 빅크런치 이론과 빅프리즈 이론이 그것이다.

빅뱅 이론은, 대략 150억년 전, 작고 엄청난 밀도의 물질점이 폭발하여 확장을 하게 되었는데, 이로 인해 우주가 생성되었다고 주장한다. 이러한 물질이 왜 그리고 어떻게 존재하게 되었고 폭발했는지, 그리고 빅뱅 이전에는 무엇이 존재하고 있었는지는 알려지지 않고 있다. 이 이론은 단지 우주가 존재하는 이유와 우주가 생성되고 그 후 팽창하게 된 이후의 역사를 설명해줄 뿐이다. 빅뱅 이론의 증거는 여러 가지 근거로부터 나온다. 1920년대, 미국의 천문학자 에드윈 허블은 멀리 떨어진 은하계들이 지구로부터 멀어지고 있다는 점을 규명했다. 또한 그의 관찰에서 더 멀리 떨어진 은하계 일수록 더 빠른 속도로 멀어지고 있다는 점이 밝혀졌다. 이는 우주 자체가 중심점으로부터 확장되고 있음을 암시해준다. 수년 후, 1960년대에, 우주배경복사의 측정으로 우주가 한 때는 현재보다 더 뜨거웠으며 현재의 냉각은 팽창 때문이라는 점이 증명되었다. 그 이후의 증거는, 이는 고성능의 현대 망원경에 의해 발견된 것인데, 우주의 형성과 관련된 가장 보편적인 이론으로써의 빅뱅 이론의 입지를 강화시켜주었다.

현재 우주의 크기가 어느 정도인지 혹은 최종적으로 얼마나 커질 것인지는 알려져 있지 않다. 그러나 우주가 어떻게 소멸될지에 대해서는 여러 가지 이론들이 경합 중에 있다. 빅크런치 이론은 중력이 너무 강력해서 우주의 팽창 속도를 느리게 하고 있다는 생각에 기반한다. 결국, 우주는 팽창을 멈추게 될 것이고 다시 처음 우주가 시작되었던 중심점을 향하여 수축하게 될 것이다. 그리고 나면, 모든 물질들이 하나로 "붕괴"되어, 우주를 파멸시키게 될 것이다. 이 이론을 지지하는 몇몇 사람들은 또 다른 빅뱅으로 대붕괴 이후 새로운 우주가 생성될 것이며, 그 결과로서, 사실상, 진동 우주가 생성될 것이라고 주장한다. 하지만, 1990년대에 우주가 지구로부터 점점 빠르게 팽창하고 있다는 것이 발견된 이래로 빅크런치 이론을 고수하는 사람들은 거의 없게 되었다.

이러한 사실 때문에 천문학자들은 보다 더 가능성이 높아 보이는 우주 종말에 대한 시나리오를 제시하게 되었다: 빅프리즈 이론이 그것이다. 이 이론에 따르면, 우주가 팽창함에 따라, 우주는 어떠한 생명체도 살아남을 수 없을 정도의 낮은 온도에 도달하게 된다. 은하계들은 충돌을 통하여 합쳐져서 은하단을 형성하게 될 것이다. 우주가 계속 팽창하면, 이러한 은하단들의 거리가 너무 멀어지게 되어서, 다른 은하단들이 관찰될 수 없을 것이다. 수십억 년이 지남에 따라, 별들은 연료를 모두 소진시키고 소멸할 것이다. 이러한 일이 발생하면, 별 주변의 행성들 역시 소멸하게 될 것이며, 그 후 여기에서 나오는 물질은 모든 은하계의 중심에 있는 블랙홀로 빨려 들어가게 될 것이다. 지금으로부터 약 1천조 년이 흐른 뒤, 새로운 별의 생성은 중단될 것이며, 별빛도 사라지게 될 것이다. 수천조 년이 더 지나면, 블랙홀도 사라지게 될 것이고, 우주 생성의 기본 단위들은 – 원자와 광자, 중성자, 그리고 전자들은 – 서로 멀리 떨어져서 다시는 뭉치질 수 없게 될 것이다. 천문학자들은 이를 암흑기라 부르면서, 이것이 무한한 시간 동안 지속될 것이라고 추측하고 있다.

하지만, 몇몇 천문학자들은 우주가 암흑기로부터 벗어날 가능성이 있다는 이론을 세우고 있다. 그들의 주장에 따르면, 아마도, 새로운 빅뱅이 나타날 것이다. 아직까지, 이 이론을 연구하는 과학자들은 신중하게도 추가적인 연구가 실시되지 않는 이상 어떠한 이론을 수립하지는 않고 있다. 우주에 대해 많은 것들이 여전히 알려지지 않은 상태이며, 두 가지 분야 – 암흑 에너지와 암흑 물질 – 에 대한 더 많은 연구가 언젠가 이들의 이론을 다시 생각해보도록 만들 것이다. 전체적으로 천문학자들이 동의하고 있는 바는, 말하자면, 어떻게 소멸되건 간에, 우주는 소멸할 것이라는 점이다.

Listening Section   p.63

Answers

1. C [Gist-Content Question]
2. A [Gist-Purpose Question]
3. A [Detail Question]
4. C [Making Inferences Question]
5. C [Understanding Function Question]
6. B [Gist-Purpose Question]
7. A [Gist-Content Question]
8. D [Detail Question]
9. A [Detail Question]
10.

	The Batch Method	The Continuous Method
A		X
B		X
C	X	
D	X	

[Connecting Content Question]

11. C [Understanding Attitude Question]

Script

| 05-02 |

W Librarian: Excuse me. I really hate to bother you, but your name is Randal Smith, isn't it?

M Student: Yes, that's me. Is there a problem or something? Uh, I don't, like, have a library fine or anything, do I?

W: No, not at all. ⁵If you had an overdue book, you would have received a notice by email reminding you to bring in the book and to pay the fine that you owed the library.

M: Oh, yeah. That's right. I'm well aware of that policy. **I've gotten a few of those notices this past semester.**

W: That's too bad. You need to remember to renew your books more often, Mr. Smith.

M: Yeah, right. Uh . . . So, anyway . . . You needed me for something?

W: Yes, that's correct. It's about these books that you have here on the desk.

M: Yeah? What about them? I checked them out from the reserve desk, so everything should be legitimate.

W: Right. That's how we found out that you had these books. The problem is, though, that you've had them checked out for too long.

M: That's impossible. I mean, I checked them out at one, and it's only three fifteen right now.

W: That's right. So, uh, technically, those three books are already overdue.

M: Huh . . . ? Oh, you're not trying to tell me that I should have returned them by three o'clock, are you?

W: Actually, yes, that's exactly what I'm saying. Books on reserve are handled differently from regular books. You can check out regular books for two weeks, but you get reserve books only for two hours.

M: Oh . . . Uh, I hadn't realized that. Isn't there any way that you can, uh, you know, let this go? I really need to use these books to study for a test I've got to take in a couple of days.

W: You know, I'd really love to help you out, but four students have come by asking for those exact books, so I'm going to have to take them back to the desk.

M: Is that so? I hadn't realized that they are so popular. I guess I don't have much of a choice but to give them back to you, do I?

W: Nope. Not at all.

M: So, is it possible at all to check out these reserve books for longer than two hours?

W: How so?

M: Well, I mean . . . Hey, I've got an idea. Could I check them out right at closing time and then return them the next morning by, say, uh, an hour after the library opens? That would work, wouldn't it?

W: Hmm . . . That's actually a pretty creative suggestion. I like it.

M: So you'll let me do it?

W: No, I won't. It's library policy not to let books on reserve out of the library. There's only one exception: If you bring in a note signed by your professor giving you permission to borrow the books for longer than two hours, then we will follow the professor's wishes. Do you think you can get a note?

M: I doubt it. Not if there are that many students looking to borrow the books.

W: I'm sorry to hear that. Anyway, may I have the books, please? I need to let some other students look at them.

Translation

W Librarian: 실례합니다. 귀찮게 해드려서 죄송하지만, *Randal Smith*씨 맞죠, 그렇죠?

M Student: 네, 전데요. 무슨 문제라도 있나요? 아, 제가, 그러니까, 도서관 연체료나 아니면 다른 해야 할 것이 없을 텐데요, 있나요?

W: 아니오, 그렇지 않아요. 기한이 지난 책이 있다면, 책을 반납하고 도서관 연체료를 지불하라는 이메일 안내문을 받았겠죠.

M: 아, 그렇죠. 맞아요. 그러한 방침에 대해 잘 알고 있어요. 지난 학기에 몇 번 안내문을 받았거든요.

W: 안되었네요. 대출 연장을 보다 자주 해야 한다는 점을 기억할 필요가 있겠어요, *Smith*씨.

M: 네, 맞아요… 음, 그런데… 제게 무언가 용건이 있으셨죠?

W: 네, 맞아요. 학생 책상에 있는 이 책들 때문이에요.

M: 네? 어째서요? 반출 불가 도서를 대출했고, 그래서 잘못된 점이 없을 텐데요.

W: 맞아요. 그래서 당신이 이 책들을 가지고 있다는 점을 알게 되었죠. 하지만, 문제는 이 책들을 너무 오랫동안 대출하고 있다는 점이에요.

M: 말도 안돼요. 제 말은, 저는 이 책들을 한 시에 대출했고, 지금은 겨우 세 시인걸요.

W: 맞아요, 그러니까, 음, 엄밀히 말하면, 이 책들은 이미 기한이 지났어요.

M: 네…? 아, 이 책들을 세 시까지 반납해야 된다는 말씀이신가요, 맞나요?

W: 네, 그래요. 제가 하려던 말이 바로 그거예요. 반출 불가 도서들은 일반 도서들과는 달라요. 일반 도서들은 2주간 대출이 가능하지만, 반출 불가 도서들은 단지 두 시간 동안만 대출이 가능해요.

M: 아… 음, 제가 잘 몰랐어요. 제가, 음, 그러니까, 계속 더 볼 수 있는 방법은 없나요? 이 책들은 이틀 후에 있을 시험 공부에 정말 필요하거든요.

W: 아시다시피, 정말로 도움이 되어드리고 싶지만, 네 명의 학생이 당장 이 책들을 요청하고 있어서, 책들을 다시 데스크에 갖다 놓아야 해요.

M: 그래요? 이 책들이 그렇게 인기가 좋은 줄 몰랐네요. 제 생각에는 당신에게 이 책들을 돌려드릴 수 밖에 없겠네요, 그렇죠?

W: 네, 그래요.

M: 그러면, 이 반출 불가 도서들을 두 시간 이상 대출하는 것이 가능하겠는데요?

W: 어떻게요?

M: 그러니까, 제 말은… 보세요, 저한테 생각이 있어요. 도서관 문을 닫기 직전에 이 책을 빌려서 다음날 아침에 반납을 하는 거죠, 그러니까, 음, 도서관 문을 열고 난 후 한 시간 뒤에요.

W: 흠… 그거 정말 꽤 독창적인 생각이네요. 마음에 들어요.

M: 그럼 그렇게 해 주실래요?

W: 아니오, 그렇게 하지 않을 거예요. 도서관 방침상 반출 불가 도서들은 도서관 밖으로의 반출이 금지되어있어요. 한 가지 예외는 있죠: 두 시간 이상의 대출을 허락하는 교수님의 사인이 있는 메모가 있다면, 저희는 교수님의 의견을 따르게 됩니다. 메모를 가져올 수 있나요?

M: 안될 것 같아요. 이 책들을 빌리려는 학생들이 그렇게 많다면 안되겠죠.

W: 안됐군요. 어쨌든, 책들을 가져가도 되겠죠? 다른 학생들도 이 책을 볼 수 있도록 해야 하니까요.

Script

| 05-03 |

W Professor: In our last few minutes, I'd like to speak about a method of neutralizing and destroying microorganisms in food, particularly, uh, milk. This method is called pasteurization, and it was developed by the French scientist Louis Pasteur. For more than a hundred years, his name has been associated with the process he developed: pasteurization. Basically, the process consists of heating a substance to a degree just below its boiling point in order to destroy or, uh, neutralize harmful pathogens such as bacteria. Today, it's most commonly used in the dairy industry, but it's also utilized for many other food products.

First, let me say a few words about Pasteur. He was a Frenchman who lived in the nineteenth century and is widely considered the father of modern microbiology. During his lifetime, the idea that small, invisible organisms could invade the human body and causes diseases was considered, uh, well, it was thought to be fantasy. Of course, now we know that to be true, and for that we have Pasteur and some other men to thank. Now, Pasteur's main work was in the field of germ theory and the treatment of diseases related to germs. [11]He achieved great success in his treatments of rabies and other diseases. He was also hailed as a hero in France and much of the world for his work in that field. But I'm getting off topic, and we're running out of time. So let's get back to pasteurization.

Pasteur's work on microorganisms led him to theorize that microorganisms could contaminate food, particularly beverages. He worked with wine and developed a pasteurization method for it with one of his colleagues, Claude Bernard, in, oh, 1862 I believe. The two men discovered that wine wouldn't spoil as fast if it had been heated to a temperature just below its boiling point. Pasteur theorized that the microorganisms that caused wine to spoil were destroyed by the heating process. Later, in the 1880s, German scientists took his methods and used them on milk. Thus drinking milk became a much safer activity. While pasteurization kills most of the microorganisms in milk, nowadays, scientists are starting to find new pathogens, some of which appear to be resistant to pasteurization. Perhaps some new methods of eliminating them will have to be developed in the future.

Today, lots of products besides wine and milk have extended shelf lives thanks to pasteurization. Let's see . . . juice, beer, and sports drinks are just three of many products. There are also two main types of pasteurization. There's high temperature/short time, or HTST, pasteurization, and there's ultra-high temperature, or UHT, pasteurization. The main differences between the two are the amounts of time that the products are exposed to heat and the degree of heat that is used. For HTST pasteurization, milk is heated to seventy-one degrees Celsius for around, say, about fifteen to twenty seconds. With UHT pasteurization, milk is heated to about 138 degrees Celsius, but this is only done for about a second. HTST pasteurized milk has a shelf life of almost three weeks whereas UHT pasteurized milk can last for up to two months.

Oh, pardon me again. There are also two main methods in which milk is pasteurized. They are the batch method and the continuous method. In the batch method, milk is placed in a vat that's surrounded by a jacket of circulating water or steam, or else there are pipes that contain circulating water or steam. The milk is then heated to the required temperature and kept in the vat for the proper amount of time, after which it gets released. At lower temperature levels, this takes a lot of time. In addition, the milk must be constantly agitated . . . uh, you know, shaken or stirred. This ensures that the heating is even throughout the entire vat of milk. As you can probably guess, this method isn't very common nowadays, so the continuous method is almost always used instead.

What's the continuous method? Well, basically, raw milk is forced through a device that has chambers heated to the correct temperature. The milk is kept at precise temperatures and times through the entire process, but it's almost constantly on the move, hence the name continuous method. There's no need to agitate the milk since it is flowing and being exposed to constant temperatures. Oh, there's a third method, called cold pasteurization, but it's not pasteurization as I've been describing it. It's a form of irradiation that uses, er, low levels of radiation to destroy microorganisms. So it's not pasteurization in the strictest sense of the word.

Today, pasteurization is required for most dairy products in the U.S. and many other countries. Creams and cheeses can also be pasteurized, and many countries have high standards and closely regulate and monitor the pasteurization process. Okay, that's all we have time for today. If there are no questions . . . Great. For our next class, please read the first half of chapter eight and be prepared for a class discussion on the topic. See you next time, everyone.

Translation

W Professor: 수업의 마지막 몇 분간은 음식물을 중화하고 그 안의 미생물들을 파괴하는 방법에 대해서 이야기해 보려고 하는데, 특히, 음, 우유에 대해서 이야기해봅시다. 이 방법은 저온 살균법이라고 불리는데, 이것은 프랑스의 과학자 루이 파스퇴르가 개발한 것입니다. 백 년이 넘는 시간 동안, 그의 이름은 그가 개발한 방법과 연관되어 있습니다: 즉, 저온 살균법이죠. 기본적으로, 이 방법은 박테리아와 같이 해로운 병원균을 파괴시키거나, 음, 중화시키기 위해서 물질을 끓는점 직전의 온도까지 가열하는 과정으로 이루어집니다. 오늘날, 이것은 낙농업에서 가장 흔히 사용되는 방법이며, 또한 다른 많은 식료품에서도 활용되고 있습니다.

먼저, 파스퇴르에 대해 몇 가지 이야기를 해보죠. 그는 19세기에 살았던 프랑스인으로 현대 미생물학의 아버지로 널리 인정받고 있습니다. 일생 동안, 작고, 눈에 보이지 않는 유기체가 인체를 공격하고 질병을 일으킬 수 있다는 그의 생각은, 음, 글쎄요, 공상이라고 여겨졌습니다. 물론, 현재 우리는 그것이 사실이라는 것을 알고 있는데, 이는 파스퇴르와 다른 인물들 덕분입니다. 자, 파스퇴르의 주된 연구는 배종설(胚種說) 분야와 세균과 관련된 질병의 치료 부분에서 이루어졌습니다. 그는 광견병 및 기타 질병들의 치료에 있어서 큰 성공을 거두었습니다. 또한 이러한 분야에서의 성공에 힘입어 그는 프랑스와 전 세계의 많은 곳에서 영웅으로 일컬어지기도 했어요. 하지만, 제가 주제를 벗어나서, 시간만 지나가고 있군요. 저온 살균법 이야기로 되돌아가기로 하죠.

파스퇴르의 미생물에 관한 연구는 미생물이 식품을, 특히 음료수를 오염시킬 수 있다는 사실을 이론화시켰습니다. 그는 포도주를 가지고 연구를 했고 그의 동료들 중 한 명인 클로드 베

르나르와 함께 저온 살균법을 개발해냈는데, 아, 제 생각에는, 1862년이었던 것 같습니다. 이 두 사람은 포도주를 끓는점 직전의 온도까지 가열하면 그렇게 빨리 상하지는 않는다는 점을 알아냈습니다. 파스퇴르는 가열 과정을 통해 포도주를 상하게 하는 미생물을 파괴할 수 있다는 이론을 확립했습니다. 그 후, 1880년대, 독일의 과학자들이 그의 방법을 받아들여 우유에 적용시켰습니다. 그래서 우유를 마시는 것이 훨씬 더 안전하게 되었죠. 저온 살균법으로 우유에 들어있는 대부분의 미생물들이 제거될 수 있지만, 오늘날, 과학자들은 새로운 병원균을 발견해 내기 시작했고, 이 중 몇몇은 저온 살균법에 대한 저항력이 있는 것처럼 보이고 있습니다. 아마도 미래에는 이것들을 제거할 수 있는 새로운 방법을 발견해내야 할 것입니다.

오늘날, 저온 살균법 덕분에 포도주나 우유 이외의 많은 제품들의 유통 기한이 길어졌습니다. 봅시다… 주스, 맥주, 그리고 스포츠 음료가 그러한 많은 제품들 중의 세 가지가 되겠네요. 또한 저온 살균법에는 두 가지의 주요한 형태가 있습니다. 고온/단시간, 또는 HTST라고 하는 저온 살균법이 있고, 초고온, 또는 UHT라고 하는 저온 살균법이 있습니다. 이 두 방법의 가장 큰 차이는 제품이 열에 노출되는 시간의 양과 사용되는 열의 온도입니다. HTST 저온 살균의 경우, 우유를 섭씨 21도 정도로, 이를테면, 대략 15초 내지 20초 정도로 가열합니다. UHT 저온 살균의 경우, 우유를 섭씨 138도 정도로 가열하지만, 대략 1초 정도만 가열합니다. HTST 방식으로 저온 살균된 우유는 유통기한이 3주에 이르는데, 반면 UHT 방식으로 저온 살균된 우유는 2개월까지 지속될 수 있습니다.

아, 다시 한 번 죄송해요. 우유의 저온 살균 방법에도 역시 주요한 두 가지가 있습니다. 일괄법과 연속법이 그것이죠. 일괄법에서는, 물이나 증기가 순환하는 덮개로 둘러싸여 있거나, 물이나 증기가 순환하는 파이프가 들어있는, 큰 통에 우유를 넣습니다. 그 후 이 우유는 필요한 온도로 가열되고 적절한 시간 동안 큰 통에 놓이게 되며, 그런 다음 추출됩니다. 낮은 온도에서는, 오랜 시간이 걸립니다. 게다가, 우유는 반드시 휘저어야 하는데… 음, 아시다시피, 흔들거나 저어주어야 합니다. 이렇게 함으로써 큰 통에 있는 우유 전체가 확실히 균일하게 가열됩니다. 추측해 볼 수 있듯이, 이 방법은 요즘에는 그리 흔한 방법이 아니며, 그래서 연속법이 거의 항상 그 대신 사용되고 있습니다.

연속법이란 무엇일까요? 음, 기본적으로, 공간을 정확한 온도로 가열할 수 있는 장치에 원유를 놓아둡니다. 우유는 전 과정에 걸쳐서 정확한 온도와 시간에 따라 보관되지만, 이것을 거의 계속적으로 움직여 주게 되는데, 그래서 연속법이라는 이름이 붙여지게 된 것입니다. 우유는 계속해서 흐르며 일정한 온도에 노출되기 때문에 휘저어 줄 필요가 없습니다. 아, 세 번째 방법, 냉저온 살균법이라고 불리는 방법이 있는데, 이것은 제가 설명해드린 것과 같은 저온 살균법은 아닙니다. 이것은, 음, 미생물을 없애기 위해서 낮은 수준의 방사선을 사용하는 방사선 요법의 한 형태입니다. 이것은 엄밀히 말해서 저온 살균법이 아닙니다.

오늘날, 저온 살균법은 미국과 다른 나라들의 대부분의 유제품 생산에 필요합니다. 크림과 치즈 역시 저온 살균할 수 있으며, 많은 국가들은 강도 높은 기준을 세워서 저온 살균의 과정을 면밀히 규제하고 감독하고 있습니다. 좋아요, 오늘의 시간을 마치도록 하죠… 질문이 없으면… 좋습니다. 다음 수업을 위해, 제 8장의 중간 부분 까지 읽어 오시고 주제에 대한 토론을 준비해 오세요. 모두들. 다음시간에 뵙도록 하죠.

Actual Test 06

Reading Section p.69

Answers

1. Ⓓ [Reference Question]
2. Ⓓ [Vocabulary Question]
3. Ⓑ [Factual Question]
4. Ⓓ [Factual Question]
5. Ⓑ [Vocabulary Question]
6. Ⓐ [Factual Question]
7. Ⓐ [Vocabulary Question]
8. Ⓒ [Vocabulary Question]
9. Ⓐ [Rhetorical Purpose Question]
10. Ⓒ [Negative Factual Question]
11. Ⓑ [Inference Question]
12. Ⓑ [Inference Question]
13.

	TEACHING METHOD
Direct Learning	Ⓑ, Ⓕ, Ⓖ
Lecture	Ⓒ, Ⓓ

[Fill in a Table Question]

Translation

교수법

학교에 다니는 모든 학생들의 목표는 배우는 것이며, 그들에게 지식을 전달하는 책임은 교사들에게 있다. 교사는 학생들에게 수업 내용을 이해시키기 위해 다양한 방법들을 사용한다. 여러 교수법들이 있지만, 가장 일반적인 세 가지로는 직접교수, 협동학습, 그리고 강의를 들 수 있다. 종종 교사들은 여러 가지 요인에 따라 각기 다른 방법들을 취하고 있다. 이러한 요인으로는 교사들이 가르치고 있는 학교의 종류, 학생들의 나이, 그리고 개별적인 수업의 목적 등이 있다.

직접교수는 교사가 학생들에게 설명을 제시해주는 것인데, 학생들은 교사가 가르치는 대로 따르게 된다. 교사가 단계적으로 설명을 해주면, 학생들은 그것을 듣고, 스스로 학습할 수 있는 기회를 갖는다. 이와 같은 방식은 일반적으로 과학 및 수학 수업 시간에 활용된다. 예를 들면, 교사가 특정 수학 문제를 설명한다. 교사는 풀이 방법을 설명해주고, 몇 차례의 문제 풀이를 통해 이를 적용시켜 주며, 학생들이 이해가 안 가는 부분에 대해 질문을 받아주고, 학생들이 배운 것을 테스트하기 위해 과제를 내준다. 직접교수의 한 가지 장점은 모든 학년에 있어서 유용하다는 점이다. 또한, 일반적으로 특별한 목적을 전제로 수업이 이루어지며, 학생들의 이해 정도를 판단하기가 용이하고, 기본적인 학습 내용을 가르치는데 폭넓게 받아들여지고 있다. 단점으로는, 교사가 수업에 대해 많은 것을 준비해야만 하며 뛰어난 언변을 구사할 수 있어야 하는데, 특히 명확한 설명을 제시해줄 수 능력이 필요하다. 그리고 이러한 방법은 사실상 선생님이나 학생들에게 있어서 창조력을 발휘시킬 수 있는 여지가 없다.

협동학습은 학생들이 그룹을 만들어 프로젝트나 과제를 함께 수행할 때 이루어진다. 그룹학습과 비교했을 때, 이러한 방법에서는 교사가 덜 관여하게 된다. 전형적으로, 교사는 과제에 대한 기본적인 것들만 설명해 주고 그룹을 편성해준다. 그리고 나서 그룹마다 돌아다니며 조언 및 설명을 제공해 주고 논쟁을 해결해 주며 감독 역할을 수행한다. 이와 같은 방법은 학생들에게 창의력을 표현할 기회를 제공해주며, 그룹 내에서의 의견 교환과 같은 사회적 기술을 익힐 수 있도록 해준다. 목적을 달성하기 위해, 그룹 내의 학생들은 서로 어울리며 상대방의 관점에 귀를 기울이는 방법을 익혀야만 한다. 하지만, 이 방법은 혼자 있고 싶어하는 학생이나 부끄러움을 타는 학생들에게는 적합하지 않으며, 공격적이거나 사고력이 뛰어난 학생들이 결국 그룹을 장악하여 다른 학생들에게 피해가 갈 수도 있다.

강의는 고등학교와 대학교에서 가장 일반적으로 사용되는 방법이다. 강의에 있어서, 교사는 잘 준비되어 있어야 하며 담당 과목에 대한 충분한 지식을 갖추고 있어야 한다. 강의를 할 때 교사들은 일반적으로 학생들 앞에 서서 다양한 주제에 관한 긴 설명을 제시해준다. 교사들은 시청각 장비를 사용하여 강의를 보충할 수도 있다. 학생들은 강의를 듣고, 필기를 하고, 그리고 명확하지 않은 부분에 대해서는 질문을 한다. 강의는 과학 수업에서 보다 예술학과 인문학 분야의 수업에서 보다 더 일반적이다. 하지만, 특히 대학에서, 이는 사실상 어떠한 유형의 수업에서도 가능할 수 있다. 안타깝게도, 강의는 교사가 말하는 동안 학생들은 듣기만 하기 때문에 주로 일방적인 편이다. 때로는, 교사가 질문을 통해 몇몇 학생들로부터 답을 이끌어냄으로써, 강의가 한 주제에 대한 토론으로 발전하는 경우도 있을 수 한다. 보다 높은 수준의 대학 수업에서는 전적으로 세미나 형식이 선호되어 강의가 이루어지지 않기도 한다. 이러한 수업의 경우, 종종 학생들은 보고서를 제출하게 되고, 이는 학생들 간의 토론 주제가 되며, 교수는 논의되는 주제에 대한 사회자이자 최종 권위자의 역할을 하게 된다.

직접교수와 강의가 많은 학생들에게 다소 지루한 것일 수도 있지만, 이들은 필요한 방법들이다. 직접교수는 교사들로 하여금 모든 수준의 학생들, 특히 집중하는 시간이 짧고 보다 많은 통제와 감독이 필요한 어린 학생들에게 지식을 전달할 수 있게 해준다. 그리고 강의는 대학에서 여전히 일반적으로 사용되는 방식이며, 학생이 많은 수업에서 사용될 수 있는 유일한 현실적인 방법이기도 하다. 협동학습의 경우, 교사들이 자신의 학생들에 대해 잘 알고 있어서 서로 어울릴 수 있고 협동할 수 있는 그룹을 편성시켜준다면, 보다 효과가 높아진다. 결국, 어떤 방법이 사용되던 간에, 목표는 항상 학생들이 배울 수 있도록 하는 것이다.

Listening Section p.75

Answers

1. Ⓑ [Gist-Content Question]
2. Ⓒ [Gist-Purpose Question]
3. Ⓐ [Understanding Attitude Question]
4. Ⓐ [Understanding Function Question]
5. Ⓒ [Making Inferences Question]
6. Ⓓ [Gist-Content Question]
7. Ⓑ [Gist-Purpose Question]
8. Ⓒ [Detail Question]
9. Ⓐ [Making Inferences Question]
10. Ⓐ [Understanding Function Question]
11. Ⓒ [Understanding Attitude Question]

Script

| 06-02 |

M1 Student: Professor Howard, are you busy right now?

M2 Professor: No, not particularly. Why don't you come on in and have a seat, uh . . . ?

M1: Ah, I'm Jason Jenkins. I'm a student in your early American history class, sir.

M2: Ah, yes. I believe that I remember seeing you sitting in the front row next to the window. Am I right about that?

M1: Yeah, wow. That's impressive. How'd you do that?

M2: Well, remembering your name would have been more impressive actually. But, then again, I don't take attendance, and we haven't had any class assignments for you to turn in yet, so it's kind of hard for me to learn students' names until after we've had a project or two completed and I start giving out grades.

M1: Yeah, that makes sense. Anyway, uh, I came here right now because of one of the projects that we're doing in class.

M2: Yes? Which one is that? The short paper?

M1: Yes, that's exactly the one that I'm talking about. You see . . . um, I decided to do my short paper on Benjamin Franklin, but I'm having trouble, well, I'm having some developing it.

M2: What exactly is the nature of your trouble?

M1: There's just so much to write about Franklin. I mean, the guy was such a towering figure in American history that I have no idea how I'm going to cram everything about him into a two-page paper.

M2: Okay, first of all, I think that you're going about this all wrong.

M1: Huh? How so, sir?

M2: This is just a short assignment, Jason. You can't possibly cover the entire life of Ben Franklin in only two pages unless you're writing an encyclopedia article, which is something that I definitely don't want you to do. Instead, why don't you focus on just a single aspect of his life? You could cover his time as . . . oh, as a diplomat in France, his work at the Constitutional Convention, or even his life as a printer.

M1: Yeah, that might work.

M2: But, Jason, you've only got two days to turn in this paper. Aren't you running a little behind on it?

M1: Yes, sir, I am. To be honest, I wasn't expecting there to be so much work in this class. I'm having trouble keeping up with all of the reading in this class, sir.

M2: [4]Well, I suppose that there is a lot of work, but I expect a lot from my students. This class is no easy A after all.

M1: Yes, I think I'm finding that out, sir.

M2: May I give you a suggestion?

M1: I'd love one, sir.

M2: The topics for your long paper are due in two days. Why don't you write about Ben Franklin for your long paper instead of the short one? It sounds like you've already done a lot of research about him. Perhaps you've done enough to write a long paper on him.

M1: Okay, but what about my short paper, sir?

M2: [5]Here . . . I've got a list of topics that I've come up with and which you might consider using. Take a look at these . . . Choose one of them, and you can write your paper on that.

M1: Oh, that's great. Thank you so much, sir.

Translation

M1 Student: Howard 교수님, 지금 바쁘세요?

M2 Professor: 특별히 그렇지는 않아요. 들어와서 앉겠어요? 어…

M1: 아, 저는 Jason Jenkins입니다. 교수님의 초기 미국 역사 수업을 듣고 있는 학생입니다.

M2: 아, 그렇군요. 앞줄 창문 옆에 앉아있는 것을 본 것 같아요. 그렇죠?

M1: 네, 대단하시군요. 어떻게 아셨죠?

M2: 음, 사실 학생의 이름이 기억났다면 더 대단했을텐데. 하지만, 나는 출석 체크를 하지 않고, 아직 제출해야 할 숙제를 내준 적도 없기 때문에, 한 두 가지 과제를 완료해서 성적을 주기 전까지는 학생들의 이름을 외우는 것이 힘들어요.

M1: 네, 이해가 가네요. 어쨌든, 음, 저는 우리가 수업 시간에 하고 있는 과제 중 하나 때문에 찾아 왔어요.

M2: 네? 어떤 것을 말하는 거죠? 짧은 보고서를 말하는 건가요?

M1: 네, 제가 말씀 드리는 것이 바로 그거예요. 아시다시피… 음, 저는 벤자민 플랭클린에 대한 짧은 보고서를 쓰려고 했는데, 문제가 생겼어요. 음, 어느 정도 쓰고 있긴 한데요.

M2: 그럼 문제의 본질이 정확히 뭐죠?

M1: 프랭클린에 대해서는 쓸 것이 너무나 많습니다. 제 말은, 그 사람이 미 역사상 너무나 위대한 인물이어서 두 장의 종이로 그에 대한 모든 것을 요약할 수 있는 방법이 떠오르지 않는다는 것이에요.

M2: 좋아요, 우선, 학생이 완전히 잘못 생각하고 있는 것 같군요.

M1: 네? 어떻게 그렇죠, 교수님?

M2: 이것은 짧은 분량의 과제예요, Jason. 백과사전식의 글을 쓰지 않는 이상, 프랭클린의 전체적인 인생을 겨우 두 페이지에다 담을 수는 없죠. 그리고 그것은 정말 학생이 하지 말아야 할 방법이에요. 대신, 그의 인생 중 한 가지 측면에 초점을 맞춰 보는 것은 어떨까요? 당신은 아마도 그의… 아, 프랑스에서 외교관으로서의, 또는 제헌 의회에서 그의 업적에 대해, 혹은 인쇄업자로서의 그의 삶을 다루어 볼 수도 있겠네요.

M1: 네, 그러면 되겠네요.

M2: 하지만, Jason, 보고서 제출까지는 이틀밖에 남지 않았어요. 너무 늦게 되는 것은 아닐까요?

M1: 네, 교수님, 그럴 것 같아요. 솔직히 말씀 드리면, 수업 시간에 해야 할 것들이 그렇게 많을 줄은 몰랐어요. 수업 시간에 읽어야 할 책들을 모두 읽는 것은 힘이 들어요.

M2: 음, 공부할 것이 많다는 것은 알겠지만, 나는 학생들에게 많은 것을 기대하고 있어요. 이 수업에서 A학점을 받기는 결코 쉽지 않을 거예요.

M1: 네, 알 것 같아요.

M2: 제안을 하나 할까요?

M1: 네, 교수님.

M2: 학생의 장문의 보고서에 맞는 주제는 기한이 이틀밖에 남지 않았어요. 짧은 분량의 보고서 대신 프랭클린에 대한 장문의 보고서를 작성해보는 것은 어떨까요? 그에 대해 이미 많은 조사를 한 것 같더군요. 아마도 그에 관한 장문의 보고서를 쓰기에는 충분할 것 같아요.

M1: 좋아요, 하지만 짧은 분량의 보고서는 어떻게 해야 하나요?

M2: 여기에… 내가 모아 놓은 주제 목록이 있는데 학생이 활용할 수 있을 것 같아요. 이것들을 보세요… 이 중 하나를 골라서 그것에 대해 보고서를 쓸 수 있을 거예요.

M1: 오, 멋져요. 정말 감사합니다, 교수님.

Script

| 06-03 |

W Professor: What we hear as sound is really just the vibration of sound waves against our eardrums. Sometimes, this sound is virtually immediate, such as, uh, such as when someone is speaking to you or when you're watching television. Other times, though, there's a slight delay from when you see an event and when you actually hear the noise caused by that event. Let's take a lighting strike as an example. I'm sure you've all seen lightning and heard thunder on numerous occasions. So, the lightning flashes, and then the thunder soon follows. Of course, sometimes you hear the thunder several seconds after seeing the lightning. The reason is that light travels much faster than sound. So, you won't hear the thunder from a lightning flash several miles away for a few seconds. However, if the flash and the thunder are practically simultaneous, well, uh, you'd better seek shelter really quickly because that means the lightning is practically on top of you.

Okay, so we understand that sound travels and that it's slower than light. How fast does it move? It depends.

M Student: Depends on what?

W: Good question. Mostly, it depends on the medium the sound is traveling through. Sound travels faster in some mediums and slower in others. The general rule is that it travels the fastest in solids, a bit slower in liquids, and the slowest in gases. In the vacuum of space, there's no sound at all. [10]Sound simply doesn't exist in a vacuum. So, any science fiction movie you watch that has spaceships shooting laser beams that make cool noises ... Well, that's just not possible in reality. Er, I suppose that's why it's called science fiction.

Now, we use the term mach . . . that's M-A-C-H . . . to describe the speed of sound. It comes from an Austrian, Ernest Mach, who was a physicist. Mach is essentially used to describe the speed of movement of an object in a fluid. In the case of aircraft, that fluid is the Earth's atmosphere. [11]Mach numbers are related to the conditions in which they take place, so they're not constant. This means that the speed of sound varies depending upon the temperature of the air. Keep that in mind, please. For airplanes, the temperature change is usually related to their altitude. The higher you go, the colder it gets. At sea level at fifteen degrees Celsius, Mach 1, which is the term used to describe the so-called sound barrier, is about 1,215 kilometers per hour. But, the higher you go, the slower the speed of sound becomes. Above ten thousand meters . . . that's higher than Mount Everest, by the way . . . and with freezing temperatures in the negatives, the speed of sound is about 1,055 kilometers per hour.

M: But we can break the sound barrier, right? I mean, planes do it all the time.

W: That's correct, John. So that's why it's something of a misnomer to call it a barrier. However, in decades past, people believed that it couldn't be breached. In the 1930s, German, British, and American scientists started working on jet propulsion and came to realize that the sound barrier was possible to break. They knew a propeller-driven craft could never achieve the speed of sound, so they turned to the principles of jet and rocket engines. The Germans were ahead of the others and actually developed both the jet and the rocket first. During World War II in the 1940s, the German air force had a rocket plane and a twin-engine jet plane. The British and Americans had jet aircraft by the end of the war, too, but none ever approached the speed of sound.

After the war, the Americans took the lead in jet research and production. The U.S. military ommissioned the Bell Corporation to build a plane that could exceed the speed of sound. Previously, pilots had tried to make propeller-driven aircraft do that, but all of them had various design flaws. The planes all had problems with their propellers, wings, or control surfaces, so they became uncontrollable and often crashed as they neared the speed of sound. The Bell X-1, however, was designed for a single purpose: to break the sound barrier. There was a lot of concern that it too would crash, so the engineers took extraordinary measures in designing and maintaining the plane.

The Bell X-1 finally achieved its goal on October 14, 1947, with test pilot Chuck Yeager at the controls. A B-29 bomber carried the plane aloft under its belly to almost 9,000 meters above sea level. Yeager then climbed into the aircraft, and it was released. His top speed on that day was Mach 1.06, which was the first recorded instance of a human exceeding the speed of sound. There were other claims to being first though. A German pilot in World War II and an American one week prior to Yeager were just two of them. However, neither claim was verified by instrument readings. Yeager's was. Nowadays, as John pointed out, exceeding the sound barrier is routine, and some airplanes have even flown faster than three times the speed of sound. In all likelihood, that speed will be exceeded in the future.

Translation

W Professor: 실제로 우리가 소리로 듣는 것은 고막에 부딪치는 음파의 진동일 뿐입니다. 때때로, 이 소리는 사실상 즉각적인 것인데, 음, 예를 들면, 누군가 여러분에게 이야기를 할 때나 여러분이 텔레비전을 시청하고 있을 때와 같은 경우입니다. 그러나, 여러분이 어떤 사건을 보는 때와 그 사건에 의해 실제 소리가 발생하는 것을 듣는 때에 약간의 시간 차가 있는 경우도 있습니다. 이러한 예로서 번개가 치는 경우를 들어 보도록 하겠습니다. 여러분들 모두 분명히 번개를 보고 천둥소리를 들어 본적이 매우 여러 번 있었을 것입니다. 그러면, 번개가 번쩍이고 나서 천둥소리가 그 뒤를 따릅니다. 물론, 때로는 번개를 보고 난 후 몇 초 후에 천둥소리를 듣게 됩니다. 그 이유는 빛이 소리보다 훨씬 더 빠르게 이동하기 때문이죠. 그래서, 여러분들은 수 마일 떨어진 곳에서 발생한 번개 섬광의 천둥소리를 몇 초 동안 들을 수가 없는 것입니다. 하지만, 섬광과 천둥소리가 거의 동시에 일어나는 경우도 있는데, 글쎄요, 음, 이 경우는 번개가 여러분 바로 위에서 치는 경우이므로 빨리 피할 곳을 찾아야겠죠.

좋아요, 그러면 우리는 소리가 이동한다는 점과 소리가 빛보다 더 느리다는 것을 이해하였습니다. 소리의 속도는 어떻게 될까요? 그것은 경우에 따라 달라지죠.

M Student: 어떤 경우를 말씀하시는 거죠?

W: 좋은 질문입니다. 일반적으로, 소리가 이동할 때 통과하는 매개체에 따라 달라집니다. 소리는 어떤 매개체를 통해서는 더 빠르게 이동하고 다른 매개체를 통해서는 더 느리게 이동합니다. 일반적인 법칙에 따르면 소리는 고체를 통과할 때 가장 빠르고, 액체에서는 조금 더 느리고, 기체에서는 가장 느립니다. 우주의 진공 상태에서는, 소리가 전혀 없습니다. 진공 상태에서는 소리가 전혀 존재하지 않습니다. 그래서, 여러분들이 본 공상 과학 영화에서 멋진 소리를 내는 레이저 광선이 발사되는 우주선이

나오는데… 음… 그것은 현실에서는 절대 불가능한 일이죠. 음, 제 생각에는 이러한 점 때문에 공상 과학 영화라고 불리는 것 같습니다.

이제, 음속을 표현하기 위해 마하… M-A-C-H… 라는 용어를 사용하겠습니다. 이것은 오스트리아의 물리학자인 에른스트 마하의 이름에서 유래되었죠. 마하는 본질적으로 유체 내에서의 물체의 이동 속도를 설명하는데 사용됩니다. 항공기의 경우, 이 유체는 지구의 대기가 됩니다. 마하 수는 그것이 발생되는 조건과 관련이 있는데, 그래서 일정하지가 않습니다. 이것은 음속이 기온에 따라서 변한다는 것을 의미합니다. 이 점을 잘 기억해 두세요. 비행기의 경우, 온도의 변화는 대개 고도와 관련이 있습니다. 더 높이 올라 갈 수록, 더 추워집니다. 해수면에서 섭씨 15도인 경우, 마하 1이란, 흔히 음속 장벽이라 불리는 것을 설명하는 용어인데, 이는 시속 1,215 km가 됩니다. 그러나, 더 높이 올라가면, 음속은 더 느려집니다. 1만 미터 고도에서는… 에베레스트 산 보다 더 높은 고도인데, 어쨌든… 섭씨 -0도 정도가 되는데, 그 때의 음속은 시속 1,055 km가 됩니다.

M: 하지만 우리는 음속을 깨뜨릴 수 있어요, 그렇죠? 제 말은, 비행기가 종종 그렇게 한다는 말인데요.

W: 맞는 말이에요, John. 그러한 점 때문에 장벽이라는 부적절한 명칭으로 불리는 것입니다. 하지만, 수십 년 전, 사람들은 음속의 장벽을 깨뜨릴 수 없다고 생각했어요. 1930년대, 독일, 영국, 그리고 미국의 과학자들이 제트 추진 기술을 연구하기 시작했고 음속 장벽을 깨뜨리는 것이 가능하다는 것을 알게 되었습니다. 그들은 프로펠러 동력기로는 음속에 도달할 수 없다는 것을 알고 있었기 때문에, 제트 엔진과 로켓 엔진의 원리로 관심을 돌렸습니다. 독일은 다른 나라보다 앞서 있었고 실제로 제트 엔진과 로켓 엔진을 개발해냈죠. 1940년대 제 2차 세계 대전 중, 독일 공군은 로켓 비행기와 쌍발 제트기를 보유하고 있었습니다. 영국과 미국도 전쟁이 끝날 무렵 제트기를 보유하게 되었지만, 아무도 음속에 도달하지는 못했죠.

전쟁이 끝나고, 미국은 제트 엔진 연구와 제작에 있어서 앞서 나가게 되었습니다. 미군은 벨 항공사에 음속을 뛰어넘을 수 있는 비행기의 제작을 의뢰했습니다. 이전에는, 조종사들이 프로펠러 동력기로 음속 돌파를 해보려고 했지만, 모두 설계의 결함을 갖고 있었습니다. 비행기들은 모두 프로펠러, 날개, 또는 조종익면에 문제가 있었고, 그래서 그것들은 통제 불가능한 상황이 되어 음속에 가까워지면 추락하는 경우가 잦았습니다. 하지만, Bell X-1은 단 한가지 목적을 위해 설계되었죠: 바로 음속을 깨뜨리는 것이었습니다. 이 비행기가 추락할 것이라는 많은 우려가 있었기 때문에, 엔지니어들은 비행기의 설계와 관리에 특별한 조치를 취했죠.

Bell X-1은 1947년 10월 14일, 시험 비행 조종사였던 척 야거의 조종 하에 그와 같은 목적을 달성하였습니다. B-29 폭격기가 이 비행기를 동체에 싣고 해발 9,000미터 상공으로 올라갔습니다. 그리고 나서 야거가 비행기에 올라탔고, 비행기는 낙하되었습니다. 그 날의 최고 속도는 마하 1.06이었는데, 이것은 인간이 음속을 돌파한, 기록상 최초의 사례였습니다. 하지만 자신들이 최초라고 하는 다른 주장도 있었죠. 제2차 세계 대전에 참전했던 독일의 한 조종사와 미국의 한 조종사는 야거보다 자신들이 1주일 앞섰다고 주장을 하기도 했습니다. 하지만, 어떤 주장도 계기판 판독으로 증명되지 못했습니다. 야거의 비행은 증명되었죠.

요즘에는, John이 지적했듯이, 음속의 돌파는 흔한 일이고, 몇몇 비행기들은 음속 보다 세 배 더 빠른 속도로 비행하기도 했습니다. 아마도, 이러한 속도조차 미래에는 깨어질 것입니다.

Actual Test 07

Reading Section   p.81

Answers

1. D [Reference Question]
2. D [Vocabulary Question]
3. B [Factual Question]
4. A [Rhetorical Purpose Question]
5. B [Inference Question]
6. A [Negative Factual Question]
7. C [Vocabulary Question]
8. D [Factual Question]
9. A [Factual Question]
10. A [Vocabulary Question]
11. C [Factual Question]
12. 3rd [Insert Text Question]
13.

	REASON FOR LIVING TOGETHER
Protection	B, E, F
Reproduction	C, G

[Fill in a Table Question]

Translation

포유류군

많은 포유류들이 떼, 군, 무리 등의 다양한 이름으로 불리는 집단을 이루어 함께 이동을 한다. 이러한 집단은 12마리 미만으로, 혹은 수천 마리까지로 이루어질 수 있다. 포유류는 실용적이고 사회적인 이유 때문에 집단 행동을 한다. 그러한 이유에는 피식자로서 제공 받게 되는 보호와 포식자로서 얻게 되는 사냥의 기회가 포함된다. 또한, 집단 행동은 종의 번식에도 도움이 되는데, 번식을 통해 동물들은 자신의 유전자를 다음 세대로 전달하는 것이 가능해진다.

피식 포유류는 포식자가 먹이감으로 사냥하는 동물들이다. 생존의 기회를 높이기 위해, 많은 포유류들이 대규모의 집단을 이루어 살고 있다. 이로써 포유류들은 포식자가 접근해 올 때 경고 시간을 늘릴 수 있게 된다. 보다 많은 눈이 위험을 탐지해냄으로써, 집단 내의 피식자들은 공격받기 전에 포식자들을 찾아낼 기회가 보다 많아지고, 따라서 생명을 보전한 채 달아날 수 있게 된다. 프레리도그가 그러한 동물 중 하나인데, 이들은 대규모의 집단을 이루어 살아간다. 각각의 프레리도그는 항상 여우, 늑대, 그리고 기타 포식자들을 찾기 위해 주위를 감시하며 매와 독수리를 찾아내기 위해 하늘을 쳐다본다. 이 중 한 마리가 다가오는, 혹은 잠재적인 위험을 감지하게 되면, 무리 내의 다른 동물들에게 경고를 해주기 때문에, 모두가 도망을 칠 수 있다. 아프리카의 커다란 포유류들 – 예를 들면, 큰 뿔 영양, 얼룩말, 그리고 영양들 – 또한 스스로를 보호하기 위해 거대한 무리를 지어 이동을 한다. 포식자들이 그 중 몇몇을 죽일 수는 있지만, 희생물이 된 동물들은 보통 그 무리에서 가장 약하고 느린 동물들이다.

포식자들 또한 무리를 이루어 살아가지만, 그들의 무리는 일반적으로 피식자들의 무리보다 더 작다. 몇몇 피식 포유류들의 무리는 수천 마리의 동물로 이루어질 수 있지만, 대부분 포식자들의 무리는 30마리를 넘지 않는 경우가 일반적이다. 아프리카의 사자 무리에 관한 연구에 따르면 사자 무리는 보통 한 마리에서 세 마리의 수컷과, 세 마리에서 여섯 마리의 암컷, 그리고 소수의 새끼들로 구성된다. 미 옐로우스톤 국립 공원의 늑대 무리에 대한 연구에 따르면 대부분의 늑대 무리는 네 마리에서 열 마리로 구성되는데 가장 큰 무리는 25마리 정도의 늑대로 구성된다. (하지만 대부분의 무리가 이보다는 작은 규모였기 때문에 이처럼 규모가 큰 무리는 비정상적인 것으로 간주되었다.) 이렇게 작은 수치로 구성되는 주된 이유는 먹이의 공급량 때문이다. 포식 동물들의 무리는 자신들이 사냥하는 영역에 표시를 해둔다. 이들의 영역 크기와 이용 가능한 먹이의 양이 집단의 크기를 제한한다. 이러한 이유 때문에, 대부분의 포식 동물들의 무리는 필사적으로 영역을 사수하며 같은 종이라도 자신의 영역을 침범하는 경쟁 상대에게는 공격을 가하게 될 것이다.

포식자들이 집단을 형성하는 주된 이유는 사냥의 성공 가능성을 높이기 위해서다. 포식자들은 수가 더 많아질수록 먹이감을, 특히 크기가 상당히 큰 먹이감을 손쉽게 둘러싸고, 공격하여, 쓰러뜨릴 수 있다. 아프리카에서는 커다란 포유류를 죽이기 위해 사자, 하이에나, 혹은 표범들이 동시에 공격하는 것을 흔히 볼 수 있다. 이와 마찬가지로, 늑대들이 물소, 엘크, 그리고 사슴들을 – 즉, 일반 늑대들 보다 몸집이 더 큰 동물들을 – 에워싼 다음, 힘이 빠져 쓰러져서 죽을 때까지 먹잇감의 다리를 무는 것을 목격할 수가 있다. 집단을 이루어 사냥하는 것의 가장 명백한 단점은 죽은 동물을 모두가 나누어야 한다는 점이다. 그 결과, 큰 집단은 끊임없이 사냥을 해서 집단의 구성원들이 굶어 죽지 않도록 해야 한다.

또한 포유류는 방어나 사냥 이외의 다른 목적을 위해 함께 살기도 한다. 많은 포유류의 무리들은 가족 단위로 이루어져 있다. 물론, 무리 내의 수 천 마리의 동물 모두가 서로 연관되어 있지는 않다. 하지만, 규모가 작은 포유류 무리 내에서는 – 포식자와 피식자의 경우 모두 – 그 구성원들이 동일한 유전자를 공유하고 있는 경우가 많다. 그 결과, 몇몇 무리들은 번식을 위해 결국 서로 합쳐지게 된다. 다른 경우, 번식의 욕구 때문에 몇몇 무리들이 와해되기도 한다. 예를 들어, 많은 늑대 무리들은 한 쌍의 짝을 이룬 늑대들에 의해 시작된다. 이 무리가 어느 정도의 크기가 되면, 몇몇 늑대들이 사냥을 하고 자신들의 짝을 찾을 새로운 영토를 찾아서 떠나게 된다. 사자의 경우에는, 암컷들이 단기간에만 배란을 하므로, 수컷과 암컷이 새끼를 낳기 위해서는 반드시 무리를 지어 다녀야만 한다. 그래서, 무리를 이루어 생활하고 이동을 함으로써, 피식자와 포식자들 모두는 번식 가능성을 증대시킬 수 있기 때문에, 따라서 종의 생존이 가능해진다.

Listening Section p.87

Answers

1. Ⓓ [Gist-Purpose Question]
2. Ⓑ [Detail Question]
3. Ⓓ [Understanding Attitude Question]
4. Ⓐ [Understanding Organization Question]
5. Ⓑ [Understanding Function Question]
6. Ⓓ [Gist-Purpose Question]
7. Ⓒ [Detail Question]
8. Ⓐ [Understanding Attitude Question]
9. Ⓒ [Understanding Organization Question]
10. Ⓑ [Making Inferences Question]
11. Ⓐ [Understanding Function Question]

Script

| 07-02 |

W Registrar's Office Employee: Next . . . Good afternoon. What can I do for you today?

M Student: Uh, yes, I need to get some copies of my transcript printed so that I can send them off to some potential employers. Is this the place where I can do that, ma'am?

W: It sure is. Did you fill out the correct form so that we can expedite your request?

M: Uh . . . Form?

W: Sure, you need to fill out the correct paperwork after all. There has to be a paper record of any and all requests that students make for copies of their tranScript. That way, we can always be sure of how many copies there are of them and who has them.

M: [5]Oh, yeah. Okay. So, uh, no . . . I didn't fill out the form. I don't need to go get one and then go to the back of the line, do I? **I'd hate to have to wait for another twenty minutes.**

W: No, no. It's all right. You seem like you're a polite young man, so I can give you the form here. If you had been rude on the other hand . . .

M: Yeah, I get what you're saying. Thanks by the way. I've got class in fifteen minutes, so I really appreciate this.

W: No problem. Anyway, here's the form for you to fill out.

M: This looks pretty simple. Name . . . Student number . . .

Address . . .

W: Oh, I need to look at your student ID in order to verify your identity.

M: Sure thing. Just let me get it out of my wallet . . . Okay, here it is.

W: Toby Martin. Okay, this picture sure looks like you. So, are you about done with that form?

M: Yes, I am. I just need to write down a couple more things.

W: So, how would you like to receive these tranScript? Shall we just give them to you and let you send them to the companies, or would you like for us to mail them directly to the companies?

M: You can do that?

W: Sure. We can do a lot of things here. In fact, that's what most students opt to do. That way, they can save money on postage. Plus, most companies prefer to get student tranScript straight from the school. That way they know that the tranScript haven't been, uh, tampered with in any way, shape, or form.

M: Good point. You know, I've been at this school for three and a half years, but I never knew that about sending tranScript. I guess I've got a lot to learn.

W: Well, what's it going to be?

M: What do you recommend?

W: It's probably best that you let us send them out. It will save you time and money and make you look better to the companies.

M: Okay, I think I'll do that. But, uh, I don't have the companies' addresses with me. I guess I'll have to come back later.

W: That's fine. Oh, and don't forget that there is a charge of three dollars per transcript. Be sure to bring either cash or a check for the proper amount.

M: Ah, okay, thanks. I didn't know that either.

W: Well, now you do. Okay, come back again when you have the time and the addresses. Have a great day.

Translation

W Registrar's Office Employee: 다음 분… 안녕하세요. 무엇을 도와드릴까요?

M Student: 음, 네, 지원할 몇 군데 회사에 보낼 성적 증명서를 인쇄해야 해서요. 여기에서 할 수 있을까요, 선생님?

W: 물론이죠. 저희가 학생의 요청을 더 신속히 처리할 수 있도록 적절한 양식을 작성해 주셨나요?

M: 음… 양식이요?

W: 네, 적절한 서류를 작성해 주셔야 해요. 학생들이 성적 증명서 사본을 요청한 모든 문서 기록들이 남겨져야 하죠. 그렇게 해야, 얼마나 많은 복사본들이 만들어졌는지, 그리고 누가 가지고 있는지 확인할 수가 있어요.

M: 아, 네, 알겠어요. 그러면, 어, 음… 아직 양식을 작성하지 않았어요. 제가, 음, 양식을 가지러 간 다음, 다시 저 줄에 서있을 필요는 없겠죠, 그렇죠? 또다시 20분 동안 기다리고 싶지는 않아서요.

W: 아니오. 아니에요. 학생이 공손해 보이니, 제가 양식을 드리도록 하죠. 반면에 만약 무례했더라면…

M: 네, 무슨 말씀인지 알겠어요. 어쨌든 감사해요. 제가 15분 뒤에 수업이 있어서요. 정말 고맙습니다.

W: 괜찮아요. 아무튼, 작성하셔야 할 양식이 여기 있어요.

M: 꽤 간단해 보이는군요. 이름… 학번… 주소…

W: 오, 신원 확인을 위해서 제가 학생의 학생증을 봐야 해요.

M: 물론이죠. 지갑에서 꺼내 드릴게요… 됐어요, 여기 있어요.

W: *Toby Martin*이군요. 좋아요, 사진이 분명 학생이군요. 그럼, 양식은 다 작성 해 가나요?

M: 네. 두 개 정도만 더 쓰면 될 것 같아요.

W: 그러면, 성적 증명서는 어떻게 받으실 건가요? 제가 학생에게 주면 학생이 회사로 보낼 건가요, 아니면 저희 쪽에서 직접 회사로 보내 드릴까요?

M: 그렇게 해주실 수도 있나요?

W: 그럼요. 여기에서는 많은 것들을 할 수 있죠. 사실, 대부분의 학생들이 그렇게 하는 것을 택해요. 그렇게 함으로써, 우편 요금을 절약할 수 있거든요. 또한, 대부분의 회사에서는 학교에서 바로 보내 주는 성적 증명서를 선호해요. 그렇게 해야 그들이, 음, 어떤 식으로든, 모양이나, 형식이 바뀌지 않았다는 점을 알 수 있죠.

M: 그렇군요. 아시겠지만, 제가 이 학교를 3년 반이나 다녔는데, 성적 증명서 발송에 대해서는 전혀 모르고 있었네요. 아직도 배울 것이 많이 있나 봐요.

W: 음, 그래서 어떻게 할 건가요?

M: 어떻게 하는 게 좋을까요?

W: 저희 쪽에서 보내 드리는 것이 아마 가장 좋겠죠. 돈도 절약되고 회사에서도 학생을 더 좋게 볼 테니까요.

M: 좋아요, 그러면 그렇게 할게요. 하지만, 음, 제가 회사 주소를 지금 모르겠는데요. 잠시 후에 다시 와야 할 것 같아요.

W: 괜찮아요. 아, 그리고 성적 증명서 한 장당 3달러의 비용이 든다는 점도 잊지 마세요. 비용에 맞는 현금이나 수표를 가져오세요.

M: 아, 네, 고마워요. 그것도 몰랐네요.

W: 음, 이제 알게 되었잖아요. 좋아요, 시간이 될 때 주소를 가지고 다시 들러 주세요. 좋은 하루 되시고요.

Script

| 07-03 |

W1 Professor: In the 1970s, there was a major transition that took place in the movie industry. It was the rise of blockbuster movies. As you likely already know, a blockbuster is any movie that achieves box office success and makes much more money than it cost to produce, advertise, and distribute. Nowadays, the benchmark for a blockbuster is a gross of over one hundred million dollars, but that may soon change since the costs of movies have skyrocketed recently. In many cases, one hundred million dollars isn't enough to let a movie break even. I mean, blockbusters such as *Avatar* and the *Harry Potter* films cost much more than that amount just to make.

    Prior to the advent of the blockbuster era in the 1970s, most movies were filmed on modest budgets and were then slowly distributed to cinemas throughout America and then overseas. Some films made lots of money, but there was no perceived race or competition to see which could earn the most. Of course, the major Hollywood studios, such as MGM, Twentieth Century Fox, and Universal, among others, were in the business of making money, but doing so was a, uh, a relatively slow process. It could take a studio months or years to recoup its investment and then earn a profit. So, at that time, much of the movie industry was geared to rolling out a movie slowly. [11]It would play in a few cities here and there, and then it would move on to another few cities. Moviegoers often had to wait months to see a film that had opened in New York or LA. Those overseas sometimes waited years.

W2 Student: No way. That must have been awful.

W1: Well, sure, from our way of looking at things, it was incredibly slow. But let me tell you now how we got from that era to today's time, in which a movie can be screened in over a hundred countries around the world on its opening night. So, this change occurred in 1975. Does anyone know the movie I'm talking about?

W2: You mean *Star Wars*, right?

W1: Well, that was most certainly a blockbuster, but it's not the movie I'm thinking about. This was a movie that made people afraid to go into the water.

W2: Was it *Jaws*?

W1: Exactly. In 1975, a young director, Steven Spielberg, of whom I'm sure you've all heard, made *Jaws*, which is widely considered to be the first real blockbuster. It's about a shark that terrorizes a small beach resort during the summer and the men who hunt it down. Well, the production of *Jaws* was a mess. It was plagued by problems, was finished six months late, and was millions of dollars over budget. Then, it got released . . . What happened next is the stuff of Hollywood legends. Not expecting a big turnout, the studio only made about a hundred copies of the movie. The first weekend, all of the shows were sold out. Positive word of mouth swiftly spread about *Jaws*, and the studio scrambled to make more prints of the movie. In the end, it grossed over 250 million dollars and became the first true blockbuster.

W2: That doesn't seem like a lot of money. I mean, some films have made 300 or 400 million dollars.

W1: Ah, good point. But if you adjust for inflation, *Jaws* earned almost a billion dollars. And that's a huge amount of money no matter which era you're in.

    Two years later came *Star Wars*, and it set new rules for filmmaking, distribution, and many other areas of the industry. *Star Wars*, which should require no introduction for all of you film majors, was the brainchild of George Lucas. He managed to get a relatively modest budget of ten million dollars for his science fiction epic. Oh, and showing what an astute businessman he was, he got the rights to all of the sequels as well as the merchandising for the movie. What a brilliant move! So, *Star Wars* went on to become the highest grossing movie ever. This record stood until *Titanic* broke it twenty years later in 1997.

    In addition to *Star Wars*' phenomenal box office numbers, it reaped millions . . . and eventually billions . . . of dollars for George Lucas thanks to all of the toys, games, comic books, posters, music, and a multitude of other products and tie-ins for the movie. Oh, and don't forget about the five sequels made so far. The studio that financed him—Twentieth Century Fox—has been kicking itself ever since it made that agreement with him. Anyway, the studios took notice of the success of *Star Wars* in the realm of merchandising. So now, virtually every movie—no matter how big or small—has some kind of commercial tie-ins. This is another change that blockbusters brought about. In fact, some movies are made specifically to sell the toys that are tied to them. Let's talk about some of those films now.

Translation

W1 Professor: 1970년대, 영화산업에 중대한 변화가 일어났습니다. 그것은 블록버스터 영화의 등장이었죠. 여러분이 아마 이미 알고 있듯이, 일부 블록버스터 영화는 엄청난 흥행이라는 성공을 거두었고 제작, 광고, 배급 비용보다 훨씬 더 많은 돈을 벌어들였습니다. 요즘에는, 블록버스터의 기준으로 총 수익이 1억 달러 이상이 되어야 하지만, 최근 영화 제작 비용이 급격하게 증가했기 때문에 이 기준은 곧 바뀌게 될 것 입니다. 많은 경우, 1억 달러의 수익은 영화의 손익 분기점을 넘기기에도 충분치 않습니다. 제 말은, *아바타*나 *해리포터* 같은 블록버스터 영화들은 제작하는 데만 그 이상의 비용이 들어간다는 것이죠.

    1970년대에 블록버스터의 시대가 도래하기 이전에는, 대부분의 영화가 저렴한 예산으로 제작되었으며 미국 내 영화관에 천천히 배급되었고 그 후에 해외로 배급이 되었습니다. 몇몇 영화들은 막대한 돈을 벌었지만, 어떤 영화가 가장 많은 수익을 남기는 지에 대한 눈에 띄는 경쟁은 없었습니다. 물론, MGM, 20세기 폭스, 그리고 유니버설 영화사와 같은 대형 헐리우드 제작사들은 수익을 남긴 기업들이었지만, 이렇게 되기까지는, 어, 음, 비교적 오랜 시간의 과정이 있었습니다. 제작사들이 투자한 만큼의 비용을 되찾고 이윤을 남기는 데는 수 개월에서 수 년이 걸리기도 했죠. 그래서, 당시에는, 대부분의 영화 산업이 영화를 천천히 제작할 수 있도록 조정되어 있었습니다. 영화는 이곳 저곳의 몇몇 도시에서 상영되었고, 그 후에 다른 도시로 이동하게 되었습니다. 영화 팬들이 뉴욕이나 LA에서 개봉된 영화를 보기 위해서는 몇 개월을 기다려야만 하는 경우도 많았습니다. 해외의 영화 팬들은 몇 년씩을 기다리기도 했죠.

W2 Student: 그럴 리가요. 분명 최악이었겠군요.

W1: 글쎄요, 물론, 우리가 바라보는 방식으로는, 엄청나게 느린 것이었죠. 그러나 이제 그 시대에서 오늘날까지 우리가 얻은 것

에 대해 이야기를 해 볼 텐데요. 어떤 영화는 하룻밤 사이에 전 세계 100여 개국 이상에서 상영될 수 있습니다. 자, 이러한 변화는 1975년에 일어났어요. 제가 지금 말하려는 영화를 아는 사람이 있나요?

W2: 스타워즈를 말씀하시는군요, 그렇죠?

W1: 글쎄요. 그 영화가 확실히 블록버스터이긴 하지만, 제가 말하고자 하는 영화는 아닙니다. 이것은 사람들이 물에 들어가는 것을 두려워하게 만든 영화였어요.

W2: 죠스인가요?

W1: 맞아요. 1975년, 여러분들이 모두 다 분명히 들어보았을, 당시 젊은 감독이었던 스티븐 스필버그가 죠스라는 영화를 만들었는데, 이 영화가 최초의 진정한 블록버스터 영화로 널리 인정받고 있습니다. 이 영화는 여름 동안 작은 휴양지를 공포에 떨게 했던 상어와 그것을 잡으려는 사람들에 관한 이야기입니다. 영화는 여러 문제들을 겪었는데, 제작 완료에 6개월이 지연되었고, 예산을 수백만 달러나 더 초과했습니다. 그리고 나서, 영화가 개봉되었는데… 그 후 일어난 일은 헐리우드의 전설적인 이야기가 되었죠. 대규모의 관객을 기대하지는 않았기 때문에, 제작사는 영화의 사본을 100개 정도만 만들었습니다. 이는 개봉 첫 주 만에, 모두 매진이 되었습니다. 죠스에 대한 긍정적인 소문이 입에서 입으로 빠르게 퍼져 나갔고, 제작사는 더 많은 영화의 사본을 만들기 위해 분주히 움직였습니다. 결국, 총 수익은 2억 5천만 달러 이상이 되었고 영화는 최초의 블록버스터가 되었죠.

W2: 그 액수가 그렇게 많은 것은 아닌 것 같은데요. 제 말은, 몇몇 영화들은 3억에서 4억 달러를 벌어들이니까요.

W1: 아, 좋은 지적입니다. 하지만 물가 상승률을 감안한다면, 죠스는 거의 10억 달러를 벌어 들인 셈입니다. 그리고 이 액수는 여러분들이 어떤 시대에 살고 있는지에 상관없이 엄청난 액수죠.

  2년 뒤에 스타워즈가 개봉되었는데, 이 영화는 제작, 배급, 그리고 영화 산업의 여러 분야에 걸쳐 새로운 원칙을 세웠습니다. 여러분같이 영화학 전공자들에게는 소개가 따로 필요 없는 스타워즈는 조지 루카스의 아이디어였습니다. 그는 자신의 장편 공상 과학 영화를 위해, 비교적 저렴한 예산인 1천만 달러의 예산을 확보할 수 있었습니다. 아, 그리고 그는 정말로 기민한 사업가였기 때문에, 모든 속편뿐 아니라 영화의 캐릭터 상품 판매에 대한 권리도 확보해 두었죠. 참으로 현명한 행동이었습니다! 그렇게, 스타워즈는 계속해서 역사상 최고의 수익을 올린 영화가 되었습니다. 이 기록은 20년 후인 1997년, 타이타닉에 의해 깨어질 때까지, 최고 기록이었습니다.

  스타워즈는 경이로운 성공 이외에도, 장난감, 게임, 만화책, 포스터, 음악, 그리고 여러 가지 다양한 제품들과 영화의 파생상품들로 인해 수백만 달러… 결국에는 수십억 달러의 돈을 조지 루카스에게 안겨주었습니다. 아, 그리고 지금까지 다섯 편의 속편이 제작되었다는 것을 잊어서는 안되겠습니다. 제작 지원을 한 영화사는 - 20세기 폭스인데 - 그와 합의를 맺은 이후로 줄곧 땅을 치며 후회했습니다. 어쨌든, 영화사들은 스타워즈의 캐릭터 상품 판매에서의 성공에 주목하게 되었죠. 그래서 이제, 사실상 모든 영화는 - 크건 작건 간에 - 어느 정도의 관련 상품들을 가지고 있습니다. 이것이 블록버스터 영화가 가져온 또 다른 변화입니다. 사실상, 몇몇 영화들은 관련된 장난감을 판매하기 위해서 특별히 제작되기도 합니다. 이제 그와 같은 영화들에 대해 논의해 보도록 하죠.

Actual Test 08

Reading Section p.93

Answers

1. Ⓑ [Negative Factual Question]
2. Ⓒ [Inference Question]
3. Ⓓ [Vocabulary Question]
4. Ⓑ [Vocabulary Question]
5. Ⓒ [Reference Question]
6. Ⓒ [Factual Question]
7. Ⓑ [Factual Question]
8. Ⓓ [Sentence Simplification Question]
9. Ⓑ [Vocabulary Question]
10. Ⓑ [Factual Question]
11. Ⓓ [Factual Question]
12. Ⓐ [Inference Question]
13. 2nd [Insert Text Question]
14. Ⓐ, Ⓑ, Ⓔ [Prose Summary Question]

Translation

유대류

  유대류는 포유류의 아강으로서, 대부분 호주와 남아메리카의 지역에서 살고 있지만, 몇몇 종은 뉴기니, 인도네시아, 그리고 중앙아메리카 및 북아메리카에서 산다. 아마도 유대류 중에서는 캥거루, 왈라비, 주머니쥐, 그리고 코알라가 가장 잘 알려져 있을 것이다. 유대류는 두 가지의 뚜렷한 방식에서 다른 포유류들과 다르다. 첫째는 그들이 새끼를 낳아서 기르는 방식인데, 이는 새끼가 초기 단계에 있는 동안 외부에 있는 주머니를 사용하는 것과 관련이 있다. (주머니를 가진 모든 동물들 중에서, 아마도 캥거루가 사람들에게 가장 친숙한 동물일 것이다.) 두 번째 차이점은 그들이 사는 곳과 관계가 있다. 먼 옛날, 유대류는 대부분의 대륙에서 살았다는 증거가 있지만, 그들은 결국 다른 포유류들과의 경쟁에서 밀려났다. 하지만, 이들은 오스트레일리아 및 남아메리카의 환경 조건 덕분에 이곳에서 번성할 수 있었다.

  유대류는 다른 포유류와 마찬가지로 생을 시작한다: 어미의 자궁 내에서 수정란으로서 시작되는 것이다. 일반적인 포유류는 전형적으로 자궁 내에서 성장하는데, 임신기간이 끝나고 바깥세상에서 생존할 수 있을 정도의 충분히 힘을 기를 때까지 이곳에서 어미로부터 양분을 얻는다. 새끼가 자라고 난 후 출산을 하는 포유류는 태반 포유류로 알려져 있다. 대부분의 포유류와는 달리, 유대류에게 있어서는 새끼가 자궁 안에서 모든 성장의 기간을 다 보내며 완전히 성장하지는 않기 때문에, 이는 태반 포유류가 아니다. 대신, 몇 주나 몇 달 후 – 정확한 기간은 종마다 다른데 – 유대류의 새끼는 미숙한 상태로 태어난다. 이것은 곧바로 어미의 외부 주머니로 기어 들어가게 되는데, 동물학자들은 이것을 육아낭이라고 부른다. 육아낭 안에는 젖꼭지가 있고, 미숙한 새끼는 이 젖꼭지에 달라 붙어서 영양분을 얻게 된다. 그곳에서, 어미의 주머니 덕분에 미숙한 유대류 새끼는 바깥 세상으로부터 보호를 받으며 성장하는 데 몇 주에서 몇 달을 더 보내게 될 것이다.

유대류가 이처럼 빨리 새끼를 낳는 주요한 이유는 이들에게 태반 자궁이 없고 난황 형태의 자궁이 있기 때문인데, 이것은 새들의 알과 보다 더 비슷하다. 태반 포유류에 있어서, 태반은 어미의 혈액이 성장하는 새끼에게 안정적으로 공급될 수 있도록 해주며, 이러한 혈액 공급으로 양분이 제공된다. 유대류의 자궁 내에서, 난황은 성장 단계의 초기 동안만 양분을 공급해준다; 따라서 새끼는 나머지 성장의 시간을 주머니에서 보낼 수 있도록 태어나야만 한다. 몇몇 동물학자들은 유대류가 왜 다른 포유류와 다른 모습을 가지게 되었는지에 대해 궁금해하고 있다. 가장 좋은 설명은 짧은 임신 기간이 긴 임신 기간에 비해 덜 위험하다는 것이다. 짧은 기간 동안만 뱃속에 새끼를 지니고 있음으로써, 어미에게는 임신과 관련된 다양한 위험이 더 적어진다는 것이다. 그러나, 단점들도 존재하는데, 그 중 하나는 새끼 유대류의 앞다리가 제한적인 움직임만을 할 수 있다는 점에 있다. 새끼는 자궁에서 기어 나와 주머니로 들어갈 수 있을 정도의 힘만을 가진, 무언가를 쥘 수 있는 앞다리를 갖고 있다. 게다가, 몇몇 종들에 있어서는, 앞다리가 생겨난 지 한참 뒤에도 발달이 이루어지지 않기 때문에 앞다리는 제한된 운동 능력만을 갖게 된다.

오스트레일리아와 남아메리카 이외의 지역에서는, 유대류가 상당히 희귀한 편이다. 하지만 항상 그와 같았던 것은 아니다. 화석 기록에 따르면 유대류는 한때 북아메리카와 유라시아 대륙에서 상당히 많이 살고 있었다. 실제로, 가장 오래된 유대류의 화석은 중국에서 발견되었는데, 이것은 유대류가 아시아에서 생겨나 그 후 다른 지역으로 이동했다는 것을 암시해준다. 하지만 현재, 유대류는 주로 두 지역에서만 발견되고 있다. 동물학자들은 다른 대륙에서 서식지와 먹이를 놓고 유대류가 태반 포유류를 따라잡지 못했다고 주장한다. 그러나, 오스트레일리아와 남아메리카 모두는 비교적 더운 기후를 가지고 있다. 이는 유대류에게 이로운 점이다. 이들은 먹지 않고도 긴 시간을 보낼 수 있고 또한 먹을 것 없이도 오랫동안 생존할 수 있다. 이러한 섬은 특히 오스트레일리아의 유대류에게 유리했는데, 이곳은 지구의 모든 대륙 중에서 가장 건조한 대륙이기 때문이다. 게다가, 해마다, 자라게 될 식물의 – 대부분의 유대류가 먹고 사는 – 양이 불확실하기 때문에, 때로 피식자들의 생존 가능성이 낮아지게 된다. 오스트레일리아의 이러한 조건 때문에, 이 대륙의 혹독한 환경 속에서 유대류가 살아남아 번성했던 반면, 신진 대사율이 높은 많은 태반 동물들은 오래 전에 사라져 버렸다. 오스트레일리아가 지리학적으로 다른 대륙들로부터 고립되어 있어서, 이곳에 새로 유입된 태반 동물들은 거의 없었으며, 따라서 유대류는 거의 경쟁에 직면하지 않았다.

Listening Section p.99

Answers

1. Ⓒ [Gist-Content Question]
2. Ⓒ [Detail Question]
3. Ⓒ [Connecting Content Question]
4. Ⓐ [Understanding Attitude Question]
5. Ⓑ [Understanding Function Question]
6. Ⓒ [Gist-Purpose Question]
7. Ⓑ [Detail Question]
8. Ⓓ [Understanding Attitude Question]
9. Ⓒ [Understanding Organization Question]
10. Ⓐ [Making Inferences Question]
11. Ⓑ [Understanding Function Question]

Script

| 08-02 |

W Professor: Okay, Ken, I think that covers everything that we need to go over concerning this recent paper of yours. Overall, I'd say that you did a great job. There were just a couple of minor points that could have been explained better.

M Student: Thanks so much for your help, Professor Kimball. You've cleared up a whole lot of things for me. Those problems were really bothering me a lot.

W: Great. I'm glad that we solved that problem. So, if there isn't anything else . . .

M: Uh . . . Actually . . . There's one more thing.

W: Uh-huh?

M: Do you remember how I spoke to you a couple of weeks ago about how I was considering changing my major?

W: Yes, I do . . . Aha. The moment of truth has arrived.

M: Yes, that's correct. I've finally made my decision.

W: And . . . ?

M: I'm going to do exactly what we talked about.

W: So, you're not going to change majors, right?

M: That's correct. I think that, by remaining in the Biology Department, I can have the best chance at getting accepted to medical school when I graduate in a couple of years.

W: You've made a wise decision I believe. I'm happy for you.

M: Yes, I think so. I really thought a lot about what you told me at our last meeting, and it made quite an impression on me. However, I've also been doing some research on my own, and I've spoken with some other professors as well, and, uh . . .

W: Go on.
M: Well, I've decided that I'm going to stay in this department, but I'm also going to add a minor . . . in chemistry. I feel that, by get a minor in chemistry, I can be more attractive to the, well, the elite medical schools to which I'm planning to apply.
W: [4]A minor in chemistry, huh?
M: Er, yes. How does that sound to you?
W: Well, even though it's just a minor, it's going to be a significant increase in your course load . . . much more than a minor in, say, history or English would be.
M: How so?
W: [5]Well, the chemistry classes that you'll have to take will all have labs, so that will basically double the number of hours you'll be in a classroom or lab each week. Do you think you're up to the challenge?
M: I'm pretty sure I can handle it. I mean, I was already planning to take five of the seven chemistry courses that I'll need to major in it anyway. So, basically, I'll only be adding two new courses, but I'll get the benefit of having a minor in chemistry on my transcript. It seems like a fair trade to me.
W: Hmm . . . When you put it that way, it does tend to make sense. Okay, I approve . . . Oh, have you spoken with someone in the Chemistry Department to be your advisor for the minor? You might want to try Professor Adelman.
M: Actually, he's the guy that I was thinking of asking.
W: Hold on. I'll give him a call right now and talk to him on your behalf. Let me just find his number.

Translation

W Professor: 좋아요, Ken, 우리는 학생의 최근 논문과 관련된 필요한 모든 것들을 다 검토해보았다고 생각해요. 대체로, 매우 잘 되어있다고 말하고 싶군요. 조금 더 설명이 잘 되어있었으면 하는 부분이 두군 데 정도 있었어요.
M Student: 도와 주셔서 감사합니다, Kimball 교수님. 저를 위해서 정말 많은 것들을 해 주셨어요. 이 문제들 때문에 정말 힘들었거든요.
W: 좋아요. 문제를 해결해서 기쁘네요. 그러면, 다른 문제가 없다면…
M: 음… 사실은, 음… 한가지가 더 있는데요.
W: 그래요?
M: 제가 2주 전쯤 전공을 바꾸는 것에 대해 말씀을 드렸던 것을 기억하시나요?
W: 네, 기억나요… 아하… 이제 결정을 내린 모양이군요.
M: 네, 맞아요. 드디어 결정했어요.
W: 그리고…?
M: 교수님과 함께 이야기했던 대로 할 예정이예요.
W: 그러면, 전공을 바꾸지 않겠네요, 그렇죠?
M: 그렇습니다. 제 생각에는, 생물학과에 남아 있으면, 2년 후 졸업을 할 때쯤에는 의대에 갈 수 있는 기회를 가질 수 있을 것 같아요.
W: 현명한 결정을 내렸군요. 잘 했어요.
M: 네, 저도 그렇게 생각해요. 지난번 뵈었을 때 말씀해 주신 것들에 대해 많은 생각을 해 보았고, 그것들은 제게 상당히 인상적이었어요. 하지만, 저 스스로도 많은 조사를 해 보았고, 다른 교수님들과도 역시 얘기를 나누어 봤는데, 그리고, 음…
W: 계속 하세요.
M: 음, 이 학과에 계속 남아 있기로 결정했지만, 부전공으로… 화학을 해볼까 해서요. 제 생각에는, 화학을 부전공으로 하면, 제가 지원하려고 하는 명문 의대에서, 음, 제가 조금 더 경쟁력 있게 보이지 않을까 해서요.
W: 화학 부전공이라, 그런가요?
M: 음, 네. 어떻게 생각하세요?
W: 글쎄요, 단지 부전공이라고 하지만 학습에 상당한 부담이 생기게 될 거에요… 가령 역사나 영어를 부전공으로 하는 것보다 훨씬 더 많은 부담이 생기겠죠.
M: 왜 그런가요?
W: 음, 학생이 받아야 할 화학 수업은 모두 실험실에서 이루어질 것이고, 매주 강의실과 실험실에서 보내게 될 시간이 기본적으로 두 배로 늘어 날 거에요. 학생이 그러한 점을 견뎌 낼 수 있을까요?
M: 할 수 있을 것이라고 확신합니다. 제 말은, 전공에 필요한 화학 수업을 5개에서 7개 정도 받을 계획을 이미 세워 놓고 있어요. 그래서, 기본적으로, 새로운 과정을 2개만 더 하면, 제 성적 증명서에 화학을 부전공으로 기입할 수 있는 이점을 얻을 수 있죠. 그러면 꽤 괜찮을 것 같아요.
W: 음… 그렇게 하겠다면, 말이 되네요. 좋아요, 승인해 줄게요… 아, 부전공에 대한 조언을 얻기 위해 화학과의 누군가와 이야기를 해본 적이 있나요? Adelman 교수님을 만나고 싶어할 것 같은데.
M: 사실, 제가 질문을 좀 해보려고 생각하고 있는 분이 바로 그 분입니다.
W: 잠시만요. 지금 전화해서 학생에 대한 말을 해둘게요. 전화번호 좀 찾고요.

Script

| 08-03 |

M Professor: Good morning, everyone. We're going to continue where we left off in our last class. We've got a busy day, so let's get started right now. Okay . . . We're talking about the growth of cities and suburbs in America during the twentieth century. Prior to and during World War II . . . that was in the 1940s for the history-challenged among you . . . many people lived in the country's urban areas. One reason was that the huge numbers of immigrants coming from Europe landed in the big eastern seaboard cities such as New York, Boston, and Baltimore, and many stayed there. Others moved to big eastern and Midwestern cities such as Pittsburgh, Philadelphia, Detroit, and Chicago. That increased these cities' populations. Also, during the war, many jobs—particularly those that required the manufacture of war materials—were found in the cities.

People went to wherever the jobs were, especially since the Great Depression was finally ending, so companies were hiring. However, after World War II, people began moving away from the cities and into the suburbs. There were many reasons for this . . . Some were economic, some were related to housing and transportation, and others were related to laws enacted by the government.

So . . . suburbs . . . They're basically areas that, um, mostly contain residential housing and are located near large urban areas. Typically, most suburbs began along railway and tram lines, which gave their residents easy access to the cities, where most of them worked. Even today, this is a notable feature of many suburbs: Most of the people who live in them don't work in them. [11]They often commute, sometimes for an hour or more a day, to jobs in different locations, most typically a large nearby city. New York is a perfect example. Up to three million people travel there every day just to work. **Can you believe that?**

During the twentieth century, this ease of transportation was made possible thanks first to cheap electric trams and then later to automobiles. Cars became essential parts of suburban life after World War II. Why afterward? Well, during the war, the car companies in Detroit were too busy making tanks, jeeps, and other war machines. After the war ended, they went back to making cars. Owning a car gave a suburbanite family freedom. They could drive wherever they wanted. Also, the Eisenhower administration planned and built the interstate highway system in the 1950s. This connected the rest of the country and gave an even greater impetus to car manufacturing and ownership. Coupled with cheap gasoline prices, unlike today, unfortunately, the highway system made traveling much easier than it had ever been.

Now, the government also wanted people to move out of the cities and into the suburbs. So two bills were passed, and thereby became laws, to encourage this. In 1934, the Federal Housing Administration, also called the FHA, was created. It offered low-interest loans to people who wanted to build or buy their own homes. The FHA was created during the Great Depression to give people the ability to own their own homes and also to stimulate the housing construction market. This, in turn, stimulated many other ancillary markets, such as those for building materials, furniture manufacturing, and home appliances. Many homes financed by FHA loans were built . . . yeah, you guessed it . . . They were built outside of the big cities, which caused many suburbs to arise.

The second important law was the GI Bill. This was passed after World War II. It gave all veteran servicemen and women access to free higher education and low-interest, no-down-payment housing loans. Almost twelve million men and women had served in the military because of the war. And over fifty percent of them took advantage of the bill and enrolled in universities, bought new homes, or, well, they did both. The higher education that these veterans received qualified them for higher-paying jobs, which meant that they paid higher taxes. Those taxes then went directly to the government and helped pay for their educations. The GI Bill is still in existence today and is one of the most successful pieces of legislation from the twentieth century. I myself made use of it many years ago.

Now, the second part of the bill was very important to our study of suburbs. Thanks to the bill, veterans qualified for those low-interest no-down-payment loans. Construction companies and architects seized on that provision and began constructing huge tracts of carbon-copy homes in beautiful countryside settings near urban areas. Take a look at picture of Levittown, near New York City . . . Constructed between 1947 and 1951, the community provided housing for over 2,000 veterans and became the standard for suburban construction for many years to come. Here's another picture I want you to look at. Notice how all of the houses look alike . . . ? Okay, I've got some more photos for us to look at.

Translation

M Professor: 안녕하세요, 여러분. 계속해서 지난 시간에 중단했던 부분부터 이어가도록 합시다. 시간이 없으니까, 바로 시작하도록 합시다. 좋아요… 우리는 20세기 미국의 도시와 교외 지역의 성장에 대해서 이야기하고 있습니다. 제2차 세계 대전 동안과 그 이전에는… 역사적으로 많은 일들이 있어났던 1940년대 무렵인데… 많은 사람들이 도시 지역에서 살았습니다. 그러한 한 가지 이유는 유럽에서 온 많은 이민자들이 뉴욕, 보스턴, 그리고 볼티모어 같은 동부 해안의 대도시에 상륙한 뒤, 그곳에 머물렀기 때문입니다. 동부의 대도시와 피츠버그, 필라델피아, 디트로이트, 그리고 시카고와 같은 중서부 지역의 도시로 이주한 사람들도 있었죠. 이 때문에 이와 같은 도시의 인구가 증가했습니다. 또한, 전쟁 도중, 많은 직업들은 – 특히 전쟁 물자의 생산에 필요한 직업들 – 도시에서 찾아 볼 수 있었습니다. 사람들은, 특히 마침내 대공황이 끝났을 때부터, 직업이 있는 곳이라면 어디든지 찾아갔고, 그래서 기업은 이들을 고용하게 되었습니다. 하지만, 제2차 세계 대전이 끝난 후, 사람들은 도시를 떠나 교외 지역으로 이주하기 시작했습니다. 여기에는 많은 이유가 있었는데…그 중에는 경제적인 것도 있었고, 주거와 교통에 관련된 것도 있었으며, 정부가 제정한 법률과 연관된 이유들도 있었습니다.

그래서… 교외 지역… 그 지역은 기본적으로, 음, 주거 지역을 포함하고 있으며 대도시 지역 근처에 위치하고 있습니다. 일반적으로, 대부분 교외 지역들은 철도와 전차 궤도를 따라 시작되었는데, 철도와 전차 궤도는 거주자들 대다수가 일을 했던 도시로의 접근을 용이하게 해주었습니다. 심지어 오늘날에도, 이는 많은 교외 지역의 주목할 만한 특징이 되고 있습니다: 교외 지역에 살고 있는 대다수의 사람들은 그곳에서 일을 하고 있지 않습니다. 그들은 다른 지역의 직장으로, 때로는 하루에 한 시간이나 그 이상이 걸리는, 출퇴근을 하는 경우가 많은데, 일반적으로 인근의 대도시로 출퇴근을 하는 경우가 많습니다. 뉴욕이 완벽한 사례가 되겠군요. 매일 3천만 명이나 되는 사람들이 단지 일을 하기 위한 목적으로 이곳에 옵니다. 믿어지시나요?

20세기에, 처음에는 요금이 저렴한 전차와 그 이후에는 자동차 덕분에, 편리한 교통이 가능해졌습니다. 제2차 세계 대전 이후, 자동차는 교외 지역의 생활에 있어서 필수적인 부분이 되었습니다. 왜 그 이후였을까요? 음, 전쟁 중에는, 디트로이트의 자동차 회사가 탱크와, 지프, 그리고 다른 군수품을 만드느라 너무도 분주했습니다. 전쟁이 끝나고 나서, 그 회사들은 다시 자동차를 만들게 되었죠. 교외 지역에 거주하는 가족들은 자동차를 소유하게 되면서 자유를 갖게 되었습니다. 원하는 어디든 갈 수가 있었죠. 또한, 아이젠하워 정부는 1950년대에 주간 고속도로를 계획했고 건설하였습니다. 이 도로가 국가의 나머지 지역을 연결시켜 주었고 자동차의 생산과 소유도 엄청나게 촉진시켰습니다. 안타깝게도 오늘날과는 다른데, 낮은 휘발유 가격과 고속도로 시스템 덕분에 여행이 이전보다 훨씬 더 쉬워졌습니다.

이제, 정부 또한 사람들이 도시를 떠나 교외 지역으로 이동하기를 원했습니다. 그래서 이를 장려하기 위한 두 가지 법안이 통과되었고 그 후 법률로 제정되었습니다. 1934년, FHA라 불리는, 연방 주거 관리국이 설립되었습니다. 이 기구는 집을 짓기를 원하거나 구입하고자 하는 사람들에게 이자가 저렴한 대출금을 제공해주었습니다. FHA는 대공황 당시 사람들이 집을 소유할 능력을 가지도록 만들고 주택 건설 시장을 활성화시키기 위해 창설되었습니다. 이 기구는, 결국, 건설 자재, 가구 제작, 그리고 가정 용품과 같은 여러 부수적인 시장 또한 활성화시켰습니다. 많은 주택들이… 네, 여러분들이 추측한 대로… FHA의 자금 지원으로 건설되었죠. 그와 같은 주택들은 대도시의 외곽에 건설되었는데, 이로써 많은 교외 지역들이 개발되었습니다.

두 번째로 중요한 법은 제대군인원호법입니다. 이는 제2차 세계 대전 이후에 통과되었죠. 이 법안은 남녀 모든 퇴역 군인들이 무료로 고등 교육을 받을 수 있도록 해주었고 낮은 이자의, 계약금이 없는, 주택 융자금을 사용할 수 있도록 해주었습니다. 거의 2천만 명의 사람들이 전쟁 때문에 군복무를 했습니다. 그리고 그들 중 50% 이상의 사람들이 이 법안을 활용해서 대학에 등록하고 새로운 집을 구입했는데, 즉, 음, 그들은 이 두 가지를 모두 했던 것이죠. 퇴역 군인들은 더 높은 수준의 교육을 받게 되면서 소득이 더 높은 직업을 갖게 되었는데, 이것은 그들이 더 높은 세금을 지불했다는 것을 의미했습니다. 이 세금은 곧바로 정부에 유입되었고 교육을 위한 정부의 지출에 도움이 되었습니다. 제대군인원호법은 오늘날에도 여전히 존재하며 20세기의 가장 성공적인 법안들 중 하나입니다. 저 자신도 오래 전에 그것을 이용했죠.

자, 이 법안의 두 번째 부분은 교외 지역에 대한 우리의 연구에 매우 중요했습니다. 이 법안 덕분에, 퇴역 군인들은 이자가 낮고 증거금이 없는 주택 융자금을 사용할 자격을 얻게 되었습니다. 건설 회사와 건축가들은 이 조항을 잘 활용해서 도시 지역 근처의 아름다운 시골에 서로 꼭 닮아 있는 집들로 이루어진 넓은 지역을 건설하기 시작했습니다. 뉴욕 시 근처의, 레비타운의 사진을 보세요… 1947년과 1951년 사이에 건설된 이 지역은 2,000명 이상의 퇴역 군인들에게 주택을 제공해주었고 오랫동안 교외 지역 건설의 모범이 되었습니다. 여기 여러분들이 보았으면 하는 또 다른 사진이 있습니다. 모든 집들이 얼마나 비슷하게 생겼는지 주목해 주세요… 좋아요, 우리가 볼 사진들을 몇 장 더 가지고 왔습니다.

Actual Test 09

Reading Section   p.105

Answers

1. Ⓐ [Vocabulary Question]
2. Ⓒ [Sentence Simplification Question]
3. Ⓑ [Factual Question]
4. Ⓓ [Vocabulary Question]
5. Ⓑ [Vocabulary Question]
6. Ⓒ [Rhetorical Purpose Question]
7. Ⓒ [Inference Question]
8. Ⓓ [Factual Question]
9. Ⓒ [Reference Question]
10. Ⓑ [Factual Question]
11. Ⓐ [Vocabulary Question]
12. Ⓒ [Negative Factual Question]
13. 3rd [Insert Text Question]
14. Ⓑ, Ⓓ, Ⓔ [Prose Summary Question]

Translation

사회의 기계화

인류 역사의 대부분 동안, 진보는 매우 천천히 이루어졌다. 이것은 주로 인간이나 동물의 힘에 의해서 노동이 수행되어 왔다는 사실 때문이었다. 시간이 흐르면서, 바퀴와 같은 특정한 장비의 발명이 이러한 부담을 덜어주는 데 도움이 되었다. 그럼에도 불구하고, 바퀴, 지레, 그리고 다른 단순한 기계들이 일을 약간 덜 수고스럽게 만들어주기는 했지만, 대부분의 작업 수행이 여전히 인간과 동물에 의존해야 한다는 사실을 바꾸어놓지는 못했다. 이 후, 18세기가 시작되면서, 기계화의 시대가 시작되었고, 이 시기 동안 기계는 인간 및 동물의 힘을 대체하기 시작했다. 이러한 기계들 덕분에, 인류의 진보는 예전보다 훨씬 더 빠른 속도로 진행되었다; 하지만, 기계화는 여러 가지 사회적이고 자연에 좋지 않은 환경 문제들을 일으켰기 때문에 단점이 없지는 않았다.

기계화란 인간의 모든 활동 영역에서 기계를 사용하여 노동을 수행하는 것이다. 이러한 영역에는 - 여기에만 제한되는 것은 아니지만 - 농업, 공업, 수송, 통신, 의학, 그리고 군사 분야들이 포함될 수 있다. 최초의 대규모 기계화는 1700년대 영국에서 이루어졌다. 제임스 와트가 증기 기관을 완성하자 마자, 영국은 산업화가 되기 시작했다. 그 결과는 경이적이었다. 농업에서는 기계의 사용으로 농부들이 더 많은 곡물을 더 많은 땅에 더 적은 일꾼들로 경작하는 것이 보다 용이해졌다. 농장에서 필요한 사람들의 수가 줄어들었기 때문에, 영국 전역에는 갑자기 생겨나기 시작한 공장에서 일자리를 찾는 대규모의 노동 시장이 형성되었다. 곧, 많은 산업들이 기계화되었고, 이 때문에 사람들은 더 많은 제품에 더 적은 비용을 소비할 수 있었고, 더 빠르고 더 효율적인 생산이 이루어졌다. 이러한 현상은 산업화 중에 있었던 영국뿐만이 아니었다; 유럽 전역의 많은 국가들과 미국에서도 산업화의 이익이 거두어졌다.

19세기가 끝날 무렵, 기계화는 새로운 단계에 접어들었다. 미국의 헨리 포드 같은 제조업자들이 조립 라인 공정을 고안해서 완성시킨 것이 바로 이 시기였다. 이 덕분에 노동자들은 제조 공정상 전문화되었고, 자동차나 다양한 설비들 같은 커다란 제품들을 생산하는데 필요한 시간조차 감소하게 되었다. 20세기에 걸쳐, 기계는 어디에서나 눈에 띄기 시작했다 – 공장, 사무실, 그리고 집과 농장 등에서 보이기 시작했다.

삶의 많은 측면에서 기계가 사람들이 훨씬 편안하게 살 수 있도록 해주었음에도 불구하고, 모든 사람이 매료된 것은 아니었다. 산업화 시대가 시작된 이후, 기계가 사람의 일자리를 빼앗아갈지도 모른다는 걱정이 나타났다. 이러한 두려움은 로봇의 발명 때문에 최근 악화되고 있다. 최근에 로봇은 전 세계에서 많은 일을 수행하고 있는 상당히 전문화된 기계이다. 공장 조립 라인에서의 업무를 포함하여, 이러한 일들 중 다수는 한때 인간이 해오던 일들이다. 현재, 인간 노동자들에게 스트레스와 지루함을 일으킬 수 있는 반복적인 업무들은 대다수의 로봇들이 수행하고 있다. 정밀 수술에 도움을 주는 업무 등을 수행할 수 있는 로봇들도 있지만, 그 수는 많지 않다. (하지만, 매년 로봇들이 보다 발전함에 따라, 로봇들은 보다 많은 전문적인 업무를 수행할 수 있게 되었다.) 하지만, 많은 사람들은 로봇 기술의 발전에 따라, 점점 더 많은 노동자들이 일자리를 잃게 될 것이라고 우려하고 있다.

기계화에는 또 다른 몇 가지 단점이 있다. 많은 공장들은 노동자들이 다치거나 심지어 죽을 수도 있는 시끄럽고, 유독하며, 위험한 장소이다. 조립 라인과 기계 주변에서 일하는 것 또한 사람에게 많은 정신적인 스트레스를 줄 수 있다. 일부 노동자들은 반복적인 일의 특성상 지루함과 따분함을 느끼게 된다. 기계화는 또한 환경에 피해를 끼치기도 한다. 대부분의 기계는 작동하기 위하여 전력을 필요로 한다. 초기의 공장들은 기계를 가동시키기 위해 필요한 증기를 만들 목적으로 석탄이나 나무를 태웠다. 요즘의 공장들은 석탄, 석유, 또는 가스를 연소시켜 전기를 만들어 낸 다음 이를 사용하는 경우가 많다. 그래서 기계의 사용은 지구의 자원을 고갈시키고 화석 연료의 연소는 더 많은 오염을 일으킨다. 이 뿐만 아니라, 공장에서 제조된 많은 제품들 또한 – 예를 들어 자동차 – 환경 오염의 주범이 되고 있다. 마지막으로, 사회의 기계화는 많은 사람이 시골 지역에서 도시 중심지로 이동하도록 만든다. 도시의 많은 인구는 인구 밀집, 범죄, 스트레스, 그리고 가족의 해체 등 다양한 사회적 문제를 일으켜왔다.

기계화는 세상에 혜택과 피해를 모두 가져오기 때문에 분명 양날의 칼이다. 하지만, 세상은 계속해서 산업화될 것이 분명하므로, 희망 사항은 이로 인해 발생한 문제에 대해 해결책을 찾아내서 이를 이행하는 것이다.

Listening Section p.111

Answers

1. D [Gist-Content Question]
2. B [Gist-Purpose Question]
3. D [Making Inferences Question]
4. C [Understanding Function Question]
5. B [Understanding Attitude Question]
6. C [Gist-Purpose Question]
7. C [Detail Question]
8. D [Understanding Attitude Question]
9.

	Polynesians	Phoenicians
A	X	
B		X
C	X	
D	X	

[Connecting Content Question]

10. D [Making Inferences Question]
11. A [Understanding Function Question]

Script

| 09-02 |

M Dean of Students: Hi there. Are you Kelly Thurston?

W Student: Yes, I am. Uh, how did you know that?

M: Well, it's two thirty right now, and you scheduled an appointment with me for that time. Combined with the fact that, uh, there's no one else in my reception room right now . . . well . . .

W: Good point. Anyway, yes, I'm Kelly Thurston. It's a pleasure to meet you, Dean Winston.

M: Yes, the feeling is mutual. Why don't you come on in to my office so that we can have a chat?

W: Thank you, sir.

M: You can have a seat right there . . . Coffee?

W: No thanks. I'm all right.

M: Okay then. What did you schedule this meeting for?

W: Well, sir, I have a huge problem. You see, I'm going to be a senior next year, but I need a large number of credits in order to be able to graduate next May. I'll have to take more than twenty hours each semester, and I know that if I do that, my grades are going to suffer.

M: ⁴In that case, you could always take an extra semester to graduate. A lot of students do that. You know, they graduate in four and a half years rather than in four. Some even take five years to graduate. **Actually, I did**

35

the same many years ago.

W: Oh, yeah, I had thought of that, but, uh, to be honest, the tuition here is brutal, and there's no way that my parents and I could pay for it. I've already taken out numerous student loans, and I work fifteen hours a week as well to help pay for school. I just can't handle another semester financially.

M: All right. Then, uh . . . what are your summer plans? Have you considered staying on campus for the summer and taking a course or two? That would ease your workload for the next academic year, and I'm sure that you could find a summer job as well. [5]We hire lots of students to work here during the summertime.

W: Oh, yes, that's exactly what I intend to do.

M: Uh, then, if I may be blunt, what's the problem? It sounds like you've got everything all worked out.

W: Well, the problem is that the school isn't allowing me to register for any summer courses.

M: Huh? Why not?

W: You see, I filled out the application form to enroll in two summer classes, and then I submitted it to the Registrar's Office. But, when I went there yesterday, they told me that they had no record of me filling out and submitting the form. They must have lost it.

M: Fill out another one then.

W: They won't let me. They said that the application date has already passed, so I'm not allowed to sign up for classes.

M: Hmm . . . Are you sure that you filled out the form?

W: Of course I am. I even photocopied it before I turned it in. Take a look . . .

M: Well, it looks like you did everything properly. And the date on this form is from last week. Let me give the Registrar's Office a call. I'll make sure that you're enrolled in these two classes for summer school.

W: You'll do that? Oh my gosh. Thank you so, so much, Dean Winston.

M: It's no problem. Now, let me have a chat with them so that I can clear this problem up. Why don't you wait outside my office while I make this call?

Translation

M Dean of Students: 안녕하세요. *Kelly Thurston* 이죠?

W Student: 네. 음, 어떻게 아셨나요?

M: 음, 지금이 2시 30분이니까, 지금 이 시간에 저와 약속을 잡으셨군요. 종합해보면, 음, 지금 제 응접실에 당신 말고는 아무도 없어요…

W: 맞아요. 아무튼, 네, 제가 *Kelly Thurston* 이예요. 만나서 반갑습니다, *Winston* 학과장님.

M: 네, 저도 그래요. 제 사무실로 들어와서 얘기를 좀 나눌까요?

W: 감사합니다, 학과장님.

M: 거기 앉아요… 커피 드실래요?

W: 아니오. 괜찮습니다.

M: 좋아요. 그럼. 왜 저와 약속을 잡았나요?

W: 음, 학과장님, 저한테 큰 문제가 생겼어요. 아시다시피, 제가 내년에 마지막 학년이 되는데요. 5월에 졸업하기 위해서는 많은 학점이 필요해요. 매 학기마다 20시간 이상을 들어야만 해서, 제가 그것을 할 수 있을지 모르겠지만, 제 학점에 문제가 생길 것 같아요.

M: 그렇다면, 졸업하기 위해서는 한 학기를 더 다닐 수도 있어요. 많은 학생들이 그렇게 하는 걸요. 그러니까, 4년이 아니고 4년 반 만에 졸업을 하는 것이죠. 어떤 학생들은 5년 만에 졸업을 하기도 해요. 사실, 저도 오래전에 그랬었고요.

W: 아, 네, 그것도 생각해 보았는데, 하지만, 음, 솔직히 말씀 드리면, 학비가 너무 비싸고, 부모님이나 저나 지불할 능력이 없어요. 이미 학자금 대출도 많이 받았고, 학비에 보태려고 일주일에 15시간씩 일을 하고 있어요. 한 학기 더 다니는데 필요한 비용 문제를 해결할 수가 없어요.

M: 좋아요. 그러면, 음… 여름에 계획이 있나요? 여름에 학교에 머무르면서 한 두 과목을 듣는 것은 어떨까요? 그렇게 하면 내년 과정이 좀 더 수월해 질 거예요. 그리고 또한 여름에는 일자리도 찾을 수 있겠죠. 여름에 여기서 일하는 학생들을 많이 고용하거든요.

W: 아, 네, 제가 하고자 했던 것이 바로 그거예요.

M: 음, 그러면, 직접적으로 말하자면, 문제가 뭐죠? 이미 모든 것을 다 해결 한 것으로 들리는데.

W: 음, 문제는 학교에서 제가 여름 수업을 듣는 것을 허락해 주지 않는다는 점이에요.

M: 네? 왜요?

W: 아시다시피, 여름 수업 두 과목에 등록하기 위해서 신청서 양식을 작성하고, 그것을 대학 사무실에 제출했어요. 그런데, 어제 갔더니, 제가 양식을 작성해서 제출했다는 기록이 없다는 거예요. 그들이 잃어 버린 것이 분명해요.

M: 그럼 하나 더 작성하면 되잖아요.

W: 그렇게 해주지 않더군요. 이미 신청 기간이 지났고, 그래서 제가 수업을 신청 하도록 해주지 않았어요.

M: 음… 양식을 작성한 것이 분명해요?

W: 물론 했어요. 제출하기 전에 사진까지 찍어두었는걸요. 여기 보세요…

M: 음, 모든 것을 적절하게 잘 해두었군요. 양식에 있는 날짜도 지난주 날짜가 맞네요. 대학 사무실에 전화를 좀 할게요. 학생이 여름 학기 수업의 두 과목에 등록할 수 있도록 해 줄게요.

W: 그렇게 해주실 건가요? 오 이럴 수가. 정말, 너무, 감사해요 *Winston* 학과장님.

M: 천만에요. 자, 그럼 이 문제를 해결하기 위해서 통화를 좀 해야겠어요. 제가 부를 때까지 밖에서 잠시 기다려 주실래요?

Script

| 09-03 |

M Professor: Much of the impetus for early astronomical observations was to attain accurate calculations of dates and for navigational purposes. We've already covered how the sun and moon are used to calculate the passage of time, so now I'd like to turn to the navigational aspects of astronomy. It's usually called celestial navigation in order to distinguish it from other types of navigation, such as, uh . . . radio direction finding and the more recent GPS, you know, global positioning systems. Celestial navigation is based on the positions of the sun, stars, and moon and their relation to the observer's position on Earth. Most of what I'd like to talk about is sea navigation. Er, by that I mean navigation as it's used on the oceans.

Now, the key to celestial navigation is the fixed positions of the stars in the night sky. While the stars appear to rise and set just like the sun does, they always occupy the same positions.

W Student: But, Professor Sagan, why can we see different stars in summer and winter?

M: Ah, that's a good question. Well, as we all know, Earth is tilted on its axis, so, here in the Northern Hemisphere, we see some stars all of the time, but other stars are hidden below the horizon, so we don't see them until the planet passes through various seasons. If the Earth were perfectly aligned on its axis, we would see the same stars in the Northern and Southern hemispheres all the time. I hope that answers your question.

Okay, so, uh, back to navigation then . . . The sun is also a fixed point, but its height over the horizon varies from place to place on Earth. This is a key aspect of navigation. The moon and planets are also useful markers. They move, but their positions in relation to the stars have been charted for centuries. Sailors often relied on almanacs and other charts to know where a planet, like, uh, Mars, would be on a certain day of the year.

Historically speaking, celestial navigation is one of the oldest forms of navigation. [11]Prior to its development, few ships made voyages away from the coastline. Doing so would have been extremely dangerous since, in the vastness of the ocean, there are no markers telling you where to go. Well, at least there weren't a thousand . . . or even a hundred . . . years ago. Don't misunderstand me though. I don't mean that no one went on long sea voyages. The Polynesians did. They were perhaps the greatest of the ancient navigators. Without compasses, charts, or any other devices, they went on voyages covering thousands of miles from island to island all around the Pacific Ocean.

W: Really? How did they pull that off?

M: Well, they used a method known as wayfinding. It basically depended upon knowledge of the stars that was passed down from generation to generation. Wayfinding relied on planning a course according to the stars as they changed positions in the sky as the Polynesians traveled. Now, it didn't just depend on observing the position of a star over an island that the Polynesians were departing. Wayfinding also took the positions of waves, the actions of seabirds, and even the odors carried by the wind into account. It was incredible, really, how they managed to do it.

Another group of people, the ancient Phoenicians, whose home was the modern-day state of Lebanon, were considered the greatest navigators of their age in the Mediterranean Sea. They sailed all around the Mediterranean, and there is even some evidence that they sailed into the Atlantic Ocean and maybe as far as to England. They typically remained in sight of land but at times relied on the, uh, the sun and stars to navigate their courses.

Well, over time, navigational methods started to become modernized, so ships could safely sail out of sight of land. These new methods introduced the terms latitude and longitude to us. They're used in concert to describe a person's or a ship's position anywhere on the planet. Latitude refers to the north-south position while longitude refers to the east-west position. Latitude can be measured by the height of the sun or by using a star that is above the horizon. Through endless observations of the sun and the stars above the horizon, it was realized that their heights varied as one went further north or south. Thus navigators learned to determine the latitude—the north-south position—of their ships. Over the centuries, various devices were used to figure out latitude. Some, such as the astrolabe and the T-staff, required an observer to spend a long amount of time staring at the sun each time they were used. Unsurprisingly, some navigators lost their sight because of this. Then, in 1731, the sextant was developed. It allowed navigators to determine their latitude much more easily and without fear of going blind. As for longitude, well, it was much harder to determine. Only in the eighteenth century, when accurate timekeeping devices were created, did navigators learn how to measure it. Here . . . Let me show you how they did it. It's actually pretty interesting.

Translation

M Professor: 초기의 천문학적인 관측에 많은 자극제가 되었던 것은 항해의 목적을 위해 날짜를 정확하게 계산해 내는 것이었습니다. 우리는 이미 태양과 달이 시간의 흐름을 계산하는데 어떻게 활용되는지를 다루어 보았고, 그래서 이제는 천문학의 항해적 측면에 대해 주제를 돌려보고자 합니다. 이것은, 예를 들면, 음... 무선 방향 탐지와 보다 최신의 GPS, 그러니까, 전 지구 위치 파악 시스템과 같은 다른 종류의 항해와 구별하기 위해 천문 항법이라고 불립니다. 천문 항법은 태양, 별, 그리고 달의 위치와 지구상에서 관측자의 위치간의 연관성에 기초를 두고 있습니다. 제가 말하고자 하는 것의 대부분은 바다에서의 항해입니다. 음, 제가 의미하는 것은 해양에서 사용되는 항해술이죠.

자, 천문 항법의 중요한 요소는 밤 하늘에 고정된 별의 위치입니다. 별은 태양과 마찬가지로 뜨고 지는 것처럼 보이지만, 항상 같은 자리에 위치하고 있어요.

W Student: 하지만, *Sagan* 교수님, 우리가 여름과 겨울에 서로 다른 별들을 볼 수 있는 이유는 무엇인가요?

M: 아, 좋은 질문입니다. 음, 우리가 알고 있듯이, 지구는 축에서 약간 기울어져있기 때문에, 여기 북반구에서, 우리는 항상 몇몇

별들을 볼 수 있지만, 다른 별들은 지평선 아래에 숨어 있어서, 우리는 여러 계절에 걸쳐 행성들이 지나갈 때까지 그것들을 볼 수 없습니다. 만약 지구가 축과 완벽하게 일직선을 이루고 있다면, 우리는 북반구와 남반구에서 항상 똑같은 별을 볼 수 있을 것입니다. 질문에 답변이 되었으면 좋겠네요.

좋아요, 자, 음, 그러면 항해로 되돌아가 봅시다… 태양도 역시 고정된 지점에 위치하고 있지만, 지평선에서의 고도는 지구상의 장소에 따라 달라집니다. 이 점이 항해에 있어서 중요한 측면이죠. 달과 행성도 또한 유용한 표지입니다. 이들은 움직이고 있지만, 별들과 연관된 위치는 수세기 동안 일정했습니다. 선원들은 행성의 위치를 알기 위해 종종 책력과 다른 해도들에 의존했는데, 이를테면, 음, 화성이 일 년 중 어떤 날에 어디에 위치하는가 하는 것이었습니다.

역사적으로, 천문 항법은 항해의 가장 오래된 형태 중의 하나입니다. 이것이 생겨나기 전에는, 해안선으로부터 멀리까지 항해를 할 수 있는 배가 거의 없었죠. 이렇게 한다는 것은 엄청난 위험이 뒤따르는 것이었는데, 광활한 바다에서, 그들이 어디로 가고 있는지를 알려줄 표지들이 아무것도 없기 때문입니다. 음, 적어도 천년… 혹은 심지어 100년… 그 이전까지는 없었습니다. 하지만 오해하지는 마세요. 먼 바다로의 항해를 아무도 하지 않았다고 하는 것은 아닙니다. 폴리네시아 인들이 그 일을 했죠. 그들은 아마도 고대 최고의 항해사들이었을 것입니다. 나침반, 해도, 혹은 다른 어떠한 장비도 없이, 그들은 태평양 전 지역의 섬들을 수 천 마일에 걸쳐 항해를 했던 것이죠.

W: 정말인가요? 그들이 어떻게 해냈나요?

M: 음, 그들은 길찾기라고 알려진 방법을 사용했습니다. 이 방법은 기본적으로 여러 세대에 걸쳐 내려온 별들에 대한 지식에 의존하고 있었죠. 길찾기는 폴리네시아 인들이 여행을 할 때 하늘의 별들의 위치 변화에 따라 별을 따라서 경로를 계획하는 방법에 의존하고 있었습니다. 즉, 폴리네시아 인들은 자신들이 출발한 섬에서 별의 위치를 관찰한 것에만 의존했던 것이 아니었죠. 또한 길찾기는 파도의 위치, 바닷새들의 움직임, 그리고 심지어 바람을 타고 오는 향기까지도 고려했습니다. 그들이 이런 일을 해냈다는 것은, 정말이지, 믿을 수 없는 일이었죠.

다른 사람들은, 지금의 레바논 지역에 살고 있었던 고대 페니키아 인들이었는데, 그들은 당시 지중해 지역에서 최고의 항해사들로 간주되었죠. 이들은 지중해의 전 지역을 항해 했으며, 대서양과 아마도 영국에 이르기까지 항해를 했다는 증거도 있습니다. 그들은 보통 육지가 보이는 곳에 머물렀지만 때로는, 음, 경로를 따라 항해하기 위해 해와 별에 의존하기도 했습니다.

음, 시간이 흐르면서 항해 기법은 현대화되기 시작했고, 배들은 육지가 보이지 않는 곳까지 안전하게 항해를 할 수 있게 되었습니다. 이 새로운 방법들로 인해 우리는 위도와 경도라는 용어를 처음으로 접하게 되죠. 사람이나 배의 위치가 지구상 어디에 있는지 그 위치를 설명하기 위해 이 두 가지가 함께 사용되고 있습니다. 위도는 북-남의 위치를 나타내는 반면에 경도는 동-서의 위치를 나타냅니다. 위도는 태양의 고도나 수평선 위의 별을 이용하여 측정할 수 있습니다. 수평선 위의 태양과 별을 지속적으로 관찰함으로써, 더 북쪽으로 혹은 더 남쪽으로 이동함에 따라 이들의 고도가 변한다는 점이 알려지게 되었습니다. 그래서 항해사들은 배의 북쪽-남쪽의 위치인 위도를 측정하는 방법을 알아냈죠. 수 세기 동안, 위도를 알아내기 위해 다양한 장비가 사용되었습니다. 천측구와 T-형 막대와 같은 몇몇 장비들은, 관측자가 그것들을 사용할 때마다 상당히 오랜 시간 동안 태양을 쳐다보고 있어야 했습니다. 짐작하겠지만, 몇몇 항해사들은 이 때문에 시력을 잃기도 했죠. 그리고 나서, 1731년, 육분의가 개발되었습니다. 이것으로 인해 항해사들은 눈이 멀게 된다는 두려움 없이 훨씬 더 쉽게 위도를 측정할 수 있게 되었습니다. 경도의 경우에는, 음, 측정하기가 훨씬 더 어려웠습니다. 정확한 시간 측정 장치가 발명되었던 18세기가 되어서야, 항해사들은 경도의 측정 방법을 알게 되었습니다. 여기… 그들이 했던 방법을 보여드리겠습니다. 이것은 정말로 상당히 흥미롭습니다.

Actual Test 10

Reading Section   p.117

Answers

1. Ⓐ [Vocabulary Question]
2. Ⓓ [Rhetorical Purpose Question]
3. Ⓒ [Vocabulary Question]
4. Ⓓ [Negative Factual Question]
5. Ⓑ [Factual Question]
6. Ⓐ [Inference Question]
7. Ⓒ [Factual Question]
8. Ⓐ [Rhetorical Purpose Question]
9. Ⓐ [Reference Question]
10. Ⓓ [Factual Question]
11. Ⓐ [Reference Question]
12. Ⓑ [Vocabulary Question]
13. 3rd [Insert Text Question]
14. Ⓑ, Ⓒ, Ⓕ [Prose Summary Question]

Translation

파도

파도는 해양이나 호수와 같은 수역에서 흔히 볼 수 있는 것으로, 파도의 높이는 불과 몇 센티미터에서 대양의 거대한 파도의 경우 30미터에 이르기까지 다양하다. 파도는 바다에서 부는 바람의 활동에 의해 형성되는데, 얼마나 높은 파도가 형성되는지는 몇 가지 요인에 의해 결정된다. 가장 큰 파도는 일반적으로 허리케인이나 태풍, 그리고 사이클론 같이 강력한 열대성 폭풍에 의해 일어나며, 이 모든 것들은 상당한 기간 동안 바다에서 강한 바람을 몰고 다닌다. 이 폭풍들은 육지 쪽을 휩쓸고 해안 지역을 범람하게 만드는 강력한 파도를 만들어 낸다. 다른 경우에는, 해저 지진에 의해 몇몇 큰 파도들이 만들어지기도 하는데, 이것들은 너무나 많은 양의 물을 움직여서 세상에서 가장 빠르고, 가장 크며, 가장 파괴적인 파도, 즉 쓰나미를 일으키기도 한다.

해당 수역의 표면에서 바람이 불면, 바람의 에너지가 물에 전달되면서 많고 작은 상호 작용들이 일어난다. 표면에서 일어나는 작은 물결은 파도가 생성되기 시작한다는 신호이다. 파도의 높이는 해역, 풍속, 바람이 부는 시간, 그리고 물의 깊이에 달려있다. 해역이란 바람이 물 위에서 일정한 방향으로 부는 거리를 말한다. 물 위로 부는 광대한 범위의 빠른 바람은 엄청나게 높은 파도를 만들어낼 수 있다. 거대한 바닷물이 펼쳐져 있는 대양은 육지로 둘러 쌓여있는 호수에서 보다 더 높은 파도를 만들어내는데, 이는 해역이 보다 길기 때문이다. 게다가, 바람이 더 오래 불수록, 더 많은 에너지가 물에 전달되며, 이것이 더 높은 파도를 만들게 된다. 바람이 짧은 시간 동안만 불면, 파도는 더 작아진다. 당연하게도, 허리케인과 같은, 몇 시간에서 며칠에 걸쳐 지속될 수 있는 바람은 막대한 크기의 파도를 만들어낼 수 있다. 거대한 폭풍이 부는 동안 북대서양의 날씨를 기록하는 부표들은 30미터 높이의 파도를 측정한 바 있다.

물의 깊이 또한 파도의 크기를 결정하는 요인 중의 하나이다. 깊은 물에서 더 큰 파도가 형성된다; 하지만, 파도가 더 얕은 물에 도달 하면, 부서져버린다. 이러한 이유는 파도의 내부 구조에 있다. 파도의 물 입자는 순환하며 움직이므로, 그것들은 처음 형성된 파도의 일부분으로 계속해서 물속에서 회전한다. 바람이 멎어도, 해양이 솟아오르면서 파도는 계속되는데, 이는 바람이 불지 않는 지역에서도 볼 수 있는 파도이다. 이 파도는 에너지가 다 없어지고 물이 잔잔해질 때까지 계속된다. 파도가 해안 근처의 수심이 낮은 곳으로 이동하게 되면, 해저와의 마찰에 의해서 불안정해져서, 파도의 입자와 파도의 에너지가 분산됨에 따라 파도는 사라지게 된다. 전 세계에서 파도가 최고조에 달했다가, 물결을 형성하고 해안선에 부딪히게 되는 이유가 여기에 있다.

파도의 크기를 결정하는 모든 요인들 중에서 가장 중요한 것은 풍속이다. 평균적으로, 풍속이 시속 1노트 증가함에 따라 파도의 높이는 두 배가 된다. 시속 30노트로 부는 바람은 평균적으로 3미터 높이의 파도를 일으키고 시속 40노트로 부는 바람은 약 6미터 높은 파도를 일으킨다. 게다가, 허리케인의 강풍의 힘은 거대한 파도를 일으킨다. (이러한 거대한 파도 중 일부는 너무나 강력해서 호화 유람선이나 심지어 군함과 같이 커다란 선박들도 피해를 입고 있다.) 파도는 파도를 일으키는 바람의 속도만큼 빠르게 이동할 때 가장 높은 높이에 이른다. 그래서 가장 강한 바람이 부는 지역에서 가장 큰 파도를 볼 수 있는 것은 놀라운 일이 아니다. 북대서양과 남인도양에서 부는 강한 바람은 평균 6미터 이상의 높은 파도를 일으킬 수 있다. 반면, 적도 근처의 잔잔한 바람은 가장 작은 파도를 일으킨다.

바람에 의해 생성된 파도의 한 가지 예외는 쓰나미이다. 쓰나미는 해저 밑에서 지진이 발생한 후에 생성되는데, 이 지진은 물의 위치를 바꿔 놓으며 쓰나미를 일으킨다. 대양에서, 쓰나미는 아주 작게 보이거나 눈에 띄지도 않지만, 이것들은 강력하며 빠르게 이동한다. 이것들은 몇 시간 내에 수천 킬로미터를 이동할 수 있으며, 해안 근처에 다다르면, 실제로 그 높이가 상승하게 된다. 육지에 상륙하면, 쓰나미는 수 미터의 높이가 될 수 있다. 2004년 12월 26일, 거대한 지진에 따른 연속적인 쓰나미가 동남아시아 전역의 해안을 강타했고 최소한 40만 명의 사람들이 목숨을 잃었다.

Listening Section　　　　　　p.123

Answers

1. B [Gist-Purpose Question]
2. C [Detail Question]
3. A [Understanding Organization Question]
4. A [Making Inferences Question]
5. B [Understanding Function Question]
6. C [Gist-Purpose Question]
7. A [Gist-Content Question]
8. A [Detail Question]
9. A [Understanding Organization Question]
10.

	Continuous Permafrost	Isolated Permafrost
A		X
B		X
C	X	
D	X	

[Connecting Content Question]

11. D [Understanding Attitude Question]

Script

| 10-02 |

W Student: Professor Powers, do you think that I could have a quick word or two with you?

M Professor: Oh, hi. Yeah, sure, but I've got to go to class in about ten minutes. It's not going to take longer than that, is it?

W: No, sir. I should only take up a few minutes of your time. Anyway, my name is Julie Johnston.

M: I know who you are, Julie. You're in my advanced film methods class . . . Don't look so surprised. I make an effort to learn all of my students' names. It's the least that I can do. Anyway, what about the class did you want to discuss? Our upcoming midterm exam?

W: Well, yes and no.

M: What do you mean?

W: Okay. I'm giving some thought to dropping this class.

M: What would possess you to do that? I remember that you made a great effort last semester to be able to enroll in this class, but now you're going to drop it? That's odd.

W: Yes, I really wanted to take this class last semester, and

I convinced the head of the Film Department to let me in, but now I think that it might have been a, uh, well . . . it might have been a mistake on my part.

M: How so? Your homework assignments have been good.

W: Well, yes, but, to be totally honest, this class is way beyond my understanding.

M: But you must have been aware of that before you signed up for it. After all, there are normally two classes that you're required to take prior to this one, but you managed to convince Professor Sanderson that you didn't need to take them. That's why he gave you permission to sign up for my class.

W: I wish that he hadn't.

M: Explain.

W: Well, I'm feeling totally overwhelmed by this class. [5]There is a lot of terminology that I simply don't understand. I assume that I would have learned these expressions had I taken the other courses.

M: You assume correctly. Go on.

W: So, even though my homework grades have been all right, I'm really concerned about the midterm exam. I just don't think that I'm going to do well on it. That's why I'm thinking of dropping the class.

M: All right. Let me suggest two possible alternatives. First, wait until after the midterm and you get your grade back. I'll grade your paper before all of the others and will then show you your grade. That way, if you do poorly on it, you'll still have enough time to drop the class before the date passes.

W: And the second option?

M: I can give you some extra assignments and . . .

W: More work?

M: Hold on. Calm down, and hear me out first. What these assignments would do is introduce you to some of the terms you need to know. Actually, they're mostly videos that you could watch, not books to read.

W: Hmm . . . That might work. Uh, how about if I do both?

M: Both?

W: Sure. Let me borrow those videos, and I'll take the midterm. If I feel like I'm improving and if I do well on the test, then I'll stay with the class.

Translation

W Student: Powers 교수님, 저랑 잠깐 말씀 좀 나눌 수 있으세요?

M Professor: 아, 안녕하세요. 네, 물론이죠. 하지만 10분 후에는 수업에 들어가야 해요. 그 이상으로 오래 이야기를 나눌 것은 아니겠죠, 그렇죠?

W: 네, 교수님. 몇 분만 시간을 내주세요. 어쨌든, 저는 Julie Johnston입니다.

M: 고급 촬영 기법 수업을 듣고 있죠… 놀라지 마세요. 내 학생들 이름을 다 알기 위해서 노력하고 있으니까요. 그 정도는 해야죠. 어쨌든, 수업에 대해 이야기하고자 하는 것은 무엇인가요? 곧 보게 될 중간고사인가요?

W: 음, 그렇기도 하고 아니기도 해요.

M: 무슨 얘기죠?

W: 좋아요. 이 수업을 취소시킬까 하는 생각이 들어서요.

M: 왜 그런 생각을 하게 되었죠? 제 기억에는 이 수업을 등록하기 위해 지난 학기에 애를 많이 쓴 것 같던데, 이제는 그만 들으려 한다고요? 이상하네요.

W: 네, 지난 학기에는 정말 이 수업을 듣고 싶었고, 영화학 학과장님을 설득해서 수업을 듣게 되었지만, 이제는 제 생각에 이것이, 어, 음, 그러니까… 제 경우에는 이것이 실수였던 것 같아요.

M: 왜요? 과제도 상당히 잘 해왔던데요.

W: 음, 네, 하지만, 솔직히 말하면, 제가 이 수업을 이해할 수가 없어요.

M: 하지만 수업 등록 전에 분명히 그럴 줄 알고 있었잖아요. 결국, 이 과목을 듣기 전에 보통은 두 과목을 미리 들어야 하지만, 학생이 Sanderson교수님을 설득해서 그 과목들을 들을 필요가 없다고 했잖아요. 그래서 학과장님이 제 수업에 등록할 수 있도록 허락해 준 것이었죠.

W: 허가해주지 않으셨으면 좋았을텐데요.

M: 설명해봐요.

W: 음, 제 생각에는 제가 이 수업에 완전히 압도당하고 있는 것 같아요. 제가 이해할 수 없는 수많은 전문 용어들이 있어요. 다른 과목을 들으면서 이 표현들을 익혀야 했어요.

M: 옳은 생각이에요. 계속 이야기해봐요.

W: 그래서, 제 과제 성적이 좋았다 할지라도, 중간고사가 정말 걱정이 되어요. 제 생각에는 제가 잘 할 수 없을 것 같아요. 이것이 제가 수업을 취소시키고자 하는 이유에요.

M: 좋아요. 제가 두 가지 가능한 대안을 제시할게요. 첫째, 중간고사를 보고 나서 성적이 나올 때까지 기다려봐요. 다른 학생들보다 먼저 성적을 매겨서 학생에게 보여줄게요. 그러니까, 성적이 좋게 나오지 않더라도, 기한이 지나기 전에 수업을 취소할 수 있는 시간은 충분하죠.

W: 그럼 두 번째 대안은요?

M: 몇 가지 다른 과제를 줄 것이고 그리고…

W: 과제를 더요?

M: 잠시만요. 진정해요, 그리고 먼저 내 말을 들어봐요. 이 과제들은 학생이 꼭 알아야 하는 용어들을 소개하는 것들이에요. 사실, 이것들은 거의 다 학생이 볼 수 있는 비디오들이며, 읽어야 할 책들은 아니에요.

W: 음… 효과가 있겠군요. 음, 제가 둘 다 하는 것은 어떨까요?

M: 둘 다요?

W: 네. 이 비디오들을 빌려주시고, 중간고사도 볼게요. 제가 실력이 향상된다는 느낌이 들고 시험도 잘 본다면, 계속 수업을 들을게요.

Script

| 10-03 |

M Professor: Okay, let's move on to another area of the world, the far north. In some places up there, there is a condition known as permafrost that affects large areas of northern Canada, Greenland, Alaska, Russia, and, to a lesser extent, Mongolia, China, and Scandinavia. The word permafrost comes from two others: permanent and frost. As you can most likely guess . . . as I hope you can guess, permafrost describes a state in which the ground is frozen to a great depth almost continuously throughout the year. Now, in the Northern Hemisphere, about, oh, twenty percent of the ground can be called permafrost. Yeah, that's a staggering amount of land when you think about it. [11]Oh, of course, in the Southern Hemisphere, the continent of Antarctica is permafrost under very thick ice sheets. Greenland up north is the same for the most part.

W Student: What causes permafrost to form, Professor Moody? Is it just the cold?

M: In a nutshell . . . yes. Permafrost exists because of almost continuous extremely cold weather conditions. Scientists consider any ground that remains at or below zero degrees Celsius for two years or longer to be permafrost. Many of the world's areas of permafrost have been in this state since, uh, since the last ice age began thousands of years ago.

We can divide the soil in permafrost areas into two zones. They are the active layer and the permanently frozen area. The active layer is the topsoil . . . Excuse me. The active layer is the topsoil that freezes and thaws with the seasons and is an area where some plants may grow. Depending on the type of permafrost, the active layer may be only a few feet thick and thus only permit small plants to grow for a short period of time, or it could be dozens of feet thick and therefore able to support trees and other large plant life. In fact, the area where trees stop growing in Alaska and Canada is called, appropriately enough, the treeline. It's not a real line, of course, but it does divide the land into areas that can sustain tree growth and areas that cannot because of their frozen conditions.

There are four main types of permafrost. These categories depend on the state of the frozen ground and the depth of freezing. The four types are continuous permafrost, discontinuous permafrost, sporadic permafrost, and isolated permafrost. The deepest areas of permafrost are considered continuous permafrost. They cover large areas of land, including parts of Siberia in Russia and northern Canada and Alaska. Continuous permafrost zones can have frozen ground that is thousands . . . yes, thousands . . . of feet thick. The active layer is just a few feet thick and can only support basic plant life such as shrubs and mosses. Places with continuous permafrost are among the world's coldest areas.

Now, in areas where the temperatures actually climb above freezing for relatively longer periods of time, you can find the other types of permafrost. Discontinuous permafrost may only be a few hundred feet thick and may have a thicker active layer that can support small trees. Sporadic and isolated permafrost zones have smaller permanently frozen areas and may have only tiny areas of frozen ground. Their active zones are very thick and can support large trees. In Mongolia, China, and Scandinavia, most of the areas that have permafrost are of the sporadic and isolated type.

Permafrost presents some unique problems for people who live in its zones, especially in the continuous zones. Let me see . . . Their construction methods have to take into consideration the fact that the active layers freeze and thaw as the seasons change, so builders often put the foundations of buildings deep in the permafrost. This takes time and requires extensive and expensive drilling. However, if a building is not anchored in the permafrost, when the active layer thaws and freezes again, it could upset the building and cause it to collapse.

So, uh, why would anyone want to live up there? Well, that's a good question. Here's one answer: The northern areas of Canada, Russia, and Alaska have immense mineral wealth in gold, diamonds, uranium, oil, and other precious natural resources. Getting these products out of the ground and shipped to markets takes a tremendous effort in the continuous permafrost zones. For instance, in some parts of northern Canada, construction workers can really only make buildings outdoors for about three months. So they have to race to get the foundations of buildings in place before the ground freezes again. Of course, living in a permafrost area is not easy. But the Eskimos, Inuits, Lapps, and many others do it. And they don't even use sophisticated construction methods like the ones I just described. But that's not the focus of today's class, so don't worry about it. I do, however, want to talk to you now about what happens to the ground when permafrost begins to melt.

Translation

M Professor: 좋습니다. 이제 세계의 다른 지역, 극북극지역으로 이동해봅시다. 이곳의 몇몇 지역에는, 북부 캐나다, 그린란드, 알래스카, 러시아의 넓은 지역, 그리고 몽골, 중국, 스칸디나비아의 좁은 지역에 영향을 미치는 영구동토층이라고 알려진 환경이 있습니다. 영구 동토층이라는 단어는 두 단어에서 유래한 것입니다: 'permanent'와 'frost'입니다. 여러분들이 분명 추측해 볼 수 있을 텐데… 여러분들이 추측할 수 있기를 바라며, 영구 동토층은 거의 일년 내내 엄청난 깊이로 얼어 있는 땅의 존재를 설명해 줍니다. 자, 북반구에서는, 아, 대략 20%의 땅을 영구 동토층이라고 부를 수 있겠네요. 네, 생각해보면 이것은 정말 어마어마한 크기의 땅입니다. 아, 물론, 남반구에서는, 매우 두꺼운 대륙 빙하 아래에 있는 남극 대륙이 영구 동토층입니다. 그린란드의 북쪽은 거의 대부분이 이와 같습니다.

W Student: Moody 교수님, 영구 동토층이 형성된 원인은 무엇인가요? 단지 추위 때문인가요?

M: 간단히 말하면… 그렇습니다. 영구 동토층은 거의 항상 극도로 추운 날씨 때문에 존재합니다. 과학자들은 2년 동안, 혹은 그 이상의 기간 동안 섭씨 0도나 그보다 낮은 온도가 유지되는 땅을 영구 동토층으로 간주합니다. 전세계의 대부분의 영구 동토층은, 음, 마지막 빙하기가 시작된 지 수천 년 전부터 지금의 상태였습니다.

우리는 영구 동토층 내에 있는 토양을 두 지역으로 분류할 수 있습니다. 활동층과 영구적으로 얼어있는 지역입니다. 활동층은 표토인데… 죄송합니다. 활동층은 계절에 따라 얼었다 녹는 표토이며 약간의 식물이 자라기도 하는 지역입니다. 영구 동토층의 유형에 따라, 활동층은 두께가 겨우 몇 피트 정도밖에 되지 않기 때문에 작은 식물이 짧은 기간 동안 자랄 수도 있고, 혹은 그 두께가 수십 피트에 이르러서 나무나 커다란 다른 식물이 자라기도 합니다. 사실, 알래스카와 캐나다의 나무가 자라지 않는 지역을, 상당히 적절한 표현인데, 수목 한계선이라고 부릅니다. 물론, 이것이 진짜 선은 아니지만, 나무의 성장이 가능한 지역과 얼어붙은 날씨 때문에 그럴 수 없는 지역을 구분해주죠.

영구 동토층에는 4가지 주요한 유형이 있습니다. 이 범주들은 동토의 상태와 얼어있는 깊이에 의해 나뉘어집니다. 4가지 유형은 연속적 동토층, 불연속적 동토층, 산발적 동토층, 그리고 고립된 동토층입니다. 영구 동토층의 가장 깊은 지역은 연속적 동토층으로 간주됩니다. 이는 러시아의 시베리아 지역과 북부 캐나다와 알래스카를 포함한 넓은 지역을 포함합니다. 연속적 동토층 지대에는 수천… 그렇습니다, 수천… 피트 두께의 얼어있는 땅이 있습니다. 활동층은 겨우 몇 피트 정도 밖에 되지 않고 관목이나 이끼 같은 기본적인 식물들만이 그곳에서 살 수 있습니다. 연속적 동토층이 있는 장소는 세상에서 가장 추운 지역 중 하나이죠.

이제, 비교적 더 긴 기간 동안 온도가 영상으로 올라가는 지역에서, 여러분들은 영구 동토층의 또다른 유형들을 찾아볼 수 있습니다. 불연속적 동토층은 겨우 몇 피트 정도의 두께이며 작은 나무들이 자랄 수 있는 더 두꺼운 활동층을 가지고 있습니다. 산발적 동토층과 고립된 동토층은 보다 작은 영구 동토 지역을 가지고 있으며 매우 좁은 지역의 동토 지대를 가지고 있습니다. 이곳의 활동층은 더 두꺼우며 여기에서는 큰 나무들이 자랄 수 있습니다. 몽골, 중국, 스칸디나비아에서, 영구 동토층이 있는 대부분의 지역은 산발적 동토층과 고립된 동토층 입니다.

영구 동토층은 이 지역에 살고 있는 사람들에게 몇 가지 독특한 문제를 안겨주는데, 특히 연속적 동토층 지역에서 그렇습니다. 봅시다… 그들의 건축 방식은 계절에 따라 활동층이 얼었다 녹는 사실을 고려해야만 하므로, 건설 업자들은 종종 영구 동토층의 깊숙한 곳에 건물의 토대를 세워야 합니다. 이것을 위해서는 많은 시간과 광범위하고 비용이 많이 드는 시추 작업이 필요하죠. 하지만, 건물이 영구 동토층에 제대로 고정되어있지 않으면, 활동층이 녹았다가 다시 얼었을 때, 건물이 흔들려서 붕괴될 수 있습니다.

그렇다면, 음, 왜 누군가는 그 지역에서 살고자 하는 것일까요? 음, 좋은 질문입니다. 한가지 답변은 다음과 같습니다: 캐나다의 북부 지역과, 러시아, 알래스카는 금, 다이아몬드, 우라늄, 석유, 그리고 다른 귀중한 천연자원들에 있어서 엄청난 광물의 가치를 지니고 있습니다. 이러한 생산물들을 획득하여 시장으로 운송하는 것은 연속적 동토층에서 어마어마한 노력이 필요합니다. 예를 들면, 북부 캐나다의 몇몇 지역에서, 건설 노동자들은 겨우 3개월 동안만 야외에서 건물을 지을 수 있을 뿐이죠. 그래서 그들은 땅이 다시 얼어붙기 전에 그곳에서의 건물의 기초를 세우기 위해 서둘러야만 합니다. 물론, 영구 동토층에서 산다는 것이 쉽지는 않습니다. 하지만 에스키모 인들, 이누이트 인들, 라프랜드 인들, 그리고 다른 이들이 그곳에서 살아가고 있습니다. 그리고 그들은 제가 설명한 것과 같이 정교한 건축 방법을 사용하지도 않습니다. 그러나 이러한 점은 오늘 수업 시간에서 주목할 만한 것이 아니므로, 신경을 쓰지 않으셔도 됩니다. 하지만, 이제 영구 동토층이 녹기 시작할 때 땅에서 발생하는 일들에 대해 알아보도록 하겠습니다.

3

Compact Actual iBT Reading & Listening has been designed to be used both in the classroom and by test takers working on an individual basis. Each compact test consists of one Reading passage, one Listening conversation, and one Listening lecture. All three of them are the standard length of actual TOEFL® iBT passages, conversations, and lectures. In addition, they all have the same number of questions and the same types of questions that are found on the actual test. By using this book, test takers will be more prepared for the test when they actually take it.

‹Compact Actual iBT Reading & Listening Book 3› Components
- Main Book
- Answers, Listening Scripts, and Translations
- Free MP3 Downloads
- For More Student and Teacher Support Materials, Free Downloads at http://www.darakwon.co.kr